Best of the Best
from
ILLINOIS

Selected Recipes from Illinois'
Favorite Cookbooks

Best of the Best from ILLINOIS

Selected Recipes from Illinois' Favorite Cookbooks

EDITED BY
Gwen McKee
AND
Barbara Moseley

Illustrated by Tupper England

QUAIL RIDGE PRESS

Recipe Collection © 1995 Quail Ridge Press, Inc.

Library of Congress Cataloging-in-Publication Data

Best of the best from Illinois: selected recipes from Illionis'
    favorite cookbooks / edited by Gwen McKee and Barbara Moseley.
        p. cm.
    Includes index.
    ISBN 0-937552-58-5 (alk. paper)
        1. Cookery. 2. Cookery—Illinois. I. McKee, Gwen. II. Moseley,
Barbara
TX714.B444 1995
641.5—dc20   95-16923
                                                                           CIP

First printing, June 1995
Second printing, September 1996

Manufactured in the United States of America
Designed by Barney and Gwen McKee

Chapter opening photos courtesy of: Northern Illinois Tourism Council; Springfield Illinois Convention & Visitors Bureau (Terry Farmer Photography, p.171); Peoria Area Convention & Visitors Bureau; The Dearborn Station; Gwen McKee. Cover photo courtesy of Illinois Department of Commerce and Community Affairs

QUAIL RIDGE PRESS
1-800-343-1583

CONTENTS

Editors Barbara Moseley and Gwen McKee on the University
of Illinois campus. Champaign-Urbana.

PREFACE

In Springfield, Illinois, on February 11, 1861, Abraham Lincoln said: "My Friends: No one, not in my situation, can appreciate my feeling of sadness at this parting. To this place, and the kindness of these people, I owe everything." And indeed, we now can readily understand why Lincoln felt this way.

Our big van took us all over Illinois, where we diligently searched for cookbooks in all the usual places, and found other little jewels in not-so-usual places (these are so much fun to discover!). We talked to people everywhere we went and found out all sorts of interesting things about cooking and food; traditions and history, old-world influence and specialty dishes, favorite restaurants and places where recipes originated. One of our most difficult decisions was choosing which road would most likely take us to our next discovery.

But it didn't seem to matter which way we turned, because everywhere we enjoyed the people, the countryside, the scenery, the architecture, the cities and towns, and certainly, the food. From the specialty dishes of the bigger cities to the simple preparation of farm-grown foods in the smallest of townships, we found the cuisine to be inviting...and delicious. We are very proud to present fifty-nine Illinois cookbooks that give written proof of this fact.

In Chicago, we were warmly greeted by Jean Marie Brownson at the Chicago Tribune. She, like so many helpful food editors throughout Illinois, gave us information about the cookbooks and foods and "flavors" of the entire state. "Southern Illinois," she commented from a recent article she had written, "is barbecue heaven." (And we later deliciously found that out for ourselves).

"Chicago was quite nostalgic for me," says Gwen, "since Barney and I lived here while he was in school. Back then, our friends' parents would delight in feeding us starving students, and I became an ardent fan of gooseberry and rhubarb pies, Italian roast beef, wilted spinach salad, white beans, stuffed pork chops, persimmon pudding—yum! We often frequented a neighborhood Greek restaurant...and oh my, how we enjoyed the wonderful Chicago pizza! And hot dogs!" Well, that was then, and this is now, but guess what? These same things are just as popular, and better than ever!

Motoring around the state, in and out of cities and hamlets, farm girl Barbara was excited when we got to Grand Detour. Inquiring about cookbooks, we were directed to Karen Stransky, who greeted us warmly into her lovely house—1840s vintage—that belonged to Leonard Andrus, who was responsible for bringing John Deere to Grand Detour to make a plow that would go through their sticky dirt. We stepped back into time there, in a setting as calming as the summer breeze gently blowing through the screen doors and open windows. The town's cookbook, done yearly by the villagers, was indeed a delight to find.

Traveling through the Land of Lincoln swelled in us our patriotic pride for our country. We could picture "Mrs. Lincoln's White Cake" being made in the very kitchen where it may have first been prepared.

Frequent stops to take pictures for the chapter openings led us onto backroads and into parks, through campuses, and past endless corn fields, ever meeting people who were interested in our quest, and eager to offer us whatever information they could.

All of this resulted in what appears in this book: a collection of recipes from fifty-nine outstanding cookbooks from all over Illinois. Many, many cookbooks were discovered in our research, and unfortunately, we could not utilize all of them. We do beg forgiveness for any books that might have been inadvertently overlooked.

We wish to thank all the cooks who are responsible for these wonderful recipes, and the authors, editors, chairpersons, and publishers for their cooperation in making this book possible. It is our hope that people will be encouraged to order these delightful books from the listing that begins on page 265.

We are thankful to the food editors from newspapers across Illinois who helped us with our research, as well as book and gift store managers, tourism and Chamber of Commerce personnel, and all the very nice people who took the time to talk to us along the way. And as in all the other volumes in this series, we are so grateful to Tupper England for her delightful artwork.

Illinois was great! We loved it, and we hope the enjoyment we found there shines throughout the pages of this book.

Gwen McKee and Barbara Moseley

Contributing Cookbooks

An Apple From The Teacher
Angiporto, Inc.
Best Recipes of Illinois Inns and Restaurants
Brunch Basket
C-U in the Kitchen
Caring is Sharing
Carol's Kitchen
A Cause for Applause
A Collection of Recipes From St. Matthew Lutheran Church
College Avenue Presbyterian Church Cookbook
Cookbook: Favorite Recipes from Our Best Cooks
Cookbook 25 Years
Cookin' With Friends
Cooking with Daisy's Descendants
The Cubs 'R Cookin'
Dawdy Family Cookbook
Decades of Recipes
Elsah Landing Heartland Cooking
The Elsah Landing Restaurant Cookbook
Family Celebrations Cookbook
Favorite Herbal Recipes Vol. III
Favorite Recipes of Collinsville Junior Service Club
First There Must Be Food
The Fishlady's Cookbook
The Fishlady's Forever Dieter's Cookbook
The Fishlady's Holiday Entertaining Cookbook
Five Loaves and Two Fishes II
Franklin County Homemakers Extension Cookbook
The French-Icarian Persimmon Tree Cookbook
Generations
Good Cookin' Cookbook

Contributing Cookbooks

Grand Detour Holiday Sampler
Herrin's Favorite Italian Recipes Cookbook
Holy Cow, Chicago's Cooking!
Home Cookin' is a Family Affair
Honest to Goodness: Honest Good Food
from Mr. Lincoln' Hometown
Inn-describably Delicious
Jubilee Cookbook
The Lucy Miele 6-5-4 Cookbook
The Lucy Miele Too Good To Be Low-Fat Cookbook
More to Love...Recipes and Reminiscence
from The Mansion of Golconda
Muffins—104 Recipes from A to Z
Noteworthy: A Collection of Recipes
from the Ravinia Festival
Old Fashioned Cooking
One Magnificent Cookbook
Opaa! Greek Cooking Chicago Style
Our Best Home Cooking
Our Cherished Recipes
Our Favorite Recipes
Pioneer Pantry
River Valley Recipes
Seasoned with Love
Soupçon I
Soupçon II
Still Gathering: A Centennial Celebration
Sugar Snips and Asparagus Tips
Thank Heaven for Home Made Cooks
Tradition in the Kitchen 2
What's Cooking "Down Home"

Appetizers

The Edwardsville Public Library

Apricot Mist Punch

1 (46-ounce) can apricot
   nectar
1 (46-ounce) can pineapple
   juice

3 (6-ounce) cans frozen
   limeade
3 (28-ounce) bottles ginger
   ale

Mix and serve. You can float an ice ring, using limes and strawberries in ring to make it fancy. You can also add vodka, gin or Grand Marnier for an alcoholic punch. Makes 50 punch cup servings.

A Cause for Applause

Ewing Manor Magnificent Punch

1 large can frozen orange juice
1 large can Hawaiian punch,
   red

1 large can pineapple juice
1 quart raspberry sherbet
1 large bottle 7-Up or Sprite

Mix juices together. Fold in sherbet. Add 7-Up at last minute. Will keep in refrigerator.

Cook Book: Favorite Recipes from Our Best Cooks

Open House Punch

This is the annual Christmas party punch. Animated conversation guaranteed after several glasses!

1 fifth Southern Comfort
6 ounces fresh lemon juice
1 (6-ounce) can frozen
   orange juice

1 (6-ounce) can frozen
   lemonade
3 quarts 7-Up

Chill ingredients; combine in punch bowl, 7-Up last. Add drops of red food coloring, if desired. Float block of ice in punch bowl.

Carol's Kitchen

Tequila-Champagne Punch

Perfect for brunch parties or luncheons.

2 quarts white wine, chilled
2 (6-ounce) cans frozen
concentrated pineapple
juice, reconstituted with
water
1 (fifth) bottle tequila

2 (fifth) bottles champagne,
chilled
2 quarts soda water, chilled
Strawberry halves or orange
slices

In punch bowl, combine wine, pineapple juice, and tequila (or mix in the proportions your punch bowl will hold). Just before serving, add champagne and soda water. Float fruits in punch. Or freeze strawberries or other fruits with water in ring mold; unmold and float in punch. Makes about 2 gallons.

Soupçon I

Sangria

1 (6-ounce) can frozen
lemonade
2 cans water
1 (1.5-litre) bottle red or
rose wine

2 apples, quartered, cored,
and unpeeled
1 orange, sliced in thin
rounds, unpeeled
Orange juice, as desired

Combine lemonade, water, and wine in punch bowl. Slice apples thinly and add to wine with the sliced oranges. To sweeten, add orange juice to taste. Cool with an ice ring. Serves 8.

C-U in the Kitchen

Bloody Mary Deluxe

1 (46-ounce) can tomato
  juice
½ cup beef broth
6 tablespoons fresh lime
  juice
¼ cup Worcestershire sauce
2 teaspoons sea salt or
  coarse salt

1 teaspoon ground pepper
1 teaspoon celery salt
1 teaspoon dill
½–1 teaspoon hot pepper
  sauce
1 teaspoon prepared
  horseradish
1–2 cups vodka

Put all ingredients except vodka in pitcher; mix well. Fill 12-ounce glasses with ice. Add 1–2 ounces vodka to each glass. Add tomato mixture. Garnish with celery sticks, cucumber sticks or slices, and lime. Makes 8–10 servings.

Soupçon II

Hot Buttered Rum

This makes a lot! Enough for Holidays! Great for a snowy eve!

1 (1-pound) box brown sugar
1 (1-pound) box powdered
  sugar
2 teaspoons cinnamon
Dash nutmeg

1 pound butter, melted
½ gallon Schwan's vanilla ice
  cream
Rum
Boiling water

Mix sugars, cinnamon and nutmeg together. Add melted butter and ice cream and freeze.

To use combine 2 tablespoons frozen mix with 1 shot of rum and enough boiling water to fill cup.
Note: Use good quality ingredients.

Grand Detour Holiday Sampler

Stephen Arnold Douglas, U.S. Senator from Illinois, achieved national fame for his series of debates (the Lincoln-Douglas debates) on the slavery issue in 1858. He was nicknamed "the Little Giant."

Wassail

2 quarts apple cider
2 sticks cinnamon
½ cup lemon juice
1 cup light corn syrup

1 (12-ounce) can pineapple
   juice
½ teaspoon nutmeg

Boil and simmer cider and cinnamon sticks for 5 minutes. Add rest of ingredients and serve hot.

Caring is Sharing

Johnny Appleseed Shakes

Kids love this and it's nutritious, too!

1 pint vanilla ice cream,
   slightly softened
1 cup apple juice

¼ teaspoon cinnamon
¼ teaspoon nutmeg

Place ice cream, apple juice, cinnamon, and nutmeg in blender container. Cover container. Blend on HIGH for 30 seconds or until smooth and well blended. Pour into glasses. Serve immediately. Yields 3 servings.

Approx. Per Serving: Cal 258; Prot 2.6gr; T Fat 15.9gr; Chol 56.2mg; Carbo 56.2gr; Sod 33.4mg; Potas 177.2mg.

River Valley Recipes

Vegetable Frittata

2 tablespoons extra virgin
  olive oil
1 onion, chopped
2 small zucchini, sliced
1 large red pepper, cut into
  strips
3 new potatoes, peeled,
  cooked, sliced

8 pitted black olives, sliced
8 eggs
⅓ cup milk
½ teaspoon salt
¼ teaspoon white pepper
½ cup freshly grated Parmesan
  cheese

In a large skillet heat olive oil and sauté onion for 5 minutes. Add zucchini and red pepper and sauté for 5 minutes or until soft. Stir in potatoes and olives. Cool. Preheat oven to 350°. In a bowl beat eggs with remaining ingredients.

Line a 9-inch square baking pan with foil. Heavily butter bottom and sides of foil. Spoon in vegetables, spreading them in an even layer. Pour egg mixture evenly over vegetables. Bake for 35–40 minutes or until puffed and golden brown. Remove from heat and cool 10 minutes.

To serve warm, use foil to lift frittata from pan. Turn down sides of foil and cut into 2-inch squares. To serve cold, chill frittata in pan, then remove and cut. Garnish top of each square as desired. Yield: 16 (2-inch) squares.

Suggested Garnishes: Asparagus tips and pimento strips; mushroom slices, white onion rings and parsley; small stuffed olives and parsley; pickle fan and black olive slices; cherry tomato slices topped with pumpkin seeds.

One Magnificent Cookbook

Zucchini Appetizers

3 cups thinly sliced unpared
zucchini (about 4 small)
1 cup baking mix (Bisquick
or homemade)
½ cup finely chopped onion
½ cup grated Parmesan
cheese
2 tablespoons snipped
parsley

½ teaspoon salt
½ teaspoon dried marjoram
or oregano leaves
Dash of pepper
1 clove garlic, finely
chopped
½ cup vegetable oil
4 eggs, slightly beaten

Heat oven to 350°. Grease oblong 13x9x2-inch pan. Mix all
ingredients; spread in pan. Bake until golden brown, about 25
minutes. Cut into pieces about 2x1-inch. Yield: 4 dozen
appetizers.

Favorite Herbal Recipes Vol. III

Artichoke Heart Quiche

2 (6-ounce) jars marinated
artichoke hearts
½ cup sliced green onion
1 tablespoon oil
4 eggs

Salt, pepper
½ pound sharp Cheddar
cheese, shredded
6 Ritz crackers, crushed
2 dashes Tabasco

Drain artichokes; cut in sixths. Sauté onions in oil. Beat
eggs; add artichokes, onion and remaining ingredients. Pour
into a greased 12x8-inch pan. Bake at 350°, 30–35 minutes.
Cut into squares; serve warm. Makes 40 pieces.

Grand Detour Holiday Sampler

Arcola in Central Illinois is known as the Broom Corn Capital of the world.
Raggedy Ann & Andy creator Johnny Gruelle was born here. It is also known
as the gateway to Amish country. About 3,000 Amish live in the rural area
West of Arcola.

Quesadillas with Morels

1 cup small morels
6 tablespoons butter
6 small flour tortillas

6 slices Monterey Jack
   cheese

Sauté morels in butter until golden about 5 minutes. In a sauté pan heat tortillas, one at a time, turning with a spatula. Place a slice of cheese on each tortilla, fold in half and continue to turn until cheese begins to melt. Top each cheese-filled tortilla with 3 tablespoons sautéed morels. Cut each tortilla in 3 pie-shaped sections and serve immediately. Yield: 6 servings.

One Magnificent Cookbook

Spinach Balls

2 (10-ounce) packages frozen
   chopped spinach, squeezed
   dry
1 cup (2 sticks) margarine,
   melted

1 (12-ounce) twin pack
   chicken flavor stuffing mix
   (mix according to directions)
6 eggs, slightly beaten
1 cup grated Parmesan cheese

In a large bowl stir together all ingredients. Form into bite-size balls and freeze uncovered on cookie sheets. When frozen remove spinach balls and store in freezer in freezer bags. When ready to serve, remove the number needed and bake while still frozen in preheated 350° oven 20 minutes. Makes 120 balls.

Family Celebrations Cookbook

Cucumber Canapés

Dainty appetizers with a zip!

CREAMY MAYONNAISE:

⅓ cup low-cholesterol egg
  substitute
1 teaspoon dry mustard
¼ teaspoon onion powder

¼ teaspoon paprika
Dash ground red pepper
2 tablespoons vinegar
½ cup corn oil

Combine egg substitute, mustard, onion powder, paprika, pepper, and vinegar in blender or food processor. Blend on medium-high speed until just mixed. Without turning blender off, add the corn oil very slowly. Continue blending until oil is completely incorporated and mixture is smooth and thick. Store in refrigerator. Makes 1 cup.

CANAPES:

¼ cup softened margarine
1 teaspoon grated onion
24 (2-inch) bread rounds
24 slices cucumber, thinly
  sliced

2 tablespoons Creamy
  Mayonnaise
3 tablespoons chopped parsley
6 cherry tomatoes, thinly sliced

Mix softened margarine and onion together. Spread on top of bread rounds. Put a cucumber slice on top and decorate each slice with a piece of cherry tomato, parsley, and a dollop (½ teaspoon each) of the Creamy Mayonnaise.

Note: Use remaining mayonnaise on sandwiches or as a base for salad dressing.

Still Gathering

Water Chestnut Appetizer

1 (8-ounce) can water
  chestnuts (whole)
½ pound bacon, slices cut
  in half

½ cup Open Pit Barbecue
  Sauce
½ cup brown sugar

Wrap bacon around water chestnuts. Bake in 350° oven for 30 minutes. Pour off grease and cool in refrigerator 4 hours (or overnight). Blend sauce and brown sugar. Dip chestnuts in sauce. Reheat in 350° oven for 20 minutes.

Caring is Sharing

Deviled Eggs with Three Fillings

12 eggs
¼ cup mayonnaise

¼ cup unsalted butter,
softened

Place eggs in a large pan in one layer. Add water to cover eggs by one inch. Bring to a full boil, cover and remove from heat. Let stand at least 20 minutes. Peel eggs and slice in half.

Put yolks in food processor work bowl with mayonnaise and butter. Process until very smooth. Add more mayonnaise or butter, if needed. Yolks should be soft, but should hold their shape. Divide into 3 small bowls.

FIRST FILLING:
2 tablespoons minced
prosciutto

1 tablespoon freshly grated
Parmesan cheese

Stir prosciutto and Parmesan into yolk mixture.

SECOND FILLING:
3 tablespoons sun-dried tomatoes, packed in oil

Drain sun-dried tomatoes and pat dry with paper towels. Chop and add to yolk mixture.

THIRD FILLING:
1 tablespoon unsalted butter
1 scallion, thinly sliced

1 large mushroom, minced

Melt butter in a small skillet, add scallion and mushroom; cook until tender. Mix in yolk mixture. Using a pastry bag, fitted with a star tip, or a teaspoon, fill 8 egg halves with each filling. Garnish eggs with sliced black olives, sprigs of fresh parsley, a shred of fresh basil leaf or chives. Cover lightly and chill.

To serve, line a basket with a brightly colored napkin. Fill halfway with fresh radish sprouts. Nest eggs in the sprouts.

GARNISH:
Sliced black olives
Sprigs of fresh parsley

Fresh basil leaves
Radish sprouts

Sugar Snips and Asparagus Tips

Croutons with Three Cheeses and Sun-Dried Tomatoes

1 French bread baguette, cut
  into ¼-inch slices
Extra virgin olive oil
¼ pound California goat
  cheese with herbs
¼ pound ricotta cheese

¼ pound mozzarella cheese,
  shredded
1 large garlic clove, minced
White pepper
18 sun-dried tomatoes,
  drained and halved

Preheat oven to 300°. Arrange bread slices on baking sheet. Brush tops with olive oil. Bake until croutons are golden brown, about 2 minutes. Remove from oven and set aside. Increase oven temperature to 350°.

Blend cheeses and garlic in a bowl. Season with pepper. Mound 1 teaspoon cheese mixture on each crouton. Top with sun-dried tomato half. Cover with an additional 1 teaspoon cheese mixture.

Bake until cheese begins to melt. Serve immediately. Yield: 36 appetizers.

One Magnificent Cookbook

Kay's Best Cheese Spread

2 (8-ounce) packages cream
  cheese
1 teaspoon garlic powder or
  garlic salt

½ cup Miracle Whip
1 pound Merkts sharp Cheddar
  cheese spread

Let cheeses soften, then mix with remaining ingredients with a mixer, or in a blender or food processor. Keep refrigerated. Serve on crackers.

Carol's Kitchen

 The Museum of Science and Industry is Chicago's most popular civic attraction, drawing more than four million visitors annually.

Potted Herb Cheese

8 ounces whipped butter
2 (8-ounce) packages cream
  cheese, softened
2 cloves garlic, pressed
1 teaspoon fresh oregano
1 teaspoon fresh dill weed

½ teaspoon fresh basil
½ teaspoon fresh thyme
½ teaspoon fresh marjoram
¼ teaspoon freshly ground
  black pepper

Mix all ingredients together and refrigerate overnight to blend flavors. Serve at room temperature in a crock along with your favorite crackers. Yield: 3 cups.

One Magnificent Cookbook

Triconas
(Hot Cheese Pastries)

FILLING:

2 (8-ounce) packages cream
  cheese, softened
½ pound Greek cheese,
  crumbled

1 egg
3 tablespoons butter or
  margarine, melted

Cream cheeses, egg, and butter in small bowl of electric mixer and beat at medium speed until well blended and smooth.

PASTRY:

1 package prepared phyllo-
  pastry or strudel-pastry
  leaves

1 cup butter or margarine,
  melted

Preheat oven to 350°. Place 2 leaves of phyllo-pastry on board; brush with melted butter. Cut lengthwise into strips about 2-inches wide. Place 1 teaspoon filling at end of a strip. Fold over one corner to opposite side, to make a triangle.

Continue folding, keeping triangle shape, to other end of strip. Arrange the filled triangle on an ungreased cookie sheet. Repeat with remaining strips. Repeat with other pastry leaves. Bake 20 minutes or until deep golden-brown. Serve hot. Yields 7 dozen.

Note: If desired, make and bake ahead. Cool; then refrigerate, covered, overnight. To serve: Arrange on cookie sheet; bake in 350° oven about 10 minutes, or until heated.

C-U in the Kitchen

Smoked Trout Cheesecake

CRUST:

2 cups roasted, finely
  chopped hazelnuts

6 tablespoons butter

Butter the sides of a 10-inch springform pan. Mix 1½ cups of the nuts with the butter and use this to line the bottom of the pan well.

FILLING:

24 ounces cream cheese,
  cubed
6 eggs
1 pint sour cream
⅓ cup sifted flour
Grated zest of 1 lemon
Grated zest of ½ lime

Grated zest of ½ orange
Juice of ½ lemon
1½ cups flaked smoked trout
1 cup chopped green onions
Salt and pepper to taste
Tabasco sauce to taste

Preheat the oven to 350°. Beat the cubed cream cheese until soft and creamy. Blend in the eggs one at a time until well blended. Add the sour cream, flour and the zests of lemon, lime and orange, and the lemon juice. Mix well. Stir the smoked trout and green onions into the cheese mixture and add the salt, pepper and Tabasco to taste.

Pour the cheese mixture into the prepared pan and bake for one hour. Turn off the heat and allow the cheesecake to remain in the oven for another hour. Cool to room temperature. Sprinkle the remaining nuts on top of the cake. Chill overnight. Serve with Sweet and Sour Red Onions (next page), whole grain mustard, diced tomatoes and cornichons.

From Maldaner's, 222 South Sixth Street, Springfield.

Best Recipes of Illinois Inns and Restaurants

Sweet and Sour Red Onions

1 cup red wine vinegar
1 cup sugar
2 red onions, sliced thin

2 tablespoons capers with
juice

Bring red wine vinegar to a boil in a non-reactive saucepan. Add the sugar and reduce by one quarter. Pour over the onions, then add the capers and let stand at room temperature, stirring occasionally. Serve with Smoked Trout Cheesecake (previous page).

From Maldaner's, 222 South Sixth Street, Springfield.
Best Recipes of Illinois Inns and Restaurants

Pumpkin Cheese Ball

1 (8-ounce) package cream
    cheese
1 (16-ounce) package
    shredded Cheddar cheese

1 (4-ounce) package chopped
    beef, cut up
½ cup pumpkin
Chopped nuts

Mix first 5 ingredients together. Shape into ball. Roll in nuts to cover. Keep refrigerated. Serve with crackers.
Franklin County Homemakers Extension Cookbook

Creamy Cheeseball

1 (16-ounce) package Cheddar
    cheese spread (such as
    Merkts brand)

1 (8-ounce) package cream
    cheese
1 tablespoon Triple Sec Liqueur
2 tablespoons powdered sugar

Mix cheese spread and cream cheese. Add Triple Sec and powdered sugar. Refrigerate 1 hour before serving; serve with crackers.

Cookin' With Friends

Cheese Ball

2 (8-ounce) packages cream
  cheese, room temperature
2 wedges Roquefort cheese,
  room temperature
1 tablespoon shredded onion

1 tablespoon Worcestershire
  sauce
¼ cup mayonnaise
Ground nuts
Parsley flakes

Mix cheeses, onion, Worcestershire sauce, and mayonnaise together. Cool. Place in refrigerator to handle. Roll into ball, then roll ball into very fine ground nuts, then roll in parsley flakes. Cover with Saran Wrap and place in refrigerator. Serve with crackers.

Good Cookin' Cookbook

Flaming Cheese #1
(Saganaki)

Pat Bruno, restaurant critic for the Chicago Sun-Times, gave The Parthenon Restaurant, in Greektown 3 stars. The Parthenon claims the creation of Saganaki, the famous flaming cheese appetizer. The waiters there can raise a tower of flame with the best.

1 egg
⅓ cup milk
4 ounces kasseri cheese cut
  in ½-inch thick squares

Flour
Vegetable oil

Beat egg until slightly foaming and light yellow. Add milk, and continue beating. Dip cheese in egg mixture, then in flour (both sides), pressing the cheese so that the flour will stick to the cheese. In a frying pan, heat oil well, so when you place cheese in pan you see a sizzle. Fry cheese on both sides, until golden brown. If you like, splash a few drops of brandy and flame, and shout Opaa! Eat it fast, though, as the pleasure diminishes as it cools off. Makes 1 serving.

Note: For best results, make sure your cheese is refrigerated for at least 1 hour before frying. Also use enough vegetable oil to cover cheese while frying.

Opaa! Greek Cooking Chicago Style

Fried Mozzarella
(Mozzarella Fritta)

Nothing more is needed with this filling appetizer than a glass of chilled white wine.

8 ounces whole milk
mozzarella cheese
¼ cup Wondra Flour
2 extra large eggs
1 teaspoon salt

½ teaspoon freshly milled
black pepper
1½ cups fine dry bread crumbs
1½ cups vegetable oil,
preferably corn

Cut mozzarella into ½-inch slices and then into ½-inch strips. Place flour in a shallow bowl. In another shallow bowl, beat eggs, salt and pepper thoroughly with a fork. Place bread crumbs in third bowl.

Dip mozzarella strips in flour, then in beaten eggs. Dredge thoroughly in bread crumbs, making sure cheese is thoroughly coated with crumbs so that it does not ooze in frying.

Arrange strips in a single layer on a large platter lined with waxed paper. Chill for at least 1 hour (chilling will prevent bread crumb coating from falling off when frying).

In a 12-inch skillet, heat vegetable oil over medium-high heat until haze forms. Fry mozzarella in 2 batches, turning once, until lightly golden on both sides. Drain on paper towels. To serve, arrange on platter and serve immediately. Serves 6–8.

Herrin's Favorite Italian Recipes Cookbook

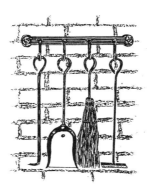

Cheese Puffs

7 or 8 slices of bread,
  crusts removed
1 cup sharp Cheddar cheese,
  grated

3 ounces cream cheese
1 stick margarine
2 egg whites, beaten

Cut each slice of bread into about 6 squares. Melt cheeses and margarine in top of double boiler over hot water. Stir well. Fold in stiffly beaten egg whites. Dip bread squares in cheese mixture, coating thoroughly. Place on lightly greased cookie sheet. Refrigerate 12–24 hours. Bake at 400° for 8–10 minutes. Serve warm. Makes 4 dozen.

Favorite Recipes of Collinsville Junior Service Club

Italian Cheese Twists

¼ cup butter or margarine,
  softened
¼ teaspoon each: basil,
  oregano and marjoram,
  crushed
¼ teaspoon garlic powder

1 (16-ounce) loaf frozen
  bread dough, thawed
¾ cup shredded mozzarella
  cheese (3 ounces)
1 slightly beaten egg
1 tablespoon water
2 tablespoons sesame seeds

In a small bowl, combine butter, basil, oregano, marjoram, and garlic powder; set aside. On a lightly floured surface, roll bread dough into a 12-inch square.

Spread butter mixture evenly over dough and sprinkle with cheese. Fold dough into thirds. With a sharp knife, cut dough crosswise into 20 (4½-inch) strips. Twist each strip twice and pinch ends to seal. Place about 2 inches apart on a greased baking sheet. Cover, let rise in a warm place until almost double, about 30 minutes.

Combine egg and water. Brush each twist and sprinkle with sesame seeds. Bake at 375° for 10–12 minutes or until golden. Yield: 24 twists.

Favorite Herbal Recipes Vol. III

Crunchy Cheese Dip

1 (8-ounce) can pineapple tidbits
2 (8-ounce) packages cream cheese, softened
1 (8-ounce) can water chestnuts, drained and chopped
3 tablespoons chopped, fresh chives
1 teaspoon salt
¼ teaspoon pepper
¼ cup chopped pecans
Fresh, chopped parsley
Assorted crackers

Drain pineapple, reserving 1 tablespoon juice. In a small bowl combine pineapple, cream cheese, water chestnuts, chives, parsley, salt, pepper, and pecans. Stir in reserved juice; mix well. Serve with crackers. Makes 3½ cups.

Old-Fashioned Cooking

Incredible Vegetable Dip

Possibly the best and easiest you'll ever use.

2 cups Hellman's mayonnaise
1 tablespoon Worcestershire sauce
1 teaspoon garlic salt
1 small onion, grated
Cracked pepper

Mix all ingredients and pour in pretty bowl in center of tray. Surround with raw vegetable fans.

Fans: Make 2 slits in each end of 2–3-inch long pieces of celery, carrot, green onions, and green pepper. Chill in ice water until they 'fan'. The fans scoop up more of this wonderful dip. Also pile radishes, cauliflorets, broccoli florets and tiny red tomatoes on the platter. Stunning—and delicious.

The Lucy Miele 6-5-4 Cookbook

Caramel Dip

2 (8-ounce) packages light cream cheese
1 cup brown sugar
1 tablespoon vanilla
¾ cup chopped nuts or nut topping

Mix ingredients together and serve with fruit such as sliced apples.

Our Cherished Recipes

Shrimp Pizza

2 (8-ounce) package cream
  cheese (softened)
1 (8-ounce) jar cocktail
  sauce

1 pound shrimp (cooked and
  cut up)
½ cup chopped green onion
1 cup shredded mozzarella
  cheese

Spread cream cheese on pizza pan. Spread cocktail sauce on top of cream cheese. Arrange shrimp on top of cocktail sauce. Sprinkle on onion and cheese. Serve with crackers or taco chips, and serve this pizza cold.

The Fishlady's Holiday Entertaining Cookbook

Tomato Phyllo Pizza

Save this recipe to try with vine-ripened summer tomatoes rather than with the out-of-season varieties that bear little resemblance to their juicy, flavorful ideal.

7 sheets phyllo dough
5 tablespoons melted
  unsalted butter
7 tablespoons freshly grated
  Parmesan cheese
1 cup shredded mozzarella
  cheese

1 cup thinly sliced purple
  onion
2 pounds vine-ripened
  tomatoes
½ teaspoon oregano
1 teaspoon fresh thyme or
  ¼ teaspoon dried thyme
Salt and pepper to taste

Layer the phyllo dough on a large buttered baking sheet, brushing each sheet lightly with butter and sprinkling all but the last sheet with 1 tablespoon Parmesan cheese. Press the layers together. Top with the mozzarella cheese and onion.

Slice the tomatoes ¼-inch thick. Arrange in a single layer over the top. Sprinkle with the remaining 1 tablespoon Parmesan cheese, oregano, thyme, salt and pepper. Bake on the center oven rack at 375° for 30–35 minutes or until golden brown. Cut into squares to serve; garnish with fresh basil or oregano. Serves 8–10.

Generations

Vegetable Pizza

1 can crescent rolls
4 ounces cream cheese
½ cup mayonnaise

½ package Hidden Valley
Original Recipe dressing

Spread rolls flat and press together on pizza pan; bake according to directions on package.

Mix cream cheese, mayonnaise and Hidden Valley dressing well. Spread on cooled crescent roll crust.

Dice choice of fresh vegetables to spread on top of mixture. (You can use diced cauliflower, green onions, broccoli flowerets, mushrooms, radishes, green pepper, celery, tomatoes, whatever you wish. Do not use cucumbers.)

Old Fashioned Cooking

Crusty Crab Points

6 ounces crabmeat
½ cup butter, softened
1 (5-ounce) jar sharp
  Cheddar cheese spread
½ teaspoon mayonnaise

½ teaspoon seasoned salt
½ teaspoon garlic powder
3 English muffins, sliced in
  half

When using canned crabmeat, drain. Combine all ingredients except English muffins with electric mixer. Spread on English muffin halves. Freeze for 1–1½ hours. Cut each muffin half into 6 wedges. Refreeze in plastic bags until ready to serve. Broil until golden brown and bubbly, about 5 minutes. Serve immediately.

Filling is also good on party rye or leave the English muffin halves uncut and serve as an openface sandwich. Makes 3 dozen points.

Honest to Goodness

Crab Puffs

1 cup water
½ cup butter
1 cup flour
4 whole eggs
1 egg, separated
2 (8-ounce) packages cream
  cheese, softened
½ teaspoon milk

2 packages frozen crab meat,
  thawed and drained (or 2 cans,
  drained)
1 teaspoon pepper
Greens of 6 green onions,
  chopped
2½ teaspoons dill weed

Preheat oven to 400°. Combine water and butter in medium saucepan; bring to a boil and add flour all at once. Stir vigorously with wooden spoon until dough leaves sides of pan and forms smooth ball. Remove from heat and beat in 4 whole eggs, one at a time, until thick dough is formed. Place level teaspoonfuls of dough 1 inch apart on foil-lined cookie sheet. Mix separated egg yolk and milk and brush dough with this mixture.

Bake for 10 minutes at 400°, then reduce heat to 300° and continue cooking for 25–30 minutes until puffs are high and golden. (Do not open oven during baking time.) Remove from oven; cool completely and slice puffs in half, but not all the way through, to prepare for filling.

Combine all remaining ingredients and stuff puffs with mixture. Yield: 50–60 puffs.

Note: Puffs may be frozen and reheated on cookie sheet for 10 minutes at 375°.

An Apple From The Teacher

Shrimply Devine

1 (8-ounce) package cream
  cheese
1 cup dairy sour cream
1 (⅝-ounce) package Italian
  Salad Dressing Mix

2 tablespoons finely chopped
  green pepper
½ cup finely chopped shrimp
1 teaspoon lemon juice

Blend cheese with remainder of ingredients. Chill at least 1 hour before serving. Makes 1⅔ cups.

A Collection of Recipes From St. Matthew Lutheran Church

Chopped Herring

1 (16-ounce) jar herring
   fillets in wine sauce,
   drained, keep juice
2 onions, sliced
3 hard cooked eggs
2 apples cored, peeled and
   sliced

¼ cup vinegar
2 slices bread or 1 matzoh,
   soaked in water, squeezed
   dry
1 tablespoon sugar
½ teaspoon cinnamon

In food processor or grinder, place herring, onions, eggs, apples, vinegar, and bread. Pulse until finely chopped. Combine sugar, juice, and cinnamon and add to mixture. Serve with rye rounds.

Tradition in the Kitchen 2

Marinated Shrimp with Orange

3 pounds large shrimp,
   uncooked, shelled, deveined
4 oranges, peeled, sectioned
4 medium white onions,
   sliced
1½ cups cider vinegar
1 cup vegetable oil
⅔ cup fresh lemon juice
½ cup ketchup

¼ cup sugar
2 tablespoons drained capers
2 tablespoons minced parsley
2 teaspoons salt
2 teaspoons mustard seeds
1 teaspoon celery seed
¼ teaspoon pepper
2 cloves garlic, crushed
Lettuce, optional

In boiling water cook shrimp 2 minutes only. Rinse with cold water until thoroughly chilled. Drain.

Combine shrimp, oranges and onions in large bowl. Mix remaining ingredients, except lettuce, and pour over shrimp mixture. Cover and refrigerate 8 hours or overnight, stirring occasionally. Serve in individual shells or on a bed of lettuce. May also be served as a luncheon dish. Serves 12.

Noteworthy

Dixon is the boyhood home of former President Ronald Reagan.

Appetizer Chicken Wings

5 pounds chicken wings
2 (4-ounce) jars strained
  baby food apricots

6 ounces soy sauce
2 teaspoons ground ginger
1 clove of garlic, minced

Disjoint wings; discard tips. Rinse well; pat dry. Place in single layer in baking pan. Pour mixture of remaining ingredients over chicken. Marinate, covered with plastic wrap, in refrigerator for 24 hours. Bake, uncovered, at 350° for 1 hour or until tender. Serve hot. Yield: 10 servings.

Approx Per Serving: Cal 520; T Fat 33g; 59% Calories from Fat; Prot 46g; Carbo 6g; Fiber <1g; Chol 145mg; Sod 1114mg.

Pioneer Pantry

Fancy Chicken Log

2 (8-ounce) packages cream
  cheese, softened
1 tablespoon bottled steak
  sauce (any kind is good)
½ teaspoon curry powder
⅓ cup minced celery

1½ cups minced, cooked
  chicken
¼ cup chopped parsley
¼ cup chopped, toasted
  almonds

Beat together first 5 ingredients and 2 tablespoons parsley. Refrigerate remaining parsley. Shape mixture into an 8-inch log. Wrap in plastic wrap and chill 4 hours or overnight. Toss together remaining parsley and almonds; use to coat log. Serve with snack crackers. Makes about 3 cups spread.

College Avenue Presbyterian Church Cookbook

Super Barbecue Meat Balls

3 pounds ground beef
2 cups quick oatmeal
1 (13-ounce) can evaporated
   milk
2 slightly beaten eggs

1 cup chopped onion
½ teaspoon garlic powder
2 teaspoons salt
½ teaspoon pepper
2 teaspoons chili powder

Mix and shape into walnut-size balls. Place in two 9x13-inch pans. Cover with sauce.

SAUCE:
4 cups catsup
3 cups brown sugar

3 tablespoons liquid smoke
1 cup chopped onion

Stir well, pour over balls and bake at 350° for 1 hour.

Family Celebrations Cookbook

Crescents 'n Sausage Snacks Italiano

1 (8-ounce) can Pillsbury
   Refrigerated Quick Crescent
   Dinner Rolls
2 tablespoons oleo, melted

¼ cup Parmesan cheese,
   grated
1–2 teaspoons oregano
8 brown-and-serve sausage links

Heat oven to 375°. Separate crescent dough into 4 rectangles; press perforations to seal. Brush each with oleo. Combine cheese and oregano. Sprinkle over dough. Cut each rectangle crosswise to form 2 squares. Place a sausage link on each square and roll up. Cut each roll into 3 or 4 pieces, and secure each with toothpick. Place cut-side-down on ungreased cookie sheet. Bake at 375° for 12–15 minutes.

Makes 2 dozen snacks. To make ahead, prepare, cover and refrigerate up to 2 hours. Bake as directed.

Herrin's Favorite Italian Recipes Cookbook

Arlington International Racecourse in Arlington Heights has world-class thoroughbred racing May through the first week in October.

Hot Dog Rolls

These are remarkably tasty, and worthy of being elevated on your hors d'oeuvre table.

1 pound hot dogs
1 pound bacon slices

1 pound brown sugar

Cut hot dogs in thirds. Cut bacon slices in halves. Wrap each hot dog third with bacon slice. Arrange in 9x13-inch baking dish. Sprinkle with brown sugar. Bake at 350° for 1 hour. Arrange on footed cake plate and spear with toothpicks.

The Lucy Miele 6-5-4 Cookbook

Popular Chicago-style hot dogs come on a poppy seed bun, with ballpark mustard, sweet relish, chopped onions, crunchy pickle and chopped tomato. Vienna hot dogs, made in Chicago, are usually recommended for authenticity.

Tortilla Temptations

1 (8-ounce) package cream
cheese, softened
1 (2¼-ounce) can ripe
olives, drained and sliced
or chopped

4 green onions, including
tops, chopped
4 small flour tortillas
Picante or salsa sauce

Combine cream cheese, olives, and green onions with an electric mixer until mixed well. Evenly spread thin layer of filling on tortillas, jelly roll fashion. Cover and refrigerate at least 2 hours until the cream cheese mixture sets. Cut each tortilla into 1-inch slices. Serve with picante or salsa sauce for dipping. Makes 24 pieces.

Honest to Goodness

Stuffed Grape Leaves
(Dolmathes Yalantzi)

Dolmathes (dol-MA-thez) are known in all of the Greek restaurants in Greektown as a medley of spices and rice wrapped in grape vine leaves, served with yogurt. Super!

1 jar vine leaves (about 3 dozen)
8 medium onions
¾ cup olive oil
1½ cups rice
1 cup parsley, finely chopped
¼ cup fresh chopped dill
½ cup pine nuts
2 tablespoons dried mint
Juice of 2 lemons
Salt and pepper

Remove vine leaves from the jar, scald with hot water, and drain. Boil onions for 4–5 minutes. Drain, peel, and chop. In a skillet, sauté onions in a ½ cup of olive oil until soft. Stir in rice, parsley, dill, pine nuts, mint, and juice of 1 lemon. Salt and pepper to taste. Cook, stirring, for 2–3 minutes over low heat. Remove from heat and let cool.

Select 6–8 grape leaves and line the bottom of a saucepan. They will protect the stuffed grape leaves from burning.

Cut off thick stems from the remaining grape leaves. Place 1 teaspoon filling on underside of each leaf near stem end and fold base of leaf over filling. Then fold sides to enclose filling; roll lightly toward point. Layer stuffed grape leaves seam-side-down on the grape leaves covering the bottom of the saucepan.

Pour in remaining ¼ cup olive oil and lemon juice. Weigh down with a heavy heat-proof plate. Cover and simmer for 10 minutes over low heat. Pour in enough boiling water to cover stuffed grape leaves and simmer for 45 minutes longer.

Though often considered an appetizer, serve along with crusty bread and imported feta cheese for a full meal. Makes 45–50.

Opaa! Greek Cooking Chicago Style

Chutney Pâté

2 (3-ounce) packages cream
  cheese, softened
1 cup shredded Cheddar
  cheese
1 tablespoon dry sherry
¾ teaspoon curry powder

¼ teaspoon salt
Dash pepper sauce
½ cup chutney
3 chopped green onions
¼ cup chopped peanuts to
  garnish

In a blender or food processor, beat cream and Cheddar cheese until smooth. Add sherry, curry, salt, and pepper sauce. Spread on a serving plate in a circle. Top with chutney, green onions, and peanuts if desired. Serve with crackers. Yield: 6–8 servings.

Holy Cow!

Marian's Sweet Pickles from Dill

1 quart commercially
  prepared hamburger dill
  slices, drained

2 cloves garlic, sliced
3 cups sugar

Drain hamburger dill slices. Discard vinegar solution. Place well drained pickles in bowl. Add sliced garlic and sugar. Stir. Let set on counter. Every few minutes give the pickles a stir. Continue stirring until all sugar is absorbed by the pickles and a sweet syrup is made. Rinse out the pickle jar and return pickles to the jar with the sweet syrup. Refrigerate.

Home Cookin' is a Family Affair

Hunker Down Popcorn

Light the fire, find a book, and hunker down with a bowl of this dynamite popcorn. It almost makes winter worthwhile.

18 cups popped corn
1 tablespoon butter or light
  margarine (Promise)
⅔ cup light corn syrup
1½–2 teaspoons vanilla

1 (3.4-ounce) package instant
  butter pecan or butterscotch
  or vanilla pudding mix
½ teaspoon salt

Preheat oven to 300°. Pam a big roasting pan. Pop corn in air popper (enough kernels to make 18 cups popped corn). Put popped corn in pan and keep warm in 300° oven. In Pyrex cup, microwave butter until melted (or melt in saucepan on stove). Stir in corn syrup, vanilla, and pudding mix with a fork. Pour syrup over popcorn and toss with wooden spoon. Sprinkle salt over corn. Toss, taste, sprinkle. Do it again until it says, "Hello!" Return to 300° oven for 8 minutes. Toss. Return to 300° oven for 8 minutes. Toss again. Determine if it needs another few minutes to make it glossy. Toss. Taste. (My oven dictates another 8 minutes, but all ovens are different. Use your infallible good taste.) Turn out on large piece of foil to cool. Break into bits. Store leftovers (if any) in covered tin box.

Servings 18 (1 cup); 1g Fat; 0mg Chol; 82 Cal

The Lucy Miele Too Good To Be Low-Fat Cookbook

Swedish Nuts

Wonderful for winter holiday times.

½ pound (about 2 cups)
  pecans
½ pound (about 2 cups)
  walnuts

1 cup sugar
Dash salt
2 stiff beaten egg whites
½ cup butter or margarine

Toast nuts in slow oven (325°) until light brown (about 20 minutes). Fold sugar and salt into beaten egg whites. Beat until stiff peaks form. Fold nuts into meringue.

    Melt butter in 15½x10½x1-inch jelly roll pan. Spread nut-meringue mixture over butter. Bake at 325° for 30 minutes. Stir every 10 minutes or until no butter is left in pan. Cool.

Jubilee

Bread and Breakfast

The peaches are delicious in Southern Illinois. Alto Pass.

Hot Rolls

1 package dry yeast
¼ cup warm water
1 teaspoon sugar
¼ cup sugar
¼ cup shortening
1 teaspoon salt
1 cup milk, scalded
1 egg
3½ cups all-purpose flour

Soften yeast in warm water with 1 teaspoon sugar. In mixer, combine ¼ cup sugar, shortening, salt, and hot milk; cool to lukewarm. Add softened yeast, egg, 2 cups flour, beat well. Gradually add remaining flour or enough to make a soft dough. Cover, let rise till doubled in size in warm place. Punch down. Make out into rolls. Let rise about 30 minutes. Bake 15–18 minutes at 350°.

Decades of Recipes

Swiss Cheese Bread

Hearty and delicious—people love it!

1 loaf French or Italian
  bread
1 pound Swiss cheese, thinly
  sliced
1 cup butter, melted
2 tablespoons minced onion
1 tablespoon poppyseed
1 teaspoon seasoned salt
1 (4-ounce) can mushrooms,
  drained
1 tablespoon dry mustard
1 tablespoon lemon juice

Slice bread loaf partly through, diagonally in both directions, making little diamonds. Stuff slices of cheese in openings. Place loaf of bread on foil on cookie sheet. Mix remaining ingredients and pour mixture over bread. Seal foil tightly around loaf.

Bake at 350° for 45–60 minutes. Check several times to be sure bottom is not browning too quickly. Serves 6–8.

Brunch Basket

 Though Illinois has thousands of acres of farmland and rural communities, 80% of Illinois' residents live in metropolitan areas.

Corn Fritters

4 cups fresh corn kernels   4 tablespoons all-purpose flour
  (about 4–6 ears of corn)   1 teaspoon salt
3 eggs   Vegetable oil

With a sharp knife, scrape kernels off the cobs. Pour into a large mixing bowl. Lightly beat the eggs and add to the bowl of kernels along with flour and salt; mix lightly. Heat vegetable oil in skillet. With a soup spoon, drop batter into hot oil. Fry like pancakes, turning once, for 5–7 minutes, or until golden brown. Drain on paper towels. Serve plain or with honey or syrup. Makes 12–16 fritters, serving 6–8.

What's Cooking "Down Home"

Sweet Potato Corn Bread

1 medium (8-ounce) sweet   ½ teaspoon salt
  potato   ¼ teapoon allspice
1 cup yellow corn meal   1½ cups buttermilk
1 cup all-purpose flour   1 egg, beaten
¼ cup sugar   3 tablespoons oleo or butter
½ teaspoon baking soda

Cook sweet potato in water until tender. Drain and mash (should have ⅔ cup). Combine all dry ingredients. Add buttermilk and egg to mashed potato until blended; blend in dry ingredients. Place margarine or butter in baking pan or iron skillet until melted. Pour in batter and bake at 400° for 25 minutes.

Old-Fashioned Cooking

41

Nutmeg Coffee Bread

3 cups sifted flour
2¼ cups firmly packed
   light brown sugar
¾ cup butter
1 cup sour cream

1½ teaspoons baking soda
2 eggs
1 teaspoon nutmeg
¾ cup chopped pecans

Preheat oven to 350°. Mix flour, brown sugar, and butter together in medium bowl until mixture is crumbly. Measure out ¾ cup of the mixture and set both portions aside. Combine sour cream and baking soda in medium bowl.

Stir eggs, nutmeg, and sour cream mixture into large portion of the reserved crumb mixture. Grease 13x9x2-inch pan. Turn batter into pan. Mix pecans and remaining crumb mixture together in small bowl. Sprinkle on batter. Bake at 350° for 40–45 minutes, or until toothpick inserted in center comes out clean. Cool in pan for 10 minutes. Cut into squares. Makes 12–15 servings.

The Elsah Landing Restaurant Cookbook

Caramel Coffee Cake

1 (6-ounce) package light
   caramels (about 21)
¼ cup water
2 cups sifted flour
½ teaspoon salt

3 tablespoons sugar
⅓ cup shortening
1 egg plus milk to make ¾ cup
½ cup pecan halves

Place caramels and water in saucepan. Switch to warm heat for 15 minutes. Stir well to blend. Sift dry ingredients together. Cut in shortening. Stir in egg and milk mixture. Beat vigorously, but briefly. (Batter will be stiff.) Place pecan halves in the bottom of a greased 5-cup ring mold. Cut through batter to marble caramel. Bake in 400° oven for 25 minutes. Loosen cake around edge of pan with knife, then turn on a plate. Let cool a few minutes, then serve warm with butter. Makes 6 servings.

Favorite Recipes of Collinsville Junior Service Club

Strawberry Bread

3 cups flour, sifted
1 teaspoon baking soda
1 teaspoon salt
2 teaspoons cinnamon
2 cups sugar

4 eggs, beaten
1½ cups vegetable oil
1 cup chopped pecans
1½ pints fresh strawberries,
    sliced

Preheat oven to 350°. In a bowl combine flour, soda, salt, cinnamon, and sugar and mix well.

Mix eggs and oil and add to dry ingredients. Stir in pecans. Fold in strawberries until moistened.

Pour into two greased 9x5-inch loaf pans and bake for 50–60 minutes or until toothpick inserted in center comes out clean. Yield: 2 loaves.

One Magnificent Cookbook

Rhubarb Nut Bread

1½ cups brown sugar
⅔ cup oil
1 egg
1 cup sour milk or buttermilk
2½ cups flour

½ cup chopped nuts
1 teaspoon soda
¼ teaspoon salt
1 teaspoon vanilla
1½ cups diced rhubarb

TOPPING:
1 tablespoon butter, melted   ½ cup sugar

In a bowl, combine sugar, oil, egg, and the rest of the ingredients. Beat until well mixed. Sprinkle with topping mixture. Bake in greased 9x5-inch loaf pan or 9x13-inch baking pan at 325° for 1 hour. Cool on rack.

The French-Icarian Persimmon Tree Cookbook

Canned Holiday Bread

Gather 6 wide mouth pint canning jars, lids, and rings. Grease jars with shortening. Place lids in pan; pour boiling water over them. Don't boil, but leave in water until ready to use. (Do this when bread is about ready to come out of oven.)

⅔ cup shortening
2⅔ cups sugar
4 eggs
2 cups shredded apple
⅔ cup water
3⅓ cups flour

1½ teaspoons salt
½ teaspoon baking powder
2 teaspoons baking soda
1 teaspoon cinnamon
1 teaspoon ground cloves
⅔ cup nuts

Cream shortening and sugar. Beat in eggs, apples, and water. Sift together flour, baking powder, baking soda, salt, and spices. Add to apple mixture, and stir in nuts. Pour batter into jars, filling about ½ full. Bake at 325° for 45–53 minutes. When done, remove one jar at a time from oven. Cut off excess, wipe edges of jar clean, put on scalded lid, and screw band tight. After cooling, you can tighten band.

Variations: (1) Two cups canned pumpkin, (2) 2 cups applesauce, (3) or 1¾ cups applesauce and ¼ cup crushed pineapple.

Seasoned with Love

Bourbon-Nut Bread

You'll love this!

8 eggs, separated	½ cup bourbon
3 cups sugar	2 teaspoons vanilla
1 pound butter	2 teaspoons almond extract
3 cups sifted flour	1 cup chopped pecans

Beat egg whites until soft peaks form. Gradually add 1 cup sugar; continue beating until stiff peaks form. Set aside. Cream butter with remaining sugar. Add egg yolks one at a time, beating well after each addition. Add flour in thirds alternately with bourbon, mixing well. Stir in both extracts and nuts. Gently fold in egg whites. Pour into 3 well greased 9x5-inch pans. Bake at 350° for 1 hour or till done. This bread freezes well!

Note: I also find it helpful to use cooking parchment or waxed paper on bottom of pans.

Carol's Kitchen

Walter's Favorite Date Nut Loaf

1 pound pitted dates	1 teaspoon salt
4 eggs	1 cup flour
1 cup sugar	4 cups pecans
½ cup oil	

Lightly dust dates in small amount of flour so they will stay separated. Combine eggs, sugar, oil, salt, and flour; beat well. Add dates and pecans. Pour into greased and floured loaf pan. Bake in slow oven at 300° for over an hour. Done when medium brown and only slightly pulled from edge of pan. Turn upside down to steam out of pan as it cools for 12 minutes. Can be iced and decorated for Christmas. Makes 2 small loaf pans.

Dawdy Family Cookbook

Banana Chocolate Chip Bread

We have seen people fight over the last loaf of this bread. It is an over-the-counter item that is brought in warm and steamy, smelling like a chocolate fantasy. It freezes well and makes marvelous gifts when baked in smaller loaf pans.

1 cup sugar
1 egg
½ cup butter
1 cup mashed ripe bananas
3 tablespoons milk
2 cups sifted flour

1 teaspoon baking powder
½ teaspoon baking soda
1 cup chocolate chips
½ cup finely chopped
   pecans

Preheat oven to 350°. Cream sugar, egg and butter together in large mixer bowl. Beat until fluffy. Set aside. Combine bananas and milk in small bowl. Set aside. Sift flour, baking powder, and baking soda together in small bowl. Stir by hand into reserved creamed mixture alternately with reserved banana mixture until flour is just moistened.

Stir in chocolate chips and pecans. Grease 1 (9x5x3-inch) loaf pan. Turn batter into pan. Bake at 350° for 1 hour, or until toothpick inserted in center comes out clean. Cool in pan for 10 minutes. Remove from pan. Cool on rack. Makes 1 (9x5x3-inch) loaf.

Elsah Landing Heartland Cooking

Raised Doughnuts or Rolls

1 package dry yeast
¼ cup lukewarm water
¼ cup shortening
1 cup boiling water
½ cup sugar

1 teaspoon salt
1 cup milk
2 eggs
1 teaspoon vanilla
6 cups flour

Soften yeast in lukewarm water; set aside. Add shortening to boiling water; add sugar and salt; add milk, eggs, and vanilla. Stir in flour until mixed well. Let rise in warm place until double in bulk. Dump on floured board, knead several minutes until it doesn't stick to the board. Roll ½-inch thick, cut with doughnut cutter. Let rise until double in bulk. Fry in deep fat at 450° until brown on both sides.

For rolls, roll ½-inch thick. Spread with melted oleo. Sprinkle with sugar and cinnamon. Roll up and cut in 1-inch slices. Place in pan and let rise until double. Bake at 350° until brown.

A Collection of Recipes From St. Matthew Lutheran Church

Norma's Surprise Breakfast Rolls

¼ cup sugar
1 teaspoon cinnamon
2 cans Pillsbury Crescent Rolls

16 large marshmallows
¼ cup butter, melted
¼ cup nuts

GLAZE:
½ teaspoon vanilla
½ cup powdered sugar

2–3 teaspoons milk

Combine sugar and cinnamon. Separate crescent rolls into 16 triangles. Dip marshmallows in melted oleo and dip in sugar and cinnamon mixture. Wrap triangle around marshmallows and seal tightly. Dip in melted butter. Place buttered-side-down in deep muffin cup. Place on foil or on cookie sheet. Bake at 375° for 10–15 minutes. Remove immediately from pan and drizzle glaze over top.

Cooking with Daisy's Descendants

Raspberry Muffins

Holy Cow! Angiporto's most famous muffin!

2 eggs
1½ cups sugar
½ cup margarine, melted
1 teaspoon baking soda
1 teaspoon cinnamon
½ teaspoon allspice

½ teaspoon cloves
Pinch of salt
2 cups flour
⅓ cup milk
2 cups raspberries

Beat the eggs, sugar, and margarine until light. Add the baking soda, cinnamon, allspice, cloves, salt, flour, and milk, and mix together until just blended. Fold in the raspberries.

Fill oiled muffin pans and top with Sinful Topping. Bake in a preheated 375° oven for 20 minutes or until the muffins are cooked in the middle. Yield: 15 muffins.

SINFUL TOPPING:
2 cups brown sugar
½ cup granulated sugar
1 cup flour
1 teaspoon cinnamon
1 teaspoon allspice

2 tablespoons melted butter
2 cups chopped pecans or
   walnuts
1 tablespoon freshly grated
   lemon peel or orange or apple

Mix everything together well—this is a hands-on operation, so dig in! Put about 1 tablespoon on each muffin—any more may sink the muffin. Freeze the rest for future toppings.
Note: Fold raspberries carefully—they're so fragile and expensive! Frozen raspberries work fairly well in a pinch—but they do tend to break up when mixed into the batter, and then the batter will turn blue and your secret will be out! Two cups finely chopped rhubarb may be substituted.

Angiporto, Inc.

In June of 1898, Chicago bakeries raised the price of bread to six cents a loaf. But three weeks later, they had to lower it to five cents because the housewives refused to pay that much for a loaf of bread.

Mandarin Orange Muffins

2 cups all-purpose flour
2 tablespoons sugar
1 tablespoon baking powder
½ teaspoon salt
1 egg

½ cup milk
¼ cup salad oil
¼ cup orange juice
1 (6-ounce) can mandarin
   oranges, drained

Preheat oven to 400°. Mix all dry ingredients with a fork in large bowl. Beat egg slightly in small bowl; add milk, salad oil, and orange juice. Add egg mixture to flour all at once. Mix until flour is moistened. Crush mandarin oranges with a fork, and add to batter mixture. Divide mixture into 12 individual greased muffin tins. Bake 20–25 minutes. Muffins should be well-risen and golden brown. Serve immediately. Makes 12 muffins.

Inn-describably Delicious

Cranberry Hazelnut Muffins

Hazelnuts, golden raisins, cranberries, cinnamon, cloves, and brandy provide a rich blend of flavors in this spicy muffin recipe.

1½ cups all-purpose flour
1 teaspoon ground cinnamon
½ teaspoon baking powder
¼ teaspoon baking soda
¼ teaspoon ground cloves
1 cup fresh cranberries
⅓ cup golden raisins

⅓ cup hazelnuts
2 eggs
¾ cup packed light brown
   sugar
½ cup orange juice
⅓ cup corn oil
1 teaspoon brandy

Heat oven to 350°. In a large bowl, sift together the flour, cinnamon, baking powder, baking soda, and cloves. In a food processor, finely chop the cranberries, raisins, and hazelnuts.

In a medium bowl, beat the eggs. Stir in the brown sugar, orange juice, corn oil, and brandy. Mix in the chopped cranberries, raisins, and hazelnuts and then pour the egg mixture into the flour mixture. Stir well. Fill the greased muffin tins. Bake for 20 minutes. Makes one dozen muffins.

Muffins—104 Recipes from A to Z

Kiwi Mango Muffins

Enjoy the exotic flavors of these muffins with the surprise kiwi centers.

2 ripe kiwis	**2 cups all-purpose flour**
2 eggs	**2 teaspoons baking powder**
½ cup mango juice	**½ teaspoon salt**
1 teaspoon coconut extract	**½ cup granulated sugar**
½ cup melted butter	**¼ cup coconut**

Heat oven to 350°. Peel the kiwis and slice them into ¼-inch thick rounds. Set aside.

In a medium bowl, whisk together the eggs and mango juice. Stir in the coconut extract and melted butter. In a large bowl, sift together the flour, baking powder, salt, and sugar. Pour the liquid ingredients into the flour mixture. Mix just until the dry ingredients are moistened.

Drop one tablespoon of batter into each greased muffin tin. Place one slice of kiwi on top of the batter and layer with one more tablespoon of batter.

Sprinkle with coconut. Bake for 15–20 minutes or until a tester inserted into a muffin comes out clean. Makes one dozen muffins.

Note: Bake the muffins on the lower oven rack so that the coconut does not burn.

Muffins—104 Recipes from A to Z

Maple Bran Muffins

1 cup sour cream	**1 teaspoon soda**
1 cup maple syrup	**1 cup bran flakes**
2 eggs	**⅓ cup raisins**
1 cup flour	**⅓ cup chopped nuts**

Combine sour cream, maple syrup and eggs. Sift flour and soda; add bran flakes, raisins, and nuts. Stir in liquid ingredients. Spoon into greased muffin tins. Bake at 400° for 20 minutes. Makes 18 muffins.

Soupçon I

Sweet Potato Muffins

2 eggs
1¼ cups granulated sugar
½ cup margarine, melted
1¼ cups cooked and mashed
  sweet potatoes
1¼ cups flour
1 teaspoon baking powder

Pinch of salt
1 teaspoon cinnamon
1 teaspoon allspice
Pinch of nutmeg
¾ cup milk
1 cup raisins
¼ cup pecans

Beat the eggs, sugar, margarine, and sweet potatoes until light and fluffy. Add the flour, baking powder, salt, cinnamon, allspice, nutmeg, and milk and mix until well blended. Fold in the raisins and pecans.

Fill oiled muffin pans to the top and sprinkle cinnamon sugar on the top of the muffins if you wish. Bake in a preheated 375° oven for 20 minutes or until the center of the muffins are done. Yield: 12 large muffins.

Angiporto, Inc.

Blueberry Orange Muffins

3 eggs
2 cups granulated sugar
½ cup margarine, melted
4 tablespoons grated orange
  (about 1 orange's rind)
4 cups flour

2 teaspoon baking powder
½ teaspoon baking soda
1 teaspoon salt
1¼ cups orange juice
1 pint blueberries

Beat eggs, sugar, and margarine along with ⅔ of the orange rind until light and fluffy. Add the flour, baking powder, baking soda, and salt, along with the orange juice, and mix until just blended. Fold in the blueberries.

Fill oiled muffin cups to the top and sprinkle the tops of the muffins with the remaining orange peel mixed with a little sugar. Bake in a preheated 400° oven for 20 minutes or until cooked in the center. Yield: 15 muffins.

Note: Try substituting cranberries if fresh blueberries are not available.

Angiporto, Inc.

Pumpkin Creme Muffins

BATTER:

2 eggs
1 cup sugar
½ cup chopped nuts
1¼ cups flour
2 teaspoons cinnamon

¾ cup oil
1 cup canned pumpkin
1 teaspoon baking soda
½ teaspoon salt

FILLING:

1 (8-ounce) package cream
   cheese

1 egg
⅓ cup sugar

STREUSEL TOPPING:

¼ cup sugar
¼ teaspoon cinnamon

3 tablespoons flour
2 tablespoons butter

Mix batter ingredients together and set aside. Blend filling ingredients until smooth and set aside. Combine streusel ingredients and set aside. Pour pumpkin batter into greased or lined muffin tins. Fill ⅔ full. Spoon heaping teaspoon creme mixture in center. Sprinkle with 1 teaspoon streusel topping. Bake at 350° for 15–18 minutes. Makes 18 muffins.

Carol's Kitchen

Corn Festival Biscuits

¾ stick butter or margarine
1½ cups Bisquick Biscuit Mix
   (no cholesterol here)

1 (8½-ounce) can cream-style
   corn

Melt the butter or margarine in a cookie sheet with sides. Stir the corn and biscuit mix together. Drop by teaspoons into the melted shortening; turn to coat the other side. Bake at 400° for 20 minutes or until nicely browned. Makes 8–10.

The French-Icarian Persimmon Tree Cookbook

David Ayres Pancakes

2 eggs, slightly beaten
½ cup flour
½ cup milk
Pinch of nutmeg
4 tablespoons butter

2 tablespoons confectioners'
   sugar
Juice of ½ lemon
Marmalade

Preheat oven to 425°. In a mixing bowl, combine eggs and beat lightly, then add flour, milk, nutmeg and beat lightly again, stopping while batter is still a little lumpy. In a 12-inch skillet with heat-proof handle, heat butter. When very hot, pour in batter and place in oven for 15–20 minutes or until golden brown. Remove from oven, sprinkle sugar over and return it very briefly to oven. Take out, sprinkle lemon juice, spread with marmalade. (Puffs high.) Be sure to use hot pads on handle of skillet for it will be very hot. Serves 2.

A Cause for Applause

Vegetable Pancakes

1 cup flour
3 tablespoons wheat germ
2 teaspoons baking powder
1 teaspoon sugar
½ teaspoon salt
1½ cups half-and-half

2 large eggs
2 tablespoons oil
1 (10-ounce) package frozen
   corn, thawed
1 cup sliced green onion tops

Mix flour, wheat germ, baking powder, sugar, and salt in a large bowl. Blend half-and-half, eggs, oil, and ½ cup corn in processor or blender and purée. Add dry ingredients; mix well. Pour into a bowl and add onion tops and rest of corn. Fry by ¼-cup ladles over medium heat on both sides until browned. Serve with syrup and fried ham slices. Yield: 8 servings.

An Apple From The Teacher

High Rise Apple Pancake

1 medium apple
1 teaspoon lemon juice
2 tablespoons sugar
1 teaspoon cinnamon
½ cup plus 2 tablespoons
  all-purpose flour

½ cup plus 2 tablespoons
  milk
3 eggs or one carton egg
  substitute
5 tablespoons butter
Powdered sugar

Preheat oven to 425°. Peel and slice apple into ¼-inch slices and place in a small mixing bowl. Toss with lemon juice, sugar, and cinnamon. In large mixing bowl, combine flour and milk and mix until just incorporated. Add eggs and mix. Batter should be slightly lumpy.

In skillet, heat butter until foamy. Remove from heat and quickly add batter. Arrange apples in a pinwheel design and place in oven. Bake for 25 minutes or until pancake is puffed up and golden brown. Sprinkle with powdered sugar and serve with warm apple sauce, syrup or jam. Yield: 2 generous servings.

Holy Cow!

Crispy Yeast Waffles

2⅔ cups all-purpose flour
1 package active dry yeast
2 tablespoons sugar
1 teaspoon salt

1¾ cups milk
¼ cup water
¼ cup butter or margarine
3 eggs

In large mixer bowl, combine flour, yeast, sugar, and salt; mix well. In saucepan, heat milk, water, and butter until very warm (120°–130°); butter does not need to melt. Add to flour mixture. Add eggs. Blend at low speed until moistened; beat 1 minute at medium speed. Cover bowl with plastic wrap and foil; refrigerate several hours or overnight.

Stir down batter. Bake on waffle iron on medium heat. Serve hot with butter and toppings.

Home Cookin' is a Family Affair

The restored mid-1800s settlement of Nauvoo, once the largest city in Illinois, was the home of Mormon leader Joseph Smith.

Overnight Caramel Toast

1 cup brown sugar
½ cup butter
2 tablespoons white corn
  syrup
6 eggs, beaten

1½ cups milk
1 teaspoon vanilla
¼ teaspoon salt
12 slices bread

In saucepan, combine brown sugar, butter, and corn syrup. Heat slowly and stir constantly as it cooks, until thickened. Spread evenly in 9x13-inch pan. Mix eggs, milk, vanilla, and salt well. Dip 6 slices of bread and place over caramel mixture. Dip 6 more and place over the first 6. Pour remaining batter evenly over bread. Cover and chill 8 hours or overnight. Bake at 350° for 35–40 minutes, or until evenly browned. Makes 4 servings.

Inn-describably Delicious

Overnight Orange French Toast

ORANGE SAUCE:
1 cup brown sugar
½ cup orange juice

2 teaspoons grated orange peel

Combine sauce ingredients in saucepan. Bring to boil and simmer until thickened, about 5 minutes, stirring frequently. Set aside.

8 (¾-inch-thick) slices
  French bread
4 eggs
1 cup milk
2 tablespoons orange juice

½ teaspoon vanilla
½ teaspoon salt
Butter
Powdered sugar

Place bread in a 13x9-inch pan. Combine eggs, milk, orange juice, vanilla, and salt. Beat well. Pour over French bread, turning to coat evenly. Cover and refrigerate overnight. Melt butter on griddle. Cook bread until brown, turn and brown other side, 4 slices at a time. Sprinkle with powdered sugar. Serve hot with Orange Sauce (warm).

Our Best Home Cooking

Crustless Quiche

5 eggs, beaten
12 ounces frozen hash brown
 potatoes, unthawed
1 chopped onion
½ cup cottage cheese
1 cup grated cheese

¼ teaspoon salt
⅛ teaspoon pepper
Dash of hot pepper sauce
Paprika to taste
6–8 slices bacon, cooked
 and crumbled

Combine all ingredients except paprika and bacon. Pour into 9 or 10-inch pie plate. Sprinkle with paprika. Bake at 350° for 25 minutes, until set. Sprinkle with bacon. Bake 5 minutes more. Let stand 5 minutes before serving. This recipe can be made the night before, and refrigerated. Makes 5–6 servings.

Inn-describably Delicious

Breakfast Pizza

12 ounces pork sausage
1 (8-count) package
 refrigerator crescent rolls
2 hash brown potato patties,
 thawed

4 eggs, beaten
2 cups shredded Cheddar
 cheese

Cook sausage in skillet until brown and crumbly; drain. Pat roll dough into lightly greased pizza pan, sealing rolls together. Sprinkle crumbled potato patties and sausage over dough. Pour eggs over top. Sprinkle with cheese. Bake at 350° for 20 minutes. Cut into wedges. May chill overnight before baking. Yields 6 servings.

River Valley Recipes

Cheese and Onion Bake

Good side dish with roasts. Also good for breakfast buffet.

2 tablespoons butter	½–¾ cup grated Swiss
2 large onions, sliced	cheese
1 (10½-ounce) can cream	Salt and pepper
of chicken soup	6 slices French bread, buttered
1 soup can milk	(preferably sourdough)

Slowly cook onions in butter until limp and golden, about 20 minutes. Place in a 2-quart casserole. Combine soup, milk, cheese, salt, and pepper. Heat. Pour ½ the mixture over the onions. Place 6 slices of bread on top (if bread is too fresh, toast slightly). Pour remaining soup mixture over bread. May be made day ahead. Bake at 350° for 1½ hours. Makes 8 servings.

Soupçon I

Cranberry Breakfast Pie

2 cups fresh cranberries	1 cup white sugar
½ cup chopped walnuts	1 teaspoon almond extract
½ cup brown sugar	1 cup flour
1 stick melted butter or	2 beaten eggs
margarine	

Grease large pie pan or 9x9-inch cake pan. Put washed cranberries in pan and sprinkle with walnuts and brown sugar. Combine butter, white sugar, almond extract, flour, and eggs, and pour over contents in pan. Bake at 350° for 45 minutes. Can be served with vanilla yogurt as a topping. Makes 8 servings.

Inn-describably Delicious

Bald Knob Cross near Alto Pass is the largest Christian Monument in all of North America. This gigantic cross, covered with white porcelain, is 111 feet tall and sits on one of the highest points in Illinois.

Three-Tiered Omelet with Wine Sauce

12 eggs, separated
1 teaspoon salt
1 teaspoon seasoned salt
Freshly-ground pepper
3 tablespoons parsley, minced

3 shallots, finely-chopped
6 tablespoons flour
4½ tablespoons white wine
   or dry vermouth

SAUCE:
¼ cup butter, melted
¼ cup flour
1 cup whipping cream
2 chicken bouillon cubes
2 teaspoons chopped chives
1 teaspoon Worcestershire
   sauce

½ cup dry white wine
1 teaspoon fresh lemon juice
1 tablespoon fresh dill or 1
   teaspoon dill weed
Dash salt

Beat egg yolks until light. Add both salts, pepper, parsley, shallots, and flour. Beat until thoroughly blended. Beat egg whites together with wine until stiff but not dry. Carefully fold whites into yolk mixture. Grease three 8-inch pie plates. Divide egg mixture between them. Bake at 350° for 15 minutes or until set.

For sauce, melt butter; stir in flour. Gradually add cream. Add bouillon cubes, chives, and Worcestershire. Cook, stirring constantly, until thickened. Stir in remaining ingredients. Simmer 10 minutes. Stir occasionally. Stack each omelet layer with sauce between; pour sauce over top. Cut in wedges. Makes 6 servings.

Variations: Use other sauces. Sprinkle grated cheese or sautéed mushrooms between layers.

Soupçon I

Sausage-Wrapped Eggs

4 hard-boiled eggs, shelled   **1 pound bulk pork sausage**

Preheat oven to 400°. Wrap each egg, using wet hands, in ¼ pound of the sausage to form a ball. Place in shallow baking dish. Bake at 400° for 30–40 minutes, or until browned. Drain. Serve with Cream Curry Sauce. Makes 4 servings.

CREAM CURRY SAUCE:
2 teaspoons Sun Brand Madras   **2 cups medium white sauce**
  Curry Powder, or to taste

Combine curry powder with white sauce in small saucepan. Cook over low heat until warm. Serve warm. Makes 2 cups sauce.

The Elsah Landing Restaurant Cookbook

Mexican Cheese Grits

Good with any meal, including breakfast. Good with roast gravy or by itself.

1 cup quick-cooking grits   **1 cup sour cream**
4 cups water   **2 cups Monterey Jack cheese**
1 teaspoon salt   **1 cup Cheddar cheese**
4–6 jalapeno peppers,
  chopped and seeded

Preheat oven to 350°. In a saucepan, bring water and salt to boiling. Slowly add grits, stirring constantly. Cook and stir until boiling. Reduce heat; cook and stir for 5–6 minutes or until water is absorbed and mixture is thick. (An alternate method is to cook grits in microwave following package directions).

Spray a 9x13-inch baking pan with non-stick vegetable spray. Layer half of the grits into pan. On top of grits, place 2 or 3 chopped peppers, then 1 layer of sour cream, then ½ of Monterey Jack cheese. Repeat the layers and top with Cheddar cheese. Bake 45 minutes. Serves 8–10.

Still Gathering

Violet Jelly

1 quart purple violet flowers,
   firmly packed
1 box fruit pectin

4 cups sugar
1 lemon, juiced

Wash and pack violets in quart jar. Pour enough boiling water to fill jar and cover violets. Place in refrigerator overnight. Pour off liquid to make 2 cups and discard violets. Add lemon juice and fruit pectin. Bring to a boil. Add 4 cups sugar; stir. Bring to a boil for 1 minute only. Skim, if necessary, and pour into 8 small baby food jars. Seal with melted parafin. Yield: 8 jars.

An Apple From The Teacher

Fried Apples

4 tablespoons butter
4–6 sliced (unpeeled)
   Jonathan apples

2 tablespoons sugar
2 tablespoons brown sugar
Dash of salt

Melt butter in heavy skillet; stir in sliced apples sprinkled with sugars and salt. Cook over medium heat about 10 minutes, stirring and turning from time to time. Serve warm.

Dawdy Family Cookbook

Winter Morning Peaches

2 (16-ounce) cans sliced
   peaches
2 tablespoons margarine or
   butter

1/3 cup brown sugar
1/2 teaspoon cinnamon
2 tablespoons cornstarch
1/4 cup cold water

In saucepan over medium heat, heat peaches, margarine, brown sugar, and cinnamon. Stir cornstarch into cold water and add to peaches. Cook and stir until thickened. Cool slightly and spoon into individual dishes. Serve warm. Makes 6–8 servings.

Inn-describably Delicious

Soups

Riverboat on the Fox River. St. Charles.

Hamburger Vegetable Soup

1–2 pounds lean ground chuck	Beef bouillon or beef broth
1 onion, chopped	Salt and pepper
½ cup water	1–2 cups chopped cabbage
1 quart tomatoes with juice	1 cup sliced celery
1 quart green beans with juice	3–4 carrots, sliced
	3–4 potatoes, diced
1 package frozen corn (or canned)	Watkins Soup and Vegetable Seasoning

Brown ground chuck with onion and water. Add tomatoes, green beans, and corn. Stir in bouillon or canned beef broth; season with salt and pepper. Cover and bring to boil while preparing vegetables.

Add cabbage, celery, carrots, and potatoes. Bring to boil again and reduce heat to simmer. May add water at this stage if needed. Sprinkle top of soup generously with Watkins Soup and Vegetable Seasoning; stir. Simmer an hour or longer. Soup is even better the next day and it freezes well.

This recipe is for a 6-quart kettle; adjust amounts for larger or smaller soup kettle.

Dawdy Family Cookbook

White Bean Vegetable Soup

1 pound Great Northern beans	2 cups peeled potatoes, diced
10 cups water	2 carrots, peeled and diced
4 cups chicken stock or canned broth	1 small head green cabbage, shredded
2 pounds smoked ham hocks	1 cup frozen lima beans, thawed
1 onion, chopped	

Soak beans overnight and drain. In large pot, put beans, water, chicken stock, and ham hocks. Cook until beans are tender, about 1½ hours. Add onion, potatoes, carrots, cabbage, and lima beans. Simmer 30 minutes longer, or until potatoes are done. Remove ham hocks and cut off meat; return meat to soup and eat.

College Avenue Presbyterian Church Cookbook

White Bean Chili

1 pound dried Great Northern
  white beans
2 pounds ground turkey
1 tablespoon olive oil
2 medium onions, chopped
4 cloves garlic, minced
2 (4-ounce) cans chopped
  mild green chilies
2 teaspoons ground cumin
1½ teaspoons dried
  oregano, crumbled

¼ teaspoon ground cloves
¼ teapoon cayenne pepper
6 cups chicken stock or
  canned broth
3 cups grated Monterey Jack
  cheese
Salt and pepper to taste
Sour cream to garnish
Salsa to garnish
Chopped fresh cilantro to
  garnish

Rinse beans and sort out any bad ones. Place beans in large heavy pot. Add enough cold water to cover by at least 3 inches and soak overnight. Cook turkey in a large heavy saucepan until cooked through; set aside. Drain beans.

Heat oil in same pot used for beans over medium-high heat. Add onions and sauté until translucent, about 10 minutes. Stir in garlic, then chilies, cumin, oregano, ground cloves, and cayenne pepper; sauté for 2 minutes. Add beans and stock and bring to boil. Reduce heat and simmer until beans are very tender, stirring occasionally, for about 2 hours.

Add turkey and 1 cup grated cheese and stir until cheese melts. Season to taste with salt and pepper. Ladle chili into bowls. Serve with remaining cheese, sour cream, salsa, and cilantro. Yield: 8 servings.

Holy Cow!

Duchess Potato Soup

6 cups fresh chicken stock,
  or 1¼ tablespoons chicken
  stock base in 6 cups water
2 medium potatoes, peeled
  and cut in large chunks
2 medium carrots, peeled and
  cut in large chunks
1 small onion, cut in large
  chunks

1 teaspoon salt
⅜ teaspoon chervil
⅜ teaspoon pepper
¼ teaspoon onion salt
1 cup Carnation evaporated
  milk
¼ cup Cheddar cheese spread
Fresh parsley sprigs

Combine potatoes, carrots, and onion with chicken stock in large pot. Cover and cook over medium heat for 30 minutes, or until vegetables are tender. Add more water if soup becomes too thick. Blend in small batches in blender.

Add salt, chervil, pepper, and onion salt. Taste and add more seasonings if desired. Add milk and cheese. Add more milk if needed to get desired consistency. Heat, but do not boil. Garnish each serving with a parsley sprig. Makes 8 servings.

The Elsah Landing Restaurant Cookbook

Dilled Tomato Soup

2 medium onions, chopped
1 clove garlic, chopped
2 tablespoons margarine
4 large fresh tomatoes,
  peeled and cubed
½ cup water

1 chicken bouillon cube
2½ teaspoons fresh dill
  or ¾ teaspoon dry dill
¼ teaspoon salt
⅛ teaspoon pepper
½ cup mayonnaise

In a 2-quart saucepan over medium heat, sauté onions and garlic in margarine for 3 minutes. Add the next 6 ingredients; cover and simmer for 10 minutes. Remove from heat and cool. Blend half in blender. Mix the second half with mayonnaise. Combine both mixtures. Cover and chill overnight. Soup is good served hot or cold. Makes 5 cups. Garnish with additional dill.

Still Gathering

Elegant Mushroom Soup

This soup is elegant enough to serve to dinner guests. Top the servings with a dollop of Crème Fraîche or sour cream and chopped parsley or green onion tops.

1 pound mushrooms, coarsely
   chopped
4 green onions with tops,
   coarsely chopped
½ cup butter
⅓ cup flour
¼ teaspoon dry mustard

2 teaspoons salt
Cayenne pepper to taste
¼ teaspoon black pepper
2 cups each chicken broth
   and whipping cream or
   half-and-half
⅓ cup sherry (optional)

Sauté the mushrooms and green onions in the butter in a saucepan for 5 minutes. Stir in the flour, dry mustard, salt, cayenne pepper, and black pepper. Stir in the chicken broth and cream gradually. Simmer until thickened and smooth, stirring constantly. Add the sherry. Serves 4.

Generations

Mushroom Wild Rice Soup

½ cup wild rice
2 tablespoons margarine
1 cup minced leek, white
   part only
⅓ cup celery, minced

1 teaspoon gingeroot, minced
1 cup mushrooms, diced
4 cups chicken broth
Salt to taste
Pepper to taste

Cook rice and drain. Heat margarine in saucepan. Add leek, celery, and gingeroot. Cook about 5 minutes on medium heat until soft. Add mushrooms; cook until they develop a juice. Add chicken broth, bring to boil, lower heat, and let simmer while covered 10 minutes. Add seasonings. Can be prepared day before. Add wild rice and seasonings immediately before serving. Makes 4–6 servings.

Tradition in the Kitchen 2

 The Chicago Board of Trade, where traders buy and sell contracts for corn, soybeans, and other commodities, is the largest commodities exchange in the world.

Cream of Broccoli-Leek Soup

Fresh broccoli florets make an attractive garnish.

1½ pounds broccoli, chopped
¾ pound leeks, sliced
½ cup butter
2 medium potatoes, peeled
  and cubed

10 cups chicken stock
1 cup whipping cream
½ teaspoon salt
¼ teaspoon white pepper

Reserve broccoli florets. In a large soup pot, sauté the broccoli stems and leeks in butter for 3–5 minutes. Add the broccoli florets and sauté the mixture for 3–5 minutes more. Add potatoes and chicken stock. Bring liquid to a boil and cook 20 minutes, or until vegetables are tender.

Purée in blender or food processor until smooth. Transfer to large saucepan; stir in cream, salt and pepper. Heat just to boiling point and serve in heated bowls.

Soup may be made ahead and reheated. Freezes well before addition of the cream. Serves 8–10.

Brunch Basket

Quick Broccoli Soup

1 (10-ounce) package broccoli,
  chopped
1 can cream of mushroom soup
  (undiluted)
1½ cups milk

2 tablespoons butter or
  margarine
⅛ teaspoon pepper
4 ounces shredded cheese

Cook broccoli in large saucepan, omitting salt; drain well. Stir in remaining ingredients. Cook over medium heat, stirring constantly until thoroughly heated.

Our Favorite Recipes

Broccoli Cheddar Soup

2 tablespoons butter
¾ cup onion, chopped
1 tablespoon chicken stock
  base with 4¼ cups water
  or (4¼ cups homemade
  chicken stock)
1 ounce American cheese,
  cubed
3¼ ounces Cheddar cheese

6 ounces fresh or frozen
  chopped broccoli
3½ tablespoons cornstarch
3 tablespoons cold water
¾ cup evaporated milk or
  ¾ cup light cream
Fresh broccoli flowerette or
  parsley sprig

Melt butter in small heavy saucepan. Add onion and sauté until translucent. Combine chicken stock base and water in large saucepan. Bring to simmer.

Add American cheese, Cheddar cheese, and sautéed onions. Stir until smooth. Add broccoli. Simmer until tender (about 10 minutes).

Mix cornstarch with cold water in small bowl. Add to soup. Simmer until smooth and creamy. Add evaporated milk. Reheat, but do not boil.

Garnish each serving with broccoli flowerette or fresh parsley sprig. Makes 8 servings.

Elsah Landing Heartland Cooking

Sweet and Sour Cabbage Soup

6 cups shredded and diced
  cabbage
1 onion, coarsely chopped
5 cups beef broth
5 cups chicken broth
2–3 cups cooked chopped meat*
1 teaspoon minced garlic
¼ teaspoon dried thyme
¼ teaspoon ground allspice

½ teaspoon ground cayenne
  (or to taste)
Salt and pepper to taste
2 cups chopped tomatoes
¼ cup tomato paste
¼ cup brown sugar
¼ cup cider vinegar
⅛ cup lemon juice

Simmer cabbage and onion in the broth until tender, about ½ hour. Add the meat, spices, tomatoes, and tomato paste, and simmer until reduced slightly and the flavors are blended. Add the brown sugar, vinegar, and lemon juice and reheat.

This soup improves with 24 hours chilling and reheating. While the recipe makes a lot of hearty soup, it freezes well. Serves 10.

*Smoked sausage, ham, beef, pork roast, pot roast—any kind of cooked meat will work in this recipe.

More to Love...from The Mansion of Golconda

Free Cabbage Soup

2 cups tomato juice
4 cups coarsely chopped
  cabbage
1 (4-ounce) can mushrooms
  drained
2 tablespoons vinegar
1 teaspoon chili powder

2 teaspoons artificial
  sweetener or 1 package
  Sweet and Low
2 cups water
2 ribs celery, diced
2 chicken bouillon cubes
2 tablespoons onion flakes

Put all above ingredients in pot and bring to boil. Reduce heat and simmer until cabbage is done.

Cookbook 25 Years

Hot and Sour Soup

¼ pound boneless, lean pork, cut in match stick pieces

1 tablespoon dry sherry or vermouth

4 cups chicken broth or Chinese pork broth

½ pound chicken breasts, skinned, boned, and cut in match stick pieces

4 medium dried Chinese mushrooms, soaked in warm water for 30 minutes, squeezed dry and cut in match stick pieces

½ cup sliced bamboo shoots, cut in match stick pieces

¼ pound firm bean curd (tofu), drained, cut in ½-inch cubes

2 tablespoons white wine vinegar

1 tablespoon soy sauce

2 tablespoons cornstarch

¼ cup water

¾ teaspoon white pepper

1 teaspoon sesame oil (preferred, but you may substitute vegetable oil)

1 egg, lightly beaten

2 whole green onions, sliced

Salt

Combine pork and sherry and marinate for 10 minutes. Heat broth to boiling point; add pork, chicken, mushrooms, and bamboo shoots. Reduce heat, cover, and simmer for 5 minutes (stir occasionally). Add bean curd, vinegar, and soy sauce; heat, uncovered, for 1 minute.

Blend cornstarch and water and add to soup. Cook, stirring, until slightly thickened. Turn off heat. Add pepper and oil. Stirring continuously, slowly pour egg into soup. Garnish with green onions and add salt to taste.

Note: It is important to cut the mushrooms, pork, chicken, and bamboo shoots the same size (and as small as match sticks). This process takes much longer than it takes to cook the soup; it may be done ahead of time with the ingredients stored in the refrigerator. Meats are easier to slice if they are partially frozen. Makes 4–6 servings.

First There Must Be Food

Illinois is French for Illini, an Algonquin word meaning "men" or "Warriors."

Polish Fresh Mushroom Soup

½ pound fresh mushrooms
3 tablespoons butter
¼ teaspoon caraway seeds
½ teaspoon paprika
1 tablespoon flour

4 cups chicken broth
1 egg yolk
1 cup sour cream
2 tablespoons chopped fresh dill

Slice mushrooms. Sauté in butter with caraway and paprika for 1 minute. Sprinkle with flour. Blend well. Add the chicken broth a little at a time. Simmer covered 30 minutes. Meanwhile, whip egg yolk with fork until creamy. Add sour cream and dill. Mix well. Pour hot soup into this mixture. Whisk it to mix thoroughly. Serve immediately. Makes 6 servings.

Soupçon II

Cream of Turnip Soup

6 cups quartered turnips
1 teaspoon sugar
1 teaspoon salt
3 cups water
2 tablespoons butter

1 tablespoon chicken stock
   base
2 tablespoons cream of wheat
2 cups evaporated milk
Buttered croutons

Peel and quarter turnips. Combine turnips, sugar, salt, and water in medium saucepan. Cover and simmer until tender—about 15 minutes. Add butter. Pour into blender jar. Purée. Return to saucepan. Add chicken stock base and cream of wheat. Stir. Simmer, stirring for 5 minutes until mixture is thickened. Add milk. Heat but do not boil. Taste for seasoning.

Garnish each serving with buttered croutons. Makes 6–8 servings.

Elsah Landing Heartland Cooking

 The Sears Tower in Chicago is the world's tallest building. At 1454 feet, it is 110 stories high.

Asparagus Soup

One of the simplest, best soups you'll ever make.

2 tablespoons butter
1 (15-ounce) can drained
  asparagus tips—reserve
  juice; or 1 pound fresh
  asparagus tips; or 1
  (10-ounce) package frozen
  asparagus pieces, thawed and
  drained—reserve juice

1 tablespoon butter
1 teaspoon curry powder
1 (10¾-ounce) can cream
  of asparagus soup
1 cup milk
Reserved asparagus juice
2 tablespoons cheap cocktail
  sherry

In saucepan melt 2 tablespoons butter. Sauté asparagus in butter; remove and set aside. In same pan, add and melt 1 tablespoon butter, add curry powder. Stir and bubble 3–4 minutes. Add cream of asparagus soup, milk, reserved asparagus juice and sherry and stir. Add the sautéed asparagus. Correct seasoning—it may need a little salt. Heat gently through. Serve with dusting of paprika on top.

The Lucy Miele 6-5-4 Cookbook

Low Cholesterol Corn Chowder

1½ teaspoons canola oil
2 large onions, chopped
2 ribs celery, chopped
1 red bell pepper, cored,
  seeded, and diced
2 cloves garlic, minced
½ teaspoon ground cumin
3½ cups defatted reduced
  sodium chicken stock

1 tablespoon fresh thyme or
  1 teaspoon dried thyme
1 bay leaf
2 cups frozen corn kernels
1 large potato, diced
2 tablespoons cornstarch
1 (12-ounce) can evaporated
  skim milk
Salt and pepper to taste
Pinch of cayenne pepper

In large heavy saucepan, heat oil over low heat. Add onions and cook for 5 minutes. Add celery, red pepper, garlic, and cumin; cook, stirring for 3 minutes more. Add chicken stock, thyme, and bay leaf and bring to a boil. Reduce heat to low and simmer uncovered for 10 minutes. Add corn and potatoes, return to a simmer and cook till vegetables are tender, about 8 minutes.

Place cornstarch in small bowl, slowly add evaporated milk, and stir until smooth. Stir milk into soup, stirring until smooth. Return soup to a simmer; cook, stirring until thickened, about 2 minutes. Remove bay leaf. Season with salt and pepper and pinch of cayenne.

Cookin' With Friends

Jack-O-Lantern Soup

2 cups unseasoned pumpkin	⅛ teaspoon pepper
3 cups chicken broth	½ teaspoon grated nutmeg
½ cup chopped onion	⅛ teaspoon ground ginger
½ cup chopped celery	⅛ teaspoon cinnamon
1 apple, peeled, chopped	3 tablespoons honey
2 tablespoons butter	Salt and pepper
½ cup light rum	1 cup heavy cream
1 teaspoon salt	2 or 3 cups milk

In a large saucepan over medium heat, bring pumpkin, broth, onion, celery, and apple to a boil. Cover, reduce heat, and simmer 20 minutes. Purée in a blender or a food processor, 2 cups at a time, or press through a sieve.

Return to saucepan and stir in butter and rum. Simmer, uncovered, 1–2 minutes, stirring constantly. Stir in seasonings and honey. Add cream and enough milk to make 8 cups of soup. Add salt and pepper to taste. Heat, but do not let boil.

To serve: Ladle into soup bowls.

To make ahead: Complete through addition of seasonings. Add cream and milk just before serving. Serves 6–8.

Family Celebrations Cookbook

Red Pepper Soup

This soup is absolutely gorgeous!!! It is not a 'hot' soup since it has sweet peppers.

4 red bell peppers, chopped	¼ teaspoon cayenne pepper
1 large onion, chopped	3 cups chicken broth
2 tablespoons margarine	½ teaspoon lemon juice
¼ teaspoon ground cumin	

Sauté the peppers and onions in the margarine until they are soft. Add the cumin and cayenne with the chicken broth and simmer until the vegetables are very soft.

Purée the solids and then run them through a strainer to eliminate the pepper skins. Return it all to the soup pot and add the lemon juice. Yield: 6 cups.

Angiporto, Inc.

Grandma Smith's Clam Chowder

We have been told by a customer, who claims to be an absolute authority on clam chowder, to be sure not to change even a grain of pepper in the recipe.

2½–3 slices bacon, diced
1 cup diced celery
3 tablespoons diced onion
3 cups water
3 medium potatoes, peeled and diced
1¾ teaspoons Worcestershire sauce
1 teaspoon salt

Pinch pepper
2 (6½-ounce) cans minced clams, undrained
¼ cup butter
6 tablespoons flour
½ cup Carnation evaporated milk and ½ cup water, or 1 cup milk
Fresh parsley sprigs

Cook bacon in skillet until crisp. Remove bacon, drain on paper towels and set aside. Reserve drippings. Sauté celery and onion in reserved drippings over low heat for 5–10 minutes, or until vegetables are translucent. Drain and set aside.

Combine potatoes, Worcestershire sauce, salt and pepper with water in medium pot. Add clams and reserved bacon and vegetables. Cover and simmer for 20–30 minutes, or until potatoes are tender.

Melt butter in heavy skillet. Blend in flour and stir over low heat for 5–6 minutes. Do not brown. Add milk slowly, stirring until mixture is smooth and thick. Add gradually to clam-vegetable mixture. Heat, but do not boil. Garnish each serving with a parsley sprig. Makes 6 servings.

The Elsah Landing Restaurant Cookbook

Crab Bisque

3 tablespoons butter
¼ cup flour
1 teaspoon salt
⅛ teaspoon pepper
3 cups milk

1 cup chicken bouillon
1 (6½-ounce) can crabmeat
1 onion, sliced
1 sprig of parsley
½ cup milk

Melt butter in saucepan. Stir in flour, salt and pepper. Add milk and bouillon. Cook until thickened, stirring constantly. Add crabmeat, onion, and parsley. Simmer, covered, for 10 minutes. Add milk. Yields 4 servings.

Approx. Per Serving: Cal 306; Prot 17.0gr; T Fat 17.4gr; Chol 102.7mg; Carbo 20.7gr; Sod 1439.2mg; Potas 434.6mg.

River Valley Recipes

Head-For-The-Border Chicken Soup

3 whole chicken breasts
1 tablespoon canola oil
2 cups onion, chopped
1 cup green pepper, chopped
2 large cloves garlic, minced
2 (14½-ounce) cans Mexican
 or chili style tomatoes
2 (15-ounce) cans pinto
 beans, undrained
¾ cup mild El Paso Chunky
 Style Salsa

1 tablespoon lemon juice
1 teaspoon chili powder
1 teaspoon ground cumin
1 teaspoon salt
1 teaspoon sugar
2 (15-ounce) cans chicken
 broth
2 tablespoons cold water
 (optional)
1 tablespoon cornstarch
 (optional)

Skin, bone and cut in 1-inch chunks the chicken breasts. Heat canola oil in heavy pot. Add chicken to pot, along with chopped onion, pepper, and garlic. Sprinkle with a little salt to draw out the juices. Sauté, stirring occasionally with a wooden spoon, until chicken turns white. Add next 9 ingredients, cover and simmer for 20 minutes. If you like your soup a bit thicker, whisk together 2 tablespoons cold water and 1 tablespoon cornstarch and add to soup mixture.

10 servings; 3g fat; 43mg cholesterol; 297 calories

The Lucy Miele Too Good To Be Low-Fat Cookbook

Chicken Curry Soup

1 chicken, cut up
6 peppercorns
2 ribs celery
1 medium onion, peeled
4 cups water
1 medium onion, finely diced
1 cup finely diced carrots
¼ cup butter

2 teaspoons curry powder
2 tablespoons cornstarch
¼ cup water
2 teaspoons salt
¼ teaspoon sugar
1 cup light cream (half-and-half)
Apple slices

Combine the chicken, peppercorns, celery, and onion with water in a large saucepan. Cover and simmer for 1 hour, or until chicken and vegetables are tender. Cool. Remove the chicken from skin and bones, cut into bite-size pieces and set aside. Discard skin and bones. Remove and strain liquid for stock.

Sauté diced onion and carrots in butter in medium saucepan over low heat for 5 minutes, or until onion is golden but not brown. Add the curry powder and sauté for an additional 10 minutes. Add reserved stock, bring to a simmer and cook over medium heat for 5 minutes.

Mix the cornstarch with the ¼ cup of water and stir this into the simmering stock. Add the salt, sugar, and reserved chicken. Add the cream, heat through, but do not boil. Adjust seasoning to taste. Garnish each serving with an apple slice. Yield: 4–6 servings.

From Elsah's Landing Restaurant, 18 La Salle Street, Elsah.

Best Recipes of Illinois Inns and Restaurants

Salads

Rock formations at Starved Rock State Park. Utica.

Cucumbers in Sour Cream

1 cucumber, peeled and
  sliced paper thin
4 thin slices onion
1 teaspoon salt

3 tablespoons sugar
3 tablespoons vinegar
Pepper
2 tablespoons sour cream

Mix together the sliced cucumber, onion, and salt. Mix with your hand to coat cucumber completely. Place in refrigerator and let stand at least ½ hour or longer.

Pour off the liquid, squeezing the pickles in your hand. Add the sugar, vinegar, and pepper. Mix thoroughly and taste. If necessary, add a little more sugar and vinegar. Stir in sour cream and serve. You may also add a bit of dill weed, if desired.

Our Best Home Cooking

Broccoli and Red Bean Salad

2 pounds broccoli, cut into
  florets and peel stems
4 cups cooked red beans,
  drained
3 stalks celery, diced
6 green onions, chopped
½ tablespoon Dijon mustard

⅓ cup vinegar (chive vinegar
  optional)
Salt and pepper
1 tablespoon fresh summer
  savory
⅔ cup olive oil

Blanch broccoli in boiling water for 5 minutes. Drain and refresh in cold water. Blend together broccoli, red beans, celery, and green onion. Combine mustard, vinegar, salt, pepper, and summer savory. Whisk in olive oil. Pour over vegetables. Marinate 3–4 hours in refrigerator.

Favorite Herbal Recipes Vol. III

Rich in history, wildlife and natural beauty, the Shawnee National Forest offers breathtaking sites and naturally quiet sounds—motor vehicles are not allowed in nearly 30,000 acres of the park. Garden of the Gods, Cave-in-Rock, Dixon Springs, Bell Smith, Ferne Clyffe, and Lake of Egypt are all as intriguing as they sound.

Crunchy Broccoli Salad

4 cups chopped broccoli
1½ cups seedless red
  grapes, halved
1 cup mayonnaise
⅓ cup sugar

2 tablespoons cider vinegar
12 slices bacon, cooked and
  crumbled
¼ cup sunflower nuts

Combine broccoli and grapes. Mix mayonnaise, sugar, and vinegar. Add to broccoli and toss. Chill. Before serving, add bacon and sunflower nuts. Toss well. Makes 6 servings. *Note:* May substitute chopped pecans for sunflower nuts, or raisins for grapes.

Honest to Goodness

Spinach and Fruit Salad

1 (1-pound) package fresh
  spinach
3 tart apples, finely cut
1 (11-ounce) can mandarin
  oranges, drained

½ of a (6-ounce) can frozen
  orange juice concentrate
½ cup mayonnaise
8 slices bacon, fried and
  crumbled
Fresh croutons

Wash spinach carefully; remove large stems and break into bite-size pieces. Toss with apples and oranges. Blend orange juice concentrate and mayonnaise. Toss with salad. Add bacon and croutons. Serves 6–8.

Still Gathering

Layered Spinach Salad

½ cup grated Romano cheese
3 slices bacon, cooked crisp
  and crumbled
1½ quarts torn spinach
2 cups mushrooms, sliced
1 cup red onion slices

1 (10-ounce) package frozen peas
½ cup mayonnaise
½ cup sour cream
1 teaspoon sugar
2 tablespoons grated Romano
  cheese

Combine ½ cup Romano cheese and crumbled bacon. Layer in large bowl spinach, cheese mixture, mushrooms, onion slices, and peas. Combine mayonnaise, sour cream, and sugar. Mix well and spread over salad to seal. Sprinkle 2 tablespoons of Romano cheese over top. Refrigerate overnight, covered.

Our Favorite Recipes

Bow Tie Spinach Salad

Combine the best of pasta and spinach salads with a zesty dressing for a salad that is pretty as well as tasty.

DRESSING:
¾ cup olive oil or vegetable
  oil
¾ cup white wine vinegar
3 cloves of garlic, crushed
2 teaspoons Dijon mustard

½ cup grated Parmesan cheese
1 tablespoon minced fresh
  oregano or 1 teaspoon dried
  oregano
Salt and pepper to taste

Combine the olive oil, vinegar, garlic, mustard, Parmesan cheese, oregano, salt and pepper in a bowl; mix well.

SALAD:
1 (16-ounce) package bow tie
  pasta, cooked, drained
1 package spinach, torn
3 tomatoes, chopped

½ cup sliced green onions
½ cup sliced black olives
¾ cup crumbled feta cheese

Combine the pasta, spinach, tomatoes, green onions, olives, and feta cheese in a salad bowl. Add the salad dressing; toss to coat well. Chill until serving time. Serves 8–10.

Generations

Summertime Salad

5 tablespoons butter
¼ cup fresh parsley, chopped
¼ cup fresh basil, chopped
2 tablespoons minced chives
1 small clove garlic, pressed
Salt to taste

1 pound fresh peas
1 teaspoon salt
1 tablespoon olive oil or
   vegetable oil
¾ pound spaghetti or linguini

Make an herb butter by combining butter, parsley, basil, chives, and garlic. Add a little salt to taste. Steam peas until tender, 5–8 minutes. Refresh under cold water and set aside.

Bring a large pot of water to boil. Add 1 teaspoon salt, 1 tablespoon oil, and pasta. Cook 3–5 minutes. Drain and toss into a warm serving dish with herb butter and peas. Serve immediately.

Favorite Herbal Recipes Vol. III

Marinated Salad

1 tablespoon Cavender's
   Greek seasoning
1 teaspoon paprika
¼ cup olive oil
¼ cup vegetable oil
¼ cup rice wine vinegar
¼ pound fresh mushrooms,
   sliced
3 slices red onion, chopped

2 medium tomatoes, chopped
1 avocado, peeled and
   chopped
½ cup chopped celery
2 tablespoons chopped fresh
   parsley
½ cup black olives
Lettuce leaves

Combine Greek seasoning and paprika with oils and vinegar in small bowl. Mix well. Add mushrooms and marinate for several hours. Add onion, tomatoes, avocado, celery, and parsley. Chill for 1 hour before serving. Add olives. Serve in bowls lined with lettuce leaves. Makes 4 servings.

The Elsah Landing Restaurant Cookbook

Pasta Salad

2 cups uncooked rotini
8 ounce chunk mozzarella
1 cup broccoli and/or
  cauliflower
1 package frozen snow peas

1 cup cherry tomato halves
¼ cup sliced green olives
2 tablespoons Parmesan
  cheese

Cook and cool rotini. Cut mozzarella into bite-size chunks. Wash and cut up broccoli and/or cauliflower. Drain veggies. Chop broccoli and cauliflower into tiny pieces or put in food processor.

Cook snow peas according to directions on box and cool. Mix everything and pour dressing over the mixture. Refrigerate overnight.

DRESSING:
½ teaspoon sugar
½ teaspoon oregano
½ cup sliced green onions
⅓ cup red wine vinegar
⅓ cup olive oil
2 tablespoons parsley

1 teaspoon garlic powder
2 teaspoons dried basil
1 teaspoon dried dill weed
1 teaspoon salt
½ teaspoon pepper

Blend well with whisk.

Family Celebrations Cookbook

Thunder & Lightning

Vine-ripened tomatoes are a requisite for this salad.

2 bell peppers, seeded and
  cut julienne
4 ripe tomatoes, cut into
  bite-size pieces

4 ribs celery, sliced
2 medium white onions, cut
  julienne

DRESSING:
1½ cups cider vinegar
1½ cups sugar
1 cup vegetable oil

1 (2-ounce) bottle hot pepper
  sauce

Prepare vegetables. Combine dressing ingredients and pour over vegetables. Chill about 20 minutes before serving. Also good to add sliced cucumbers to this salad.

More to Love...from The Mansion of Golconda

Caesar Salad

2 heads romaine lettuce,
  washed and dried
½ cup Parmesan cheese

1 can anchovies
Croutons

DRESSING:
1 coddled egg (boiled 1½
  minutes)
¼ cup olive oil
¼ cup salad oil
Juice of 1 lemon

1 tablespoon Worcestershire
  sauce
2 garlic cloves, pressed
½ teaspoon mustard powder
Salt and pepper, to taste

In a large salad bowl tear lettuce into bite-size pieces. Combine all ingredients for dressing, beat well and pour over salad. Sprinkle with Parmesan cheese and toss. Add cut up anchovies and croutons and toss again lightly. Serve immediately. Serves 8–10.

C-U in the Kitchen

German Potato Salad, Cold
(Kartoffelsalat)

8–10 potatoes, boiled the
  day before
½–¾ cup stock or beef
  bouillon (2 beef cubes)
1 large onion, finely chopped
3 tablespoons oil

5–6 tablespoons cider vinegar
Salt
Pepper
"Maggi" liquid seasoning
  (several shakes)
Chives or parsley

Boil washed potatoes in their skins in salted water until done. Drain and peel when lukewarm. Put potatoes covered in frig overnight—they don't fall apart as much. Thinly slice potatoes into large bowl next day. Pour hot bouillon over potatoes and let sit for ½ hour; stir gently to cover all potatoes. Add chopped onion.

Make salad dressing with remaining ingredients, shake or beat well. Pour dressing over potatoes and gently mix. Let stand for 2–3 hours. Potato salad should be moist. Garnish with chives or parsley. Serve with fish.

Our Cherished Recipes

Thelma's Bed and Breakfast Meals by Request Slaw

1 medium head cabbage,
  chopped
1 small onion, chopped

2 stalks celery, chopped
½ green pepper, chopped
Some red pepper

Combine chopped vegetables in a bowl.

DRESSING:
1 envelope plain gelatin
⅓ cup cold water
2 cups sugar

¾ cup vinegar
1 teaspoon salt
⅔ cup salad oil

Soften gelatin in cold water. Bring to a boil. Add sugar, vinegar, and salt. Let cool. Add salad oil. Stir and pour over vegetables. Let stand overnight or longer.

Our Cherished Recipes

Lisa's Cabbage Salad

You may know this versatile vegetable as celery cabbage, but it's neither celery nor cabbage. It's actually a member of the mustard family. The flavor is cabbage-like but more delicate—mild and sweet. Like celery, Chinese cabbage (Nappa) grows in long slender heads, white to pale yellow-green in color. You'll love the crispness of finely sliced Chinese cabbage in a tossed salad. Or, shred it for slaw, adding cucumber to the dressing. It's equally tasty as a cooked vegetable—buttered or creamed.

1 large head Nappa cabbage,
   chopped
3 green onions, chopped
1 package chicken Ramen
   noodles

¼ cup butter
1 package slivered almonds
   (or sliced)
⅓ cup sesame seeds

Mix chopped cabbage and onions. Crush Ramen noodles and brown with seasoning package with butter, almonds and sesame seeds. Add noodle mixture to cabbage mixture.

DRESSING:
1 tablespoon soy sauce
½ cup oil
¼ cup rice wine vinegar or
   white vinegar

⅓ cup sugar
Salt and pepper to taste
½ teaspoon sesame oil (not
   a cooking oil—it's flavoring)

Shake together in a jar. Serve over Cabbage Salad.

What's Cooking "Down Home"

Skinny Cole Slaw

⅓ cup low-cal mayonnaise
2 tablespoons vinegar
1 teaspoon salt
¼ teaspoon pepper
¼–½ teaspoon curry powder

Artificial sweetening to
   equal 1 tablespoon sugar
4 cups cabbage, shredded

Mix first 6 ingredients together and pour over shredded cabbage.

Note: For Fat Cole Slaw, use Miracle Whip in place of the low-cal mayonnaise, real sugar instead of artificial sweetening, and then crumble real bacon bits on top.

The Lucy Miele 6-5-4 Cookbook

Beet Root Salad

4–6 large beets (or use
  2 (#303) cans
1 onion, sliced
½ cup mayonnaise

2 teaspoons tarragon vinegar
¼ cup heavy cream, whipped
  (can use sour cream)

Mix beets and onions lightly in salad bowl. Mix mayonnaise and tarragon vinegar; fold in whipped cream. Pour sauce over salad and serve on chopped lettuce. Or mix lightly and serve in a bowl.

What's Cooking "Down Home"

Jackson Salad

¼ small onion, chopped
3 tablespoons cider vinegar
2 teaspoons spicy brown
  mustard
½ teaspoon sugar
½ teaspoon salt
¼ teaspoon pepper
1 cup vegetable oil

2 bunches romaine lettuce,
  torn into bite-size pieces
1 can hearts of palm,
  quartered
1 can water-packed artichoke
  hearts, quartered
4 ounces blue cheese, crumbled
½ pound bacon, crumbled

Purée onion with vinegar in blender. Transfer to medium bowl. Using electric mixer, blend mustard, sugar, salt and pepper. Gradually add oil in thin, steady stream and continue beating until thick.

Mix lettuce, hearts of palm, artichokes, blue cheese and bacon in serving bowl. Toss with dressing to taste. Makes 8 servings.

Jubilee

Mary Kay's Marinated Chicken Rice Salad

2 packages Uncle Ben's Wild
  Rice Mix (cook with ½ cup
  less water; cool)

4–5 whole chicken breasts,
  cooked, cooled and cut into
  chunks

Mix rice and chicken together.

1 package Good Season's
  Italian (made as directed)
1 can of artichokes, drained
  and cut up
2 cups chopped celery

1 (4-ounce) jar pimento, sliced
1 cup chopped green pepper
1 cup mayonnaise
1 pound fresh mushrooms,
  sliced

When Italian dressing is made, let artichoke hearts marinate in it awhile. Add next 4 ingredients and mix with rice and chicken. Let marinate overnight. About 1 hour before serving, slice 1 pound fresh mushrooms and toss gently with chicken-rice mixture. Serves 12–16.

Carol's Kitchen

Chicken Salad

2 chickens, cooked, boned
  and diced
1 cup seedless white grapes,
  halved
1 cup mandarin oranges
½ cup mayonnaise
½ cup sour cream
2 tablespoons finely chopped
  parsley

¾ cup diced celery
2 tablespoons finely chopped
  onion
1 tablespoon lemon juice
½ teaspoon salt
½ teaspoon pepper
½ teaspoon Herb Italian spices
¼ cup toasted slivered
  almonds

Mix all ingredients together; toss lightly. Chill before serving. Serve with lettuce, rolls, olives, etc.

Cookbook 25 Years

Froelich Memorial Home-Made Hot Chicken Salad

2 cups chicken, cooked, cubed
2 cups celery, thinly sliced
2 teaspoons grated onion
1 (8-ounce) can water chestnuts, sliced
½ teaspoon salt
1 box frozen peas, thawed
1 cup mayonnaise
2 tablespoons lemon juice
1 can black olives, sliced
½ cup grated American cheese

Preheat oven to 450°. Mix all ingredients except cheese. Pour into 9x11-inch baking dish. Cover with cheese. Bake for 20–30 minutes, until hot and bubbly.

Variations: Add 4–6 ounces cork screw pasta, cooked, and 1 (4-ounce) jar sliced pimento. Or ½ cup slivered almonds and 1 (4-ounce) can sliced mushrooms; top with crushed potato chips.

Cook Book: Favorite Recipes from Our Best Cooks

Wong's Chinese Chicken Salad

This ultimate Chinese chicken salad recipe comes directly from Hong Kong.

4 whole chicken breasts, halved
2 quarts cooking oil, preferably peanut oil
3¾ ounces cellophane noodles
11 ounces (8 or 9 squares) frozen won ton wrappers, cut into ⅛-inch strips

1 cup nuts (dry roasted peanuts, almonds, or cashews)
1 head iceberg lettuce, shredded
1 cup scallions, cut diagonally into 1½ strips
½ cup chopped parsley

MARINADE:
6 tablespoons dry mustard
3 tablespoons Oriental sesame oil

1½ cups soy sauce

Poach or steam chicken breasts 20 minutes or until barely tender. Do not overcook. Discard skin and bones; shred chicken with fingers into 2-inch pieces.

Heat oil to 350°. Test oil temperature by dropping in a cellophane noodle. It should become opaque and "explode" instantly. Drop noodles, in small amounts, into oil. Upon "explosion," remove immediately with slotted spoon to drain on paper towels. Using same oil, cook won ton strips in small amounts until lightly browned. Remove with slotted spoon to drain on paper towels. Drop nuts in same oil; cook until lightly browned. Remove with slotted spoon to drain on paper towels.

To prepare marinade, place mustard in small bowl. Gradually add sesame oil while stirring to eliminate lumps. Add soy sauce. Mix well. Marinate chicken in 1 cup marinade for 20 minutes only.

Arrange shredded lettuce on large flat platter. Layer won ton strips over lettuce followed by cellophane noodles. Layer marinated chicken over noodles. Sprinkle with scallions, nuts, and desired amount of remaining marinade. Garnish with chopped parsley and serve immediately.

Noodles may be prepared several days in advance and stored in airtight container. Serves 8.

Noteworthy

Fresh Tuna Salad

1 pound tuna steaks
½ cup chopped celery
6 chopped egg whites
1 tablespoon lemon juice
½ cup chopped cucumber
¼ teaspoon pepper

½ cup chopped onion
1 cup reduced calorie salad
  dressing
Halved green grapes or chopped
  sweet pickles, optional

Poach tuna in skillet, covering steaks with water. Simmer tuna until turns light in color and is very flaky. Drain and let tuna cool. Flake into a bowl and add rest of ingredients. Mix and chill.

Serve on wheat or rye bread with lettuce or just scoop tuna onto a leaf of lettuce.

Note: You can also use canned white tuna, water packed.

Nutritional value (per serving): 495 calories, 10 grams

The Fishlady's...Forever Dieter's Book

Salmon Salad

1 pound cooked salmon
8 ounces cooked rotini
  noodles (drained)
1 cup Italian dressing
1 teaspoon pepper

1 teaspoon seasoned salt
2 large chopped fresh tomatoes
1 large chopped green pepper
½ cup chopped green onion

Combine all ingredients and chill 1 hour before serving. It's great on crackers or on a leaf of lettuce.

The Fishlady's Holiday Entertaining Cookbook

 Celebrated soloists from around the world perform each summer at the prestigious Ravinia Festival in Highland Park. Starlight nights, picnic baskets, candlelight, and radiant faces—all a part of the unique pleasure of a Ravinia evening.

Fake Crab Salad

2 (12-ounce) packages of
  fake crab
1 (10-ounce) package frozen
  peas, cooked and drained
1 cup celery, chopped
1 small onion, chopped
¾ cup mayonnaise

1 teaspoon lemon
⅛ teaspoon curry powder
1 teaspoon soy sauce
⅛ teaspoon garlic powder
1 (3-ounce) can chow mein
  noodles
½ cup toasted almonds

Thaw the crab; cut into ½-inch pieces. Cook; drain and add the peas. Chop celery and onion; add to mixture. Mix the mayonnaise with the seasonings. Add to salad and toss. Add the chow mein noodles and toasted almonds last before serving.

A Cause for Applause

Apricot Jello Salad

2 (3-ounce) boxes apricot Jello
1 (20-ounce) can crushed
  pineapple
1 egg
1 tablespoon butter or
  margarine

½ cup sugar
1 tablespoon flour
1 (3½-ounce) package
  Philadelphia cream cheese
1 (5-ounce) carton Cool Whip

In 9x13x2-inch (glass) pan, prepare Jello according to directions. Add crushed pineapple that has been drained (should have one cup or a little less juice). Let set until firm. In a small saucepan, combine the cup of pineapple juice with the egg, butter, sugar, and flour. Cook until thick like pudding. Cool. Add Philadelphia cream cheese and Cool Whip; spread on the firm Jello.

Cookbook 25 Years

Frozen Fruit Salad

Easy enough for children to make.

1 large can crushed
  pineapple
1 (10-ounce) package frozen
  strawberries, thawed

1 (21-ounce) can apricot or
  peach pie filling
½ cup sugar
1 cup whipping cream, whipped

Mix all ingredients together and pour into 9x9-inch pan. Freeze several hours. Cut into squares and serve each on lettuce leaf. Keeps well in freezer if covered. Serves 9.

Brunch Basket

Jensen's Drug Store in Momence is the oldest drugstore in Illinois. It originally opened for business in 1861 around the start of the Civil War and it has been in operation ever since.

Spring Parfait Salad

2 (3-ounce) packages lemon
  Jello
1 cup boiling water
3 cups diced celery
⅔ cup diced green bell
  pepper
⅓ cup diced carrot

2 cups diced cucumber
½ cup sliced radishes
1 cup salad dressing
½ cup drained crushed
  pineapple
Juice of 1 lemon

Dissolve Jello in boiling water in bowl. Chill until partially set. Combine celery, green pepper, carrot, cucumber, and radishes in bowl. Add salad dressing; mix well. Add pineapple and lemon juice; mix well. Add to Jello. Pour into mold. Chill until set. Yields 8 servings.

Approx. Per Serving: Cal 251; Prot 3.5gr; T Fat 12.9gr; Chol 15.0mg; Carbo 33.0gr; Sod 318.1mg; Potas 424.mg.

River Valley Recipes

Cucumber Mousse

1 package lime flavored
  gelatin
1 cup boiling water
1 teaspoon salt
2 tablespoons vinegar or
  lemon juice
1 cup sour cream

¼ cup mayonnaise
1½ cups finely cut, drained
  cucumber
3 tablespoons minced green
  onions and tops
1 tablespoon green pepper

Dissolve gelatin in water. Add salt and lemon juice. Cool to room temperature and add sour cream and mayonnaise. Chill until syrupy, and fold in cucumber, onion and green pepper. Chill until firm in 8-inch ring mold. Needs no additional dressing.

Editors Note: Good on crackers as appetizer or in lettuce cups for salad.

Five Loaves and Two Fishes II

Raspberry Pretzel Salad

2 cups pretzels, crushed
3 tablespoons sugar
¾ cup butter or margarine, melted
1 (8-ounce) package cream cheese, softened
½ cup confectioners' sugar

1½ cups Cool Whip
2 cups miniature marshmallows
2 (3-ounce) packages raspberry Jello
2 cups boiling water
2 (10-ounce) packages frozen raspberries

Crush pretzels; mix with sugar and butter. Press into 13x9-inch pan and bake at 350° for 15 minutes. Set aside to cool. Cream softened cheese; add sugar and beat well. Fold in Cool Whip and marshmallows. Spread this mixture over cooled crust. Dissolve Jello in water and stir in raspberries, breaking up as to thaw them. Chill until thick. Spread this over cream layer. Chill and put into the refrigerator until served.

Cooking with Daisy's Descendants

Gooseberry Salad

2 cups frozen or fresh gooseberries, (can use 2½ cups)
1 cup sugar
½ cup water

2 packages lemon Jello
¼ cup sugar
½ cup orange juice
2 cups celery, cut fine
½ cup walnuts, optional

Cook berries, 1 cup sugar and water for 15 or 20 minutes and cool. Dissolve Jello and ¼ cup sugar in 2½ cups boiling water and chill. Add orange juice. Add berries, celery and optional walnuts. Refrigerate till ready to serve. Serves 8.

Five Loaves and Two Fishes II

 Galena, founded by lead miners and steamboaters in the 1820s, was a boomtown in the 1850s—home of Ulysses S. Grant and eight other Union generals (Chetlain, Parker, Rawlins, Rowley, John E. Smith, John S. Smith, Duer, and Maltby).

Taffy Apple Salad

Use both red and green apples for a more colorful salad. Garnish the top with additional peanuts.

1 (16-ounce) can crushed pineapple	1½ tablespoons white vinegar
4 cups miniature marshmallows	8 ounces whipped topping
1 tablespoon flour	2–3 cups coarsely chopped unpeeled apples
½ cup sugar	1 cup chopped Spanish peanuts
1 egg, beaten	

Drain the pineapple, reserving the juice. Combine the pineapple with the marshmallows in a bowl; set aside.

Combine the reserved juice with the flour, sugar, egg, and vinegar in a saucepan; mix well. Cook until slightly thickened, stirring constantly. Cool to room temperature. Fold in the whipped topping, marshmallow mixture, apples, and peanuts. Chill for several hours. Serves 6–8.

Generations

Pina Colada Salad

2 cups cold milk	1 (20-ounce) can crushed pineapple, drained
1 can frozen pina colada mix	2 cups coconut
½ cup pineapple juice	1 (8-ounce) carton Cool Whip
1 small package instant vanilla pudding	
1 small package instant coconut cream pudding	

Combine milk, pina colada mix, pineapple juice. Add puddings; beat 5 minutes. Fold in pineapple, coconut, and Cool Whip. Pour into dish; chill several hours. Can use a mold. Garnish with pineapple and maraschino cherries.

Decades of Recipes

Thanksgiving Jello Salad

2 cans black cherries, cut up
1 large can crushed pineapple
2 (3-ounce) packages
  strawberry Jello
1 (8-ounce) package cream
  cheese

2 cups red or green
  maraschino cherries
1 cup English walnuts
2 (6-ounce) bottles cola

Drain juice from cherries and pineapple. Dissolve Jello with boiled juice. While hot, whip cream cheese until soft and add with Jello; beat good. Add rest of ingredients with cheese and Jello mixture. Put in large 13x9-inch dish. Chill in refrigerator. Serve with turkey.

Our Favorite Recipes

Vegetables

*Dearborn Station, one of the oldest metropolitan railroad stations
in the US (1885). Chicago.*

Baked Spinach and Ham Frittata

8 eggs or 2 (8-ounce) cartons of frozen egg product, thawed
¼ teaspoon dried basil, crushed
⅛ teaspoon pepper
¼ cup chopped onion
1 tablespoon margarine

1 (10-ounce) package frozen chopped spinach, thawed and well drained
4 ounces thinly sliced, fully cooked ham, chopped
1 tablespoon grated Parmesan cheese

In a medium bowl, combine eggs or egg product, basil, and pepper. Beat until combined. Set aside. In a 10-inch oven-proof skillet, cook onion in hot margarine until tender but not brown. Remove from heat. Stir in spinach and ham. Add egg mixture. Bake at 350° for 15 minutes or until a knife inserted in the center comes out clean. Sprinkle with cheese, cover and let stand for 5 minutes.

Favorite Herbal Recipes Vol. III

Poz Noz
(Spinach)

6 eggs
2 pounds cottage cheese
1 package chopped spinach, well drained
2 tablespoons margarine, melted

⅓ cup flour
½ cup chopped onion
1 teaspoon salt
½ cup grated Cheddar cheese

Beat eggs. Add cottage cheese and well drained spinach (press water out of spinach). Into margarine, stir flour and onion. Put all together; add salt and grated cheese. Bake at 350° for 1 hour.

College Avenue Presbyterian Church Cookbook

Berghoff Creamed Spinach

2 slices bacon, diced
2 tablespoons butter
1½ tablespoons flour
1 cup half-and-half, scalded

1 large onion, diced and sautéed
　until soft, but not brown
1 pound cooked spinach, chopped
　fine (frozen is okay–just thaw)
Salt, pepper and nutmeg to taste

Sauté bacon in Dutch oven 'til crisp. Reduce heat to medium low and add butter. When melted, whisk in flour to make roux. Cook 2 minutes, stirring constantly. Mixture should be golden. Be sure not to overcook. Slowly add hot half-and-half, whisking constantly 'til sauce is smooth and thickened. Blend in remaining ingredients and heat through, adding salt, pepper and nutmeg to taste.

Grand Detour Holiday Sampler

Spinach with Rice
(Spanakoryso)

In Chicago, every Greek restaurant has a spinach and rice dish that you won't believe! The secret is fresh spinach and tomatoes. An easy dish to prepare. Frugal, too!

1 pound fresh spinach	½ teaspoon oregano
½ cup olive oil	½ cup rice
½ stick butter	1 cup water
1 onion, chopped fine	Salt and pepper to taste
1 tablespoon dried dill	1 cup fresh chopped tomatoes

Remove and discard coarse stems of spinach. Wash leaves well and sprinkle lightly with salt. Stir to spread salt evenly. After 20 minutes, rinse off salt and squeeze out excess water. Cut up spinach.

In a heavy pot, heat olive oil and butter and sauté onions until soft. Add dill and oregano. Stir well. Add rice and stir until grains are well coated. Add water, salt, and pepper and cook for 10 minutes. Add spinach and tomatoes; cook till rice is tender.

Accompany with feta cheese and crusty bread. I have enjoyed this spinach dish as a main dish many times. Makes 4 servings.

Opaa! Greek Cooking Chicago Style

Carrots and Cheese

2 pounds carrots	2 cups shredded sharp
2 tablespoons butter,	Cheddar cheese
softened	½ teaspoon salt
1 medium onion, grated	⅛ teaspoon pepper

Preheat oven to 350°. Pare and slice carrots ¼-inch thick. Boil in water to cover until tender (about 10 minutes). Drain well. Mash carrots. Add butter, onion, cheese, salt, and pepper; blend thoroughly. Pour mixture into a lightly greased 1½-quart baking dish. Bake for 40 minutes or until hot and bubbly. Serves 6.

First There Must Be Food

Garden Casserole

4 medium-size potatoes,
  peeled
2 onions, sliced
1 medium-size zucchini
4 or 5 tomatoes
3 carrots, pared

1 cup chicken broth
Salt and pepper
¼ cup butter, melted
1 cup small bread cubes
2 cups grated Cheddar cheese

Slice potatoes thin and spread over bottom of a medium-size, ungreased casserole. Place onions, in rings, over potatoes. Cut zucchini in half, remove seeds, and cut in small chunks. Spread over previous layer. Cut tomatoes in small chunks. Place over squash. Slice carrots thin and place throughout casserole. Pour chicken broth over entire casserole. Add salt and pepper to taste. Cover dish and bake at 375° for 1 hour or until vegetables are softened, but crisp.

Mix bread cubes with melted butter until all are coated. Sprinkle grated cheese and bread cubes over entire casserole. Return to oven. Bake, uncovered, for 15 minutes longer. Serves 8.

Five Loaves and Two Fishes II

Sautéed Asparagus

2 pounds fresh asparagus
½ medium-size onion,
  finely chopped
1 garlic clove, chopped

2 tablespoons vegetable oil
2 tablespoons butter
Salt and pepper to taste

Wash the asparagus thoroughly in cold water to eliminate any sand. Snap off the tough bottom portion of the asparagus stalks and discard. Parboil the asparagus in a small amount of lightly salted boiling water for 5 minutes. Drain.

In a skillet, sauté the onion and garlic in the oil and butter for about 3–5 minutes over medium heat. Add the asparagus. Cover and cook to the desired tenderness (5–10 minutes). Turn once, being careful not to break the stalks. Add salt and pepper to taste, and serve at once.

Caring is Sharing

Crazy Casserole

1 pound fresh mushrooms,
  sliced lengthwise
1 small onion, grated
½ cup butter
¼ cup flour
½ teaspoon pepper
1 teaspoon salt
1 teaspoon monosodium
  glutamate, (MSG)
3 cups milk

¾ pound sharp Cheddar
  cheese, grated
⅛ teaspoon Tabasco
1 tablespoon soy sauce
1 package frozen artichoke
  hearts
1 package frozen French
  green beans
1 package frozen lima beans
1 can water chestnuts
1 can French onion rings

Sauté mushrooms and onion in butter for 5 minutes. Blend flour and seasonings and add to mushroom mixture. Stir in milk and cook, stirring constantly until thickened and smooth. Then add grated cheese, Tabasco sauce and soy sauce. Stir until cheese is melted. Meanwhile, cook the vegetables as packages instruct. Blend cooked vegetables into cheese mixture. Add water chestnuts, mixing lightly to avoid mashing vegetables. (¼ cup white wine will do wonders for the taste— a glass won't hurt the cook either.)

Turn mixture into a buttered 2-quart casserole. Bake in preheated 350° oven for 30 minutes. Crumble one can French onion rings and sprinkle over top of casserole. Return to oven to bake 10 minutes longer. Serves 8–10.

Grand Detour Holiday Sampler

Hundred Dollar Broccoli Casserole

2 packages frozen broccoli
1 (8-ounce) package cream
  cheese
1 envelope Lipton Dry Onion
  Soup Mix
1 (8-ounce) carton sour cream
1 small can water chestnuts,
  drained and sliced
Sharp grated cheese
Ritz cracker crumbs

Cook broccoli until tender in the amount of water called for on one package and drain. Have cream cheese out of refrigerator at least 3 hours to soften. Mash together soup mix, cream cheese, sour cream, and chestnuts. Add to drained broccoli and stir well. Place in lightly buttered casserole dish and top with grated cheese and cracker crumbs; dot with butter. Bake at 275° for 30–35 minutes. Serves 8–10.

Our Favorite Recipes

Broccoli Soufflé Restauranteur

Very elegant.

¼ cup butter
¼ cup flour
½ cup whipping cream,
  scalded
½ cup rich chicken broth
3 egg yolks
1 teaspoon grated onion
1 teaspoon chopped parsley
1 teaspoon Worcestershire
  sauce
1 teaspoon finely chopped chives
Salt, pepper, nutmeg
1½ cups cooked chopped
  broccoli
⅓ cup grated Cheddar cheese
4 egg whites, stiffly beaten

Melt butter; stir in flour. Gradually stir in scalded cream mixed with chicken broth. Cook, stirring constantly, until mixture thickens. Remove from heat. Beat egg yolks with onion, parsley, Worcestershire sauce, and chives. Add salt, pepper, and nutmeg to taste. Stir a little hot mixture into the egg yolks; combine with remainder. Add broccoli and cheese. Fold in egg whites. Turn into 2-quart buttered souffle dish. Bake at 400° for 25 minutes. Makes 6 servings.

Soupçon II

Oven-Roasted Vegetables

Quick and easy to prepare!

10 unpeeled new potatoes,
   cut into quarters
1 cup peeled baby carrots
1 small onion, cut into wedges
¼ cup olive oil
3 tablespoons lemon juice
3 cloves of garlic, minced

1 tablespoon minced fresh
   rosemary or 1 teaspoon dried
1 teaspoon salt
½ teaspoon pepper
½ small eggplant, cut into
   ½-inch slices
1 medium red or green bell
   pepper, cut into ½-inch strips

Arrange the new potatoes, carrots, and onion in a 9x13-inch baking dish. Drizzle with a mixture of olive oil, lemon juice, garlic, rosemary, salt and pepper. Bake at 450° for 30 minutes, stirring occasionally. Stir in the eggplant and bell pepper. Bake for 15 minutes.

Generations

Skillet Squash

2 slices bacon, diced
1 small onion, sliced or diced
2 medium summer squash or
   zucchini

Seasoned salt
1 teaspoon sugar
5 or 6 slices American cheese

Brown bacon and onion in skillet. Add sliced or diced squash or zucchini. Sprinkle seasoned salt and 1 teaspoon sugar. Cover, cook over medium heat. Turn once or twice, until tender-crisp. Lay slices of cheese on top. Cover and turn off heat until cheese is melted.

Decades of Recipes

Onion Pie

½ cup butter, melted
30 soda crackers, crushed
3 cups sliced onions,
   browned in ¼ cup butter
½ pound cheese, grated

1½ cups milk
3 eggs
¼ teaspoon salt
½ teaspoon pepper

Melt butter and pour on crackers in casserole dish. Mix and press down. Brown onion slices in ¼ cup butter and pour on crackers. Combine cheese, milk, eggs, salt and pepper. Scald and pour over other ingredients. Bake at 350° for 30 minutes.

Our Cherished Recipes

Onion Shortcake

An epicurean delight!

2 large onions, sliced thin
⅓ cup butter or margarine
1 cup sour cream
½ teaspoon dried dill
¼ teaspoon salt
1 cup grated Cheddar cheese
   (8-ounces)

1 (15-ounce) can creamed
   corn, undrained
⅓ cup milk
1 (8½-ounce) package corn
   muffin mix
1 egg, slightly beaten
4 drops red pepper sauce or
   to taste

Preheat oven to 425°. Sauté onions in butter or margarine. Stir in sour cream, dill weed, salt, and half the Cheddar cheese. In a separate bowl, combine corn, milk, dry muffin mix, egg, and hot pepper sauce. Put corn mixture in buttered 10-inch ovenproof dish. Spread onion mixture over the top. Sprinkle with remaining Cheddar cheese. Bake for 30–40 minutes or until cheese is golden brown. Serves 6.

Still Gathering

 Cahokia Mounds preserves the remains of the central section of the only prehistoric Indian city north of Mexico. Covering nearly 4,000 acres, the Cahokia site was first inhabited around 700 A.D. and grew to a population of nearly 20,000 by 1100 A.D. Near Collinsville.

Stuffed Tomato with Feta Cheese

It is important that you use the ripest tomatoes. If tomatoes aren't quite ripe, place them in a brown paper bag and keep in a dark place for a couple of days to ripen.

5 ripe, medium tomatoes
3 tablespoons finely chopped
  scallions, use most of the
  green stem

3 tablepoons finely chopped
  parsley
¾ cup feta cheese, crumbled
½ cup bread crumbs
4 tablepoons olive oil

Carefully cut tops off tomatoes. Using a spoon, carefully scoop out pulp and seeds. Save pulp and discard seeds. Coarsely chop the tomato pulp. Combine pulp, scallions, parsley, feta cheese, bread crumbs, and olive oil. Mix well. Spoon mixture into the hollowed-out tomatoes. Preheat oven to 350°. Place tomatoes right-side-up on baking sheet and bake for 15–20 minutes. Makes 5 servings.

Opaa! Greek Cooking Chicago Style

Swiss Style Green Beans

2 tablespoons butter
2 tablespoons flour
Salt
¼ teaspoon pepper
1 teaspoon sugar

1 cup sour cream
4 cups (2 cans) French style
  cut green beans
½ pound Swiss cheese, grated
1 small onion, cut up

Melt butter; stir in flour, salt, pepper, and sugar. Add sour cream gradually, stirring constantly. Fold in green beans, grated cheese, and onions. Pour into buttered 1½-quart casserole. Mix cracker crumbs with melted butter and put over top. Bake 20 minutes at 350°. Serves 6–8.

A Collection of Recipes From St. Matthew Lutheran Church

In addition to his home, there are many Carl Sandburg sites in Galesburg, a town he grew up in and loved. The Pulitzer Prize winner for poetry and history writes about many of these places in his autobiography, *Always the Young Strangers.*

Corn & Tomato Casserole

3 strips bacon
½ medium onion, finely
chopped
¼ cup finely diced green
pepper
3 large ears sweet corn or 1
(16-ounce) package frozen
sweet corn

2 tablespoons brown sugar
½ teaspoon salt and dash
pepper
1 teaspoon dried sweet basil
2–2½ cups canned
tomatoes, drained and
chopped

TOPPING:
¾ cup herb flavored stuffing
mix or ¾ cup crushed
tortilla chips

2 cups shredded Cheddar
cheese

In large skillet, fry bacon until crisp. Save drippings in skillet. Crumble bacon into greased 1½-quart casserole. Set aside.

Sauté onion and green pepper in bacon drippings until tender.

Cut corn off cobs; add to onion mixture along with brown sugar, salt, pepper, basil, and tomatoes. Cook 10–15 minutes. Pour over bacon in casserole. Top with stuffing mix or crushed tortilla chips and cheese. Bake at 350° for 25–30 minutes. Makes 6 servings.

Cookin' With Friends

New Salem Corn Casserole

1 (16-ounce) can whole
kernel corn, drained
1 (16-ounce) can cream style
corn
2 eggs, slightly beaten
½ teaspoon salt

½ cup margarine, melted
1 cup sour cream
1 (8½-ounce) box corn muffin
mix
1–2 cups grated Cheddar
cheese (optional)

Mix together all ingredients except cheese. Add 1 cup Cheddar cheese if desired. Pour into greased 9x13-inch pan. Bake at 350° for 40 minutes or until set. If more cheese is desired, add additional ½–1 cup Cheddar cheese on top of casserole when set. Bake another 5 minutes or until cheese melts. Makes 10–12 servings.

Honest to Goodness

Illinois is the birth state of an exceptionally large number of entertainers, many of whom began their career at the popular Chicago caberet theater, Second City. A small sampling of Illinois-born entertainers includes: Jack Benny, Richard Pryor, Betty White, Gene Krupa, Marilu Henner, George Wendt, Burl Ives, Dan Fogelberg, Grace Slick, David Ogden Stiers, Frankie Laine, Karl Malden, Eddie Albert, Fred MacMurray, Darryl Hannah, Lou Rawls, Harvey Korman, John Malkovich, Lawrence Tero (Mr. T.), Ken Berry, McLean Stevenson, Howard Keel, Charlton Heston, Don McNeill, Pat Sajac, Robert Reed, Tom Bosley, Robert Young, Tom Berenger, Ken Olin, Mandy Patinkin, William Christopher, Susan Dey, Jim Jordan and Marian Driscoll (Fibber McGee and Molly), Bill Murray, Louella Parsons, Benny Goodman, Bobby Christian, Harrison Ford, Sam Shepard, Buddy Ebsen, Donna Mills, Clayton Moore, Betty Thomas, Morey Amsterdam, Karen Black, Kim Novak, Robin Williams, Gary Coleman, Mitzi Gaynor, Elizabeth McGovern, Martin Mull, Mary Astor, Bruce Dern, and Bob Fosse.

Escalloped Corn
(Microwave)

1 #2 can cream-style corn
1 #2 can whole kernel corn,
  drained
1 cup cracker crumbs

1 (5¾-ounce) can evaporated
  milk
1 egg, slightly beaten
2 tablespoons butter

Combine corns, crumbs, and milk in 1-quart casserole. Mix well. Stir in egg. Dot with butter. Cover. Microwave 7 minutes, 30 seconds on '8' or until set. Let stand 3–5 minutes covered. Garnish with paprika, if desired.

Cookbook 25 Years

Fried Cauliflower with Cheese Sauce

1 large head cauliflower
1 (12-ounce) can beer, at
  temperature

1¼ cups flour
Vegetable oil for deep frying

Wash cauliflower; cut into small flowerets. Cook, covered, in a small amount of water in saucepan for 8–10 minutes or until tender-crisp; drain.

Combine beer and 1¼ cups flour in bowl; mix well. Dip cauliflower in batter. Deep-fry in 375° oil until golden brown; drain. Serve cheese sauce with cauliflower. Yield: 6 servings.

CHEESE SAUCE:
2 tablespoons butter
2 tablespoons flour
1 cup milk

1½ cups shredded Cheddar
  cheese

Melt butter in heavy skillet. Add 2 tablespoons flour, stirring until smooth. Cook for 1 minute, stirring constantly. Add milk gradually. Cook over medium heat until thickened, stirring constantly. Remove from heat. Add cheese, stirring until melted.

Approx Per Serving: Cal 316; T Fat 15g; 44% Calories from Fat; Prot 13g; Carbo 29g; Fiber 3g; Chol 46g; Sod 237mg. Nutritional information does not include oil for deep frying.

Pioneer Pantry

White Bean Bake

What can represent Southern Illinois better than white beans!

8 cups seasoned cooked navy
  beans
1 cup golden raisins
2 cups chopped onions
1 cup sour cream
1 cup light brown sugar,
  packed
2 (3-ounce) packages cream
  cheese, room temperature

2 (4-ounce) cans chopped
  mild green chilies
8 cooked sausage patties,
  crumbled (1 pound)
3 tablespoons Dijon mustard
2 cups grated provolone cheese
4 green onions, chopped
  fine (use some green tops)
½ cup seasoned bread crumbs

Place navy beans, raisins, and onions in large bowl. Combine sour cream, brown sugar, and cream cheese and blend well. Add to beans. Add chilies, sausage, and mustard, and mix well. Pour into 10x15-inch baking pan. Bake at 350° about 45 minutes, until bubbly. Remove pan from oven and top with provolone cheese, green onions, and bread crumbs. Return to oven and bake 5 minutes more to melt cheese. Serve at once.

More to Love...from The Mansion of Golconda

Mushrooms in Marjoram Butter

1 pound mushrooms, washed
½ cup butter

2 teaspoons marjoram
½ teaspoon salt

Melt butter in large skillet, add mushrooms, sauté over medium-high heat for 10 minutes, stirring constantly until golden. Sprinkle with marjoram and salt; stir, remove from heat. Serve at once. Makes 6 servings.

Elsah Landing Heartland Cooking

Cavoli in Agrodolce
(Cabbage in Sweet and Sour Sauce)

3 tablespoons olive oil
½ cup thinly sliced onions
1½ pounds cabbage, cut into
    ¼-inch strips (about 8 cups)
3 large tomatoes, peeled, seeded
    and coarsely chopped

2 tablespoons wine vinegar
2 teaspoon salt
Freshly ground black pepper
1 tablespoon sugar

Heat the olive oil in a heavy 10–12-inch skillet, add the onions and cook them over moderate heat, stirring constantly, for 2 or 3 minutes. When they are transparent but not brown, stir in the cabbage, tomatoes, vinegar, salt and a few grindings of pepper.

Simmer uncovered, stirring frequently, for 20 minutes, or until the cabbage is tender. Then stir the sugar into the cabbage and cook 1 or 2 minutes longer. Serve in a heated bowl, either as a vegetable accompanying a fish or meat course, or as a separate dish preceding the main course. Serves 4–6.

Herrin's Favorite Italian Recipes Cookbook

Holiday Mashed Potatoes

12 medium potatoes, cooked
    and mashed
1 (8-ounce) package cream
    cheese, cut in chunks
¼ cup margarine

½ cup sour cream
½ cup milk
2 eggs, slightly beaten
1 teaspoon salt
¼ cup onions, finely chopped

Mash potatoes. Add cream cheese and margarine. Combine sour cream and milk. Add to potato mixture. Add beaten eggs, salt and onion. Put in greased casserole. (May be prepared the day before serving and refrigerated in greased casserole.) Bake uncovered at 350° for 45 minutes.

A Cause for Applause

Party Potatoes

2 pounds frozen Ore-Ida Hash
  Browns
1 can cream of celery soup
8 ounces sharp Cheddar
  cheese, shredded

1 small onion, chopped
1 small carton sour cream
1 stick margarine, melted
1 sleeve Hi-Ho crackers,
  crushed

Mix all ingredients except the margarine and crackers. Put mixture in a 9x13-inch dish. Cover top with melted margarine and crushed crackers. Bake at 350°, uncovered, for 1 hour.

Good Cookin' Cookbook

Potatoes Boulangère

8 medium potatoes
1 clove garlic
Butter
1 teaspoon salt
¼ teaspoon black pepper

1½ cups shredded gruyère
  or Swiss cheese
6 tablespoons butter,
  divided
1 cup chicken broth

Preheat oven to 425°. Peel potatoes, or leave skins on, and slice thin. Place in cold water to prevent discoloring.

Rub a 9x13-inch baking dish with garlic clove and butter generously. Drain potatoes thoroughly and dry on paper toweling. Arrange half of sliced potatoes in baking dish. Sprinkle with half of the salt, pepper, and cheese; dot with 3 tablespoons of butter. Repeat with remaining potatoes, salt, pepper, cheese, and butter. Pour chicken broth over casserole.

Place oven rack in high position (upper ⅓ of oven). Bake uncovered for 30 minutes or until potatoes are tender and crust is golden brown. Serve immediately. Quick and elegant! Serves 6.

First There Must Be Food

Golden Parmesan Potatoes

6 large potatoes (3 pounds)
¼ cup sifted flour
¼ cup grated Parmesan
   cheese
¾ teaspoon salt
⅛ teaspoon pepper
⅓ cup butter
Parsley

Peel potatoes; cut into quarters. Combine flour, cheese, salt and pepper in a bag. Moisten potatoes with water and shake a few at a time in bag, coating potatoes well. Melt butter in a 13x9-inch pan. Place potatoes in a layer in pan. Bake at 375° for 1 hour, turning once. When golden brown, sprinkle with parsley.

Home Cookin' is a Family Affair

Dilled Potatoes

5 unpeeled potatoes
2 tablespoons margarine
2 tablespoons flour
1 cup milk
½ cup mayonnaise
¼ teaspoon dillweed
2 tablespoons chopped onion
¼ teaspoon pepper

Cook potatoes in water in saucepan until tender. Peel and slice. Cool. Melt margarine in saucepan. Add flour. Cook until bubbly. Add milk. Cook until thickened, stirring constantly; remove from heat. Add mayonnaise, dillweed, chopped onion, and pepper; mix well. Pour over potatoes; mix well. Pour into buttered casserole. Bake, covered, for 30 minutes. Yields 6 servings.

Approx. Per Serving: Cal 349; Prot 5.9gr; T Fat 20.4gr; Chol 18.8mg; Carbo 36.9gr; Sod 184.2mg; Potas 840.2mg.

River Valley Recipes

Potato Latkes I
(Pancakes)

4 large potatoes	1 teaspoon grated onion
2 eggs	½ cup flour, scant
1 teaspoon salt	½ teaspoon baking powder
Dash pepper	Vegetable oil for frying

Peel potatoes and grate on a fine grater. Pour off half the liquid that accumulates and add rest of ingredients. Drop batter by tablespoonsful onto a well greased hot frying pan. Fry, browning both sides. Serve hot with applesauce, sugar, or sour cream. Serves 4.

C-U in the Kitchen

Sweet Taters and Apples

6 medium sweet potatoes	⅓ cup light brown sugar
6 medium cooking apples	½ teaspoon nutmeg
½ cup melted butter	

Bake the potatoes in their skins in hot oven, 400°, 1 hour or until tender. When cool, peel and slice ¼–½-inch thick. Peel, core and slice apples. Layer sliced apples and potatoes alternately in a 9x9x2-inch baking dish, applying melted butter, brown sugar, and nutmeg over each layer. Cover and bake (350°) 30–35 minutes, until bubbling.

Cook Book: Favorite Recipes from Our Best Cooks

Pasta, Pizza, Etc.

World renowned for its architecture, the Baha'i House is the only temple in North America for the universal religion of Baha'i. Wilmette.

Pasta with Chicken

Different and very easy.

1 pound green spinach
  noodles
4 tablespoons olive oil
8 tablespoons butter
1 cup finely chopped onion
1 teaspoon minced garlic
4 whole chicken breasts, cubed

½ pound zucchini, cubed
4 cups cherry tomatoes
2 teaspoons salt
Few grindings pepper
1 teaspoon basil
1 teaspoon oregano
2 cups shredded Swiss cheese

While pasta is cooking, heat oil and 4 tablespoons butter in skillet over high heat. Add onion and garlic and cook until onion is golden. Turn down heat and add chicken. Cook until chicken is white, about 5 minutes. Add zucchini, tomatoes, salt, pepper, basil, and oregano. Mix hot, drained pasta with remaining butter. Add chicken mixture and toss gently. Sprinkle with cheese and serve. Makes 6 servings.

Soupçon II

Spaghetti Pie

6 ounces spaghetti
2 tablespoons butter or
  margarine
⅓ cup grated Parmesan
  cheese
2 well-beaten eggs
1 cup cottage cheese (8 ounces)
1 pound ground beef
½ cup chopped onion

¼ cup chopped bell pepper
1 clove chopped garlic
1 (8-ounce) can tomatoes, cut
1 (6-ounce) can tomato paste
1 teaspoon sugar
1 teaspoon oregano
½ teaspoon garlic salt
½ cup shredded mozzarella
  cheese

Cook spaghetti; drain. Stir butter into hot spaghetti. Stir in Parmesan cheese and eggs. Form mixture into a crust in a buttered 10-inch pie plate. Spread cottage cheese over crust. In a skillet, cook ground beef, onion, pepper, and garlic until browned. Drain fat. Stir in undrained tomatoes, paste, sugar, oregano, and garlic salt. Heat through. Turn meat mixture into spaghetti crust. Bake, uncovered, at 350° for 20 minutes. Sprinkle mozzarella on top. Bake 5 minutes longer. Yield: 6 servings.

Favorite Herbal Recipes Vol. III

Special Manicotti

½ pound link Italian sausage
1 pound ground chuck
2 medium onions, chopped
5 garlic cloves, minced
2 (15-ounce) cans tomato
  sauce
1 (16-ounce) can tomatoes,
  chopped and undrained
1 (12-ounce) can tomato paste
1½ teaspoons dried whole
  oregano
1¼ teaspoons dried whole basil
1 teaspoon sugar
½ teaspoon salt
½ teaspoon pepper
½ teaspoon dried whole thyme
½ teaspoon dried whole
  rosemary
¼ teaspoon dried whole
  marjoram
⅛ teaspoon red pepper
16 manicotti shells
1 (8-ounce) package cream
  cheese, softened
1 (3-ounce) package cream
  cheese with chives, softened
4 garlic cloves, crushed
½ teaspoon pepper
½ teaspoon dried whole thyme
½ teaspoon dried whole oregano
1 (16-ounce) carton ricotta
  cheese
4 cups shredded mozzarella
  cheese (1 pound)
½ cup grated Parmesan cheese

Remove Italian sausage from casing; crumble. Combine sausage, beef, onions and garlic in a large Dutch oven. Cook over medium heat until beef is browned, stirring to crumble meat; drain well. Add tomato sauce and next 11 ingredients; bring sauce to a boil. Cover, reduce heat, and simmer 2½ hours, stirring occasionally.

Cook manicotti shells according to package directions. Combine cream cheeses and next 7 ingredients in a large bowl; stuff mixture into shells.

Spoon half of sauce into a lightly greased 14x12-inch baking dish or 2 lightly greased 2½-quart shallow casseroles. Arrange stuffed shells over sauce. Spoon remaining sauce over shells. Bake at 350° for 30–40 minutes or until heated. Let stand 5 minutes before serving. Makes 8 servings.

A Cause for Applause

Illinois was Frank Lloyd Wright's first residence and workplace. Springfield's Dana-Thomas House is the best preserved and most complete of his early "prairie houses," having over 100 pieces of original Wright furniture, 250 art-glass doors and windows, and nearly 100 art-glass light fixtures.

Cheesy Biscuit Lasagna

1 pound ground beef
1½ cups water
1 (8-ounce) can tomato sauce
1 (6-ounce) can tomato paste
1 teaspoon garlic powder
1 teaspoon ground oregano
1 teaspoon basil leaves,
  divided
½ teaspoon pepper

1½ cups (6 ounces)
  shredded mozzarella cheese
½ cup cottage cheese
1 tablespoon parsley flakes
½ teaspoon instant minced
  onion
1 (7.5-ounce) can refrigerated
  biscuits
Grated Parmesan cheese

Heat oven to 375°. In large skillet brown meat, drain. Stir in water, tomato sauce, tomato paste, garlic, oregano, ½ teaspoon basil, and pepper. Cover and simmer for 15–20 minutes. In a small bowl, combine mozzarella and cottage cheeses, parsley, onion, and remaining ½ teaspoon basil leaves.

Separate dough into 10 biscuits. Press each biscuit to a 4-inch circle. Place approximately 1½ tablespoons of cheese mixture on each circle. Fold dough in half over filling. Press edges with fork to seal. Pour hot mixture into 13x9-inch baking dish. Arrange filled biscuits on top. Sprinkle with Parmesan cheese. Bake at 375° for 30 minutes or until golden brown. Makes 5–6 servings.

Cookin' With Friends

Mexican Lasagna

1½ pounds hamburger
1 package taco seasoning
1 cup water
1 can pitted black olives
1 (8-ounce) can tomato sauce
1 (6-ounce) can tomato paste

2 eggs
8 ounces sour cream
1 brick Monterey Jack cheese
Soft tortilla shells
Dorito chips

Brown hamburger; drain. Add seasoning, water, chopped olives, tomato sauce, and tomato paste. Simmer 10 minutes. Mix eggs and sour cream. Spray a 9x13-inch pan with Pam. Put 4 or 5 shells on bottom of pan, ½ of meat mixture, then ½ of the sour cream mixture. Repeat for second layer starting with 4 or 5 shells. Cut up slices of Monterey Jack cheese; lay over top. Crunch up ½ bag of Dorito chips; spread over top. Bake, uncovered, at 350° for 30 minutes.

College Avenue Presbyterian Church Cookbook

Barb's Burritos

1½–2 pounds ground beef
2 tablespoons oil
2 cans refried beans
1 can green chilies, chopped
1 can tomatoes and chilies, chopped

1 cup thick and chunky Old
    El Paso Salsa
½–1 teaspoon red chilies
½–1 teaspoon garlic salt
Tortillas (about 10 large size)

Brown hamburger; drain. Set aside. Put about 2 tablespoons oil in pan. Add refried beans and other ingredients. Cook until dried out. Add hamburger. Put on heated tortilla. Top with cheese, sour cream, lettuce, chopped onions, tomatoes, salsa, etc.

Cooking with Daisy's Descendants

Rockford is Illinois' second largest city. It was once a shallow place in the river where stagecoaches crossed on their way from Chicago to Galena.

Taco Pie

1 deep-dish frozen pie crust
1 pound ground beef
1 medium onion, chopped
1 package taco seasoning mix
1 can refried beans
1 jar taco sauce, divided

2 cups shredded Cheddar
  cheese
12 nacho chips, crushed
Chopped lettuce
Chopped tomatoes
Sour cream

Preheat oven to 400°. Thaw pie crust 10 minutes. Prick bottom and sides of pie crust with fork. Bake pie crust for 10 minutes. Remove from oven and reduce temperature to 350°.

In skillet, brown hamburger and onion until brown. Drain fat. Add taco seasoning mix. In small bowl, combine refried beans and ⅓ cup taco sauce.

Layer ½ of refried bean mixture into pie crust; cover with ½ hamburger mix, then 1 cup Cheddar cheese and crushed nacho chips. Repeat layers, except nachos. Bake an additional 20–25 minutes. Remove from oven and top with lettuce, tomato, and additional taco sauce or sour cream.

Our Best Home Cooking

Turkey Lasagna Florentine

1 (8-ounce) package (9 pieces) rippled edge lasagna
1 (9-ounce) package frozen chopped spinach
2–3 cups cooked, diced turkey or chicken
2 cups shredded American or Cheddar cheese
1 (10¾-ounce) can cream of mushroom soup
1 cup dairy sour cream
1 (4-ounce) can sliced mushrooms, drained
⅓ cup minced fresh onion
½ teaspoon salt
¼ teaspoon pepper
½ cup grated Parmesan cheese

Cook lasagna; drain. Cook spinach according to package directions; drain well. Combine diced meat, 1½ cups shredded cheese, cream of mushroom soup, sour cream, mushrooms, minced onion, salt, pepper, and spinach. Toss till well blended.

Butter bottom and sides of 11½x7½x1½-inch baking dish. Arrange meat mixture and lasagna strips in layers, with 2 tablespoons Parmesan sprinkled on each layer. Top with remaining lasagna, ½ cup shredded Cheddar, and ¼ cup Parmesan. Cover with foil. Bake at 350° for 30 minutes. Uncover. Bake 10 minutes longer till brown. Let stand 15 minutes before cutting.

Dawdy Family Cookbook

Alla Panna
(Alfredo Sauce)

2 cups whipping cream
½ cup unsalted butter
½ cup Parmigiano
1 tablespoon freshly ground pepper

In medium saucepan, heat cream over low heat, watching that it does not come to a boil. Add butter and cheese, heating slowly until all is melted and mixture is of rich consistency. This could take 20 minutes or more. Cook pasta and add to heated sauce. Serve immediately over Pastificio fettuccini, linguine, or angel hair (Cappelli d'angelo). Add steamed vegetables to this for a marvelous primavera sauce.

Caring is Sharing

Swiss Chicken Pie

1 (10¾-ounce) can condensed cream of mushroom soup
⅓ cup milk
2 whole skinless, boneless chicken breasts, cooked and cubed
1 (10-ounce) package frozen cauliflower, thawed and drained
1 (10-ounce) package frozen broccoli spears, thawed, drained, and cut up
1½ cups shredded Swiss cheese
Salt and pepper, to taste
Herbs as desired
Pastry for a single crust pie

In bowl, stir together soup and milk. Fold in remaining ingredients. Spoon into 9-inch pie crust. Bake in a 400° oven for 40 minutes or until pie is golden brown and vegetables hot. Makes 6 servings.

College Avenue Presbyterian Church Cookbook

Chicken Pecan Quiche

1 (9-inch) pie crust, baked and cooled
1 cup cooked chicken, finely chopped
1 cup grated Swiss cheese
¼ cup chopped onion
1 tablespoon flour
½ cup chopped toasted pecans, divided
2 eggs, beaten
1 cup milk
½ teaspoon Dijon mustard

Preheat oven to 325°. Mix chicken, cheese, onion, flour, and ¼ cup pecans. Spread into pie crust.

Mix eggs, milk, and mustard; pour over chicken mixture. Top with remaining ¼ cup pecans.

Bake for 50 minutes or until knife inserted in center is withdrawn clean. Cool on wire rack. Serve warm.

Hint: This casserole may be frozen and defrosted the night before baking. Makes 6 servings.

Sugar Snips and Asparagus Tips

Crustless Crab Quiche

½ cup chopped onion
1 pound mushrooms, chopped
2 tablespoons butter
4 eggs
1 cup sour cream
1 cup small curd cottage
  cheese

1 cup freshly grated
  Parmesan cheese
¼ cup flour
4 drops hot red pepper sauce
2 cups shredded Monterey
  Jack cheese
6 ounces crabmeat, drained

Preheat oven to 350°. In a large saucepan, sauté onions and mushrooms in butter.

In a mixing bowl combine eggs, sour cream, cottage cheese, Parmesan cheese, flour, and pepper sauce. Add mushroom and onion mixture, Monterey Jack cheese and crabmeat. Stir to combine.

Pour mixture into a buttered 10-inch quiche dish and bake 40 minutes until golden brown. Let stand 15 minutes before serving. Yield: 6 servings.

One Magnificent Cookbook

Mock Spinach Quiche

2 eggs, well beaten
1 cup milk
1 stick margarine, melted
½ package spinach, cooked
  to package instructions,
  very well drained

8 ounces Cheddar cheese,
  shredded
1 cup flour
1 teaspoon salt, scant
1 teaspoon baking powder
¼ cup onion, minced

Mix eggs, milk, butter. Stir well and add other ingredients. Pour into well greased 9x13-inch pan. Bake at 350° for 30–35 minutes. Allow to cool before cutting into 1-inch squares. Serve warm, not hot. If glass pan, bake at 325°.

Caring is Sharing

Though Chicago is nicknamed "the Windy City," it is actually ranked 16th windiest in the U.S.

Neapolitan Vegetable Cheesecake

Far from being a dessert, this "cheesecake" is an excellent accompaniment to broiled meat or chicken. The name is derived from the texture, which resembles the dessert.

3 cups packed coarsely
  grated zucchini
1 teaspoon salt, divided
1 onion, chopped
1 tablespoon butter
3 cloves garlic, finely
  minced
1 cup coarsely grated
  carrots
3 tablespoons flour
½ teaspoon basil
½ teaspoon oregano
¼ cup packed chopped
  parsley

1½ tablespoons lemon juice
4 eggs
3 cups ricotta cheese
½ pound mozzarella cheese,
  grated
¾ cup grated Parmesan
  cheese, divided
Salt to taste
Freshly ground pepper to taste
⅓ cup fine bread crumbs
5–6 plum tomatoes, thinly
  sliced
Rolled anchovies, optional

Sprinkle grated zucchini with ½ teaspoon salt. Place in sieve and let drain 15 minutes. Squeeze out all moisture.

In large skillet combine onion, butter, and remaining ½ teaspoon salt. Sauté 3–4 minutes. Add zucchini, garlic, carrots, flour, basil, and oregano. Stir over medium heat 5–6 minutes. Remove from heat. Add parsley and lemon juice.

In large bowl combine eggs, ricotta, mozzarella, and ⅔ cup Parmesan cheese. Beat well. Add vegetable mixture and blend thoroughly. Stir in salt and pepper.

Butter 10-inch springform pan and sprinkle a few bread crumbs on bottom. Pour mixture into pan. Bake uncovered in preheated 375° oven 30 minutes. Remove from oven. Decorate with tomato slices; dredge in remaining bread crumbs and optional anchovies. Sprinkle with remaining Parmesan cheese.

Reduce oven temperature to 350° and bake additional 30 minutes. Turn oven off, open door, and leave "cake" inside 15 minutes. Remove from oven. Cool on rack 10 minutes before serving. Serves 8.

Noteworthy

Fried Rice

4 tablespoons vegetable oil, divided
¼ cup chopped green onion
¼ cup chopped carrots
2 eggs, slightly beaten
2 tablespoons soy sauce
2 teaspoons sugar
¼ teaspoon garlic powder

Cayenne pepper (optional)
2 cups cooked long grain rice
2 cups fresh bean sprouts, (optional)
1 cup frozen green peas, thawed
1 (8-ounce) can sliced water chestnuts, drained (optional)
½ cup sliced fresh mushrooms

Heat 2 tablespoons vegetable oil in large skillet. Add onion and carrots. Sauté over moderate heat until tender. Stir in eggs. Cook, stirring constantly, until set but moist. Remove egg mixture from skillet; set aside. Combine remaining 2 tablespoons vegetable oil, soy sauce, sugar, garlic powder, and cayenne (optional) in small bowl. Mix rice, bean sprouts, peas, water chestnuts, and mushrooms in large skillet. Add soy sauce mixture. Cook over moderate heat, stirring occasionally, 5–8 minutes or until mushrooms are tender. Stir in egg mixture. Makes 6 servings.

Seasoned with Love

Ham and Rice Casserole

SAUCE:
3 tablespoons butter
3 tablespoons flour
1½ cups milk

1½ teaspoons lemon juice
1 cup sour cream

Melt butter in saucepan. Stir in flour. Add milk gradually, stirring constantly. Cook and stir over heat until thickens and begins to boil. Stir in lemon juice and sour cream (can use low-fat yogurt).

2 (10-ounce) package frozen broccoli
2 cups cubed ham

½ cup grated Cheddar cheese
1½–2 cups cooked rice
Pepper

Cook and drain broccoli. Place in greased casserole. Top with ham and half of cheese. Spoon on rice and pour sauce over all. Top with pepper and rest of cheese. Bake at 400° for 20–25 minutes.

Dawdy Family Cookbook

Chicago Deep Dish Pizza

2½–3 cups flour
¼ cup cornmeal
1½ teaspoons salt
1 teaspoon sugar
1 package dry yeast

1 cup very hot water
2 tablespoons salad oil
Assorted pizza toppings
Prego Pizza Sauce
Mozzarella cheese

In mixer bowl, combine ½ cup flour, cornmeal, salt, sugar, and yeast. Mix well. With mixer at low speed, gradually add hot water and oil. Increase speed to medium and beat 1 minute. Stir in enough flour to make soft dough.

On lightly floured board, knead 5 minutes. Place in oiled bowl, turning dough to oil top. Cover and let rise until doubled, about 45 minutes. Punch down, and let rest 10 minutes.

Preheat oven to 400°. Roll out dough and fit into deep dish pizza pan, or any ovenproof pan. Prick with fork. Bake dough about 4 minutes and brush lightly with 1 tablespoon olive oil. Cover with sauce, toppings and cheese, and bake about 20 minutes more.

Our Best Home Cooking

Chicago-Style Pizza

Chicago is famous for its wonderful, thick, gooey, deep-dish pizzas.
The special method was developed by Uno's Pizzeria in the 1950s.

CRUST:

1 package dry yeast
1¼ cups warm water
1 tablespoon sugar
1½ teaspoons salt

¼ cup oil
3 cups flour
2 tablespoons cornmeal

Dissolve yeast in water. Add sugar, salt, and 2 tablespoons oil. Stir in flour to make a soft dough. Turn out onto well-floured board. Knead about 3 minutes. Put in greased bowl; cover and let rise in warm place until doubled in bulk, about 1½ hours.

SAUCE AND TOPPING:

1 (28-ounce) can Italian
  pear tomatoes, well drained
  and chopped
1 tablespoon oregano
1 teaspoon sugar

1 pound mozzarella or Scamorza
  cheese, thinly sliced
1 pound mild Italian sausage,
  broken up, cooked and drained
½ cup grated Parmesan cheese

Combine tomatoes, oregano, and sugar. Set aside.

Brush a 14-inch, deep-dish pizza pan with 2 tablespoons oil; sprinkle with cornmeal. Punch dough down; press in bottom of pan. Let rise about 30 minutes. Arrange cheese over dough. Place sausage over cheese. Spread with tomato sauce. Sprinkle with Parmesan cheese. Place pizza in a 500° oven. Immediately reduce heat to 450° and bake 20–25 minutes or until cheese is melted and crust is golden. Makes 4 (2-slice) servings.

Soupçon II

The legend of the Chicago Fire: After 3 months without rain, Chicago was as dry as a tinderbox. On the night of October 8, 1871, Mrs. O'Leary, a boarding housekeeper, went to the barn to milk her cow. She left her lighted lantern in the barn and the cow kicked it over, igniting straw in the stall. Destroying 65 acres per hour, in 27 hours the fire killed 250 people and destroyed much of the North Side of Chicago, leaving only the pumping station and the Old Water Tower of the Chicago Water Company remaining. They stand today as reminders of the past.

The Springfield Horseshoe

The Springfield Horseshoe Sandwich was created at the Old Leland Hotel in 1928 by Joe Schweska and Steve Tomko. For years the only recipe that existed was "a pinch of this and a little of that."

It wasn't until a Christmas edition of the State Journal Register in 1939 that Chef Schweska finally revealed the secret. The name "horseshoe" was derived from the shape of the cut of ham used in the original sandwich. The French fries represent the nails of the shoe and the sizzle platter represents a hot anvil.

The sandwich is made by laying two pieces of toast on a pre-heated platter, then placing the meat on the toast, covering the entire sandwich with cheese sauce, circling the platter with French fries. Add a dash of paprika for color and you have created a horseshoe.

As a result of the popularity of the original ham version, Chefs Schweska and Tomko produced endless variations including ham and egg, all egg, hamburger, ham and chicken, chicken, bacon, shrimp, turkey, corned beef. The possibilities are limited only by the chef's imagination.

While the ingredients can vary from the original, all the experts (and there are many of them) agree that the key is the sauce.

The secret is a sharp Old English Cheddar or a good Colby Longhorn cheese, Worcestershire sauce and Tabasco for the adventurous.

THE SAUCE IS THE THING...

2 egg yolks
½ cup beer
2 tablespoons butter
3 cups grated sharp Old English Cheddar or Colby Longhorn cheese
1 teaspoon Worcestershire sauce
¼ teaspoon dry mustard
½ teaspoon salt
Dash of cayenne pepper

Beat the egg yolks and beer together. Melt the butter and cheese over boiling water, stirring in one direction only with a wooden spoon.

Add the seasonings. Stirring constantly, add the beer and egg mixture a little at a time. Keep the mixture piping hot as you stir; but don't let it bubble. Constant stirring and the very best cheese will yield a smooth, uncurdled mixture. Serves 4.

Cook Book: Favorite Recipes of Our Best Cooks

Horseshoes

½ cup butter or margarine
¼ cup flour
1 teaspoon salt
½ teaspoon freshly ground
  black pepper

2 cups light cream or
  half-and-half
½ teaspoon cayenne pepper
2 cups shredded Cheddar
  cheese, sharp or mild

Melt butter in saucepan. Blend in flour and cook over low heat until mixture is smooth and bubbly. Remove from heat; stir in salt, pepper, cream, cayenne, and cheese. Return to heat, stirring constantly to make a smooth sauce. Keep warm until sandwiches are assembled.

8 slices bread, toasted
Cooked French fries

Sliced or shaved ham, chicken,
  or turkey or cooked ground
  beef patty

Place 2 slices of toast on serving plate; top with meat of your choice and cover with cheese sauce. Mound French fries on top. Serve immediately.

Note: A smaller sandwich, using only 1 slice of toast, is a Ponyshoe.

Honest to Goodness

Stroganoff Steak Sandwich

⅔ cup beer
⅓ cup cooking oil
1 teaspoon salt
¼ teaspoon garlic powder
¼ teaspoon pepper
2 pounds (1-inch thick) flank
  steak

2 tablespoons butter
½ teaspoon paprika
4 cups sliced onions
12 slices French bread, toasted
1 cup sour cream
½ teaspoon prepared horseradish

In shallow dish, combine beer, oil, salt, garlic powder, and pepper. Marinate steak in covered dish in refrigerator overnight, or at room temperature for several hours.

Drain. Broil steak 3 inches from heat 5–7 minutes on each side for medium rare.

Melt butter in saucepan and blend in paprika and a dash of salt. Add onion. Cook until tender, but not brown.

Thinly slice meat diagonally across grain. For each serving, arrange meat slices over two slices of bread. Top with onions. Combine sour cream and horseradish; spoon onto each sandwich. Sprinkle with paprika. Yield: 6 servings.

An Apple From The Teacher

Ooh! Soo! Good! Baked Bean Sandwiches

2 cups canned baked beans
½ cup tomato paste
½ cup chopped onion
⅓ cup sweet pickle relish
1 tablespoon prepared
  mustard

1 tablespoon brown sugar
½ teaspoon salt
8 toasted bread slices
4 partially fried thick bacon
  slices

Mix baked beans, tomato paste, onion, relish, mustard, sugar, and salt. Spread to edges of each toast slice. Top with half bacon slice. Broil 4 inches from heat until bacon is crisp. Delicious served with mugs of hot chocolate (cocoa). Makes 8 servings.

Cookin' With Friends

Strombolis
(Italian Sloppy Joes)

1 pound ground beef
1 tablespoons chopped onion
 (or more to taste)
½ cup ketchup
3 tablespoons grated
 Parmesan cheese
⅓ teaspoon garlic powder

¼ teaspoon fennel seed,
 crushed (a must ingredient)
¼ teaspoon dried oregano
6–8 hamburger buns
Garlic Spread
6–8 slices mozzarella cheese

Brown meat; drain fat. Add onion, ketchup, Parmesan cheese, garlic powder, fennel seed, and oregano. Simmer for 20 minutes.

Split hamburger buns. Spread about 1 teaspoon Garlic Spread on each bun top. Divide meat mixture evenly on bun bottoms. Top meat mixture with a cheese slice. Top with bun top. Wrap each sandwich in a square of foil. Bake in 350° oven for 15 minutes, or until heated through. Yield: 6–8 sandwiches.

Note: These can be frozen for up to 1 month. Partly thaw, then bake.

GARLIC SPREAD:
2 tablespoons butter,
 softened

¼ teaspoon garlic powder
¼ teaspoon paprika

Combine butter, garlic powder, and paprika; mix well.

Herrin's Favorite Italian Recipes Cookbook

Reuben Sandwich Casserole

1 large onion
1 small (1-pound) head
  cabbage
2 tablespoons salad oil
¼ teaspoon salt
½ cup water
⅓ cup mayonnaise
⅓ cup chili sauce
¼ cup milk

1 tablespoon sweet pickle
  relish
½ pound thin sliced deli
  corned beef
¼ pound thin sliced Swiss
  cheese
½ (8-ounce) loaf party
  pumpernickel bread slices

Cut onion into thick slices. Cut cabbage into thin wedges. In a large skillet heat oil and add onions; cook until tender. Remove onions. Add cabbage wedges and brown. Add salt and water. Over high heat, heat to boiling. Cover and reduce heat to low. Simmer 10 minutes until cabbage is tender.

In small bowl combine mayonnaise, chili sauce, milk, and relish. Stir until well blended.

In a 13x9-inch dish, arrange onions, cooked cabbage, corned beef, cheese, and top with slices of bread. Spread mayonnaise mixture evenly on top of bread slices. Cover and bake at 375° for 20–25 minutes. Serves 8.

Franklin County Homemakers Extension Cookbook

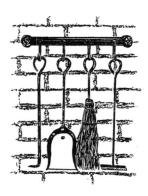

Turkey Mornay

2 (10-ounce) packages frozen broccoli spears, cooked until tender-crisp
¼ pound thinly-sliced prosciutto
1 pound sliced cooked breast of turkey
¼ cup butter
¼ cup flour
1 cup rich chicken broth

1 cup light cream
2 tablespoons grated Parmesan cheese
2 tablespoons grated Swiss cheese
2 tablespoons sherry
Salt to taste
Dash cayenne
¼ cup grated Parmesan cheese

Drain broccoli and arrange it in a baking dish. Cover with the prosciutto, then with the turkey. Melt butter and blend in flour. Stir in the chicken stock and cream; cook, stirring constantly, until smooth and thick. Stir in cheeses, sherry, salt, and cayenne. Heat just until cheese is melted. Pour sauce over turkey; sprinkle with ¼ cup grated Parmesan. Bake at 350° until the sauce is hot and the cheese brown and bubbly, about 30 minutes. Makes 6 servings.

Soupçon I

Healthy Italian Beefless

½ whole turkey breast
Water (to cover)
Beef bouillon cubes
¼ cup white vinegar
1 medium onion, chopped
1 green pepper, seeded and sliced

2 cloves garlic, minced
1 teaspoon oregano
1 tablespoon Worcestershire sauce
Tabasco to taste
1 package brown gravy mix

Simmer the turkey breast in water to cover; add 1 bouillon cube for each cup of water. Bring to boil; reduce heat and simmer 4–5 hours. Remove turkey from broth and string the meat. Add remaining ingredients, except the gravy mix, to the broth and cook another 1–2 hours. Stir the brown gravy mix into ½ cup water and add it to the broth; cook 20 minutes. Serve on hard rolls. Serve with onion slices and pepperoncini.

Cooking with Daisy's Descendants

Open-Faced Crab Sandwich

2 pounds crab meat
¼ cup chopped parsley
1 tablespoon lemon juice
½ cup mayonnaise
¼ cup sour cream
½ teaspoon garlic salt

12 unbaked rectangular-
 shaped party rolls
¼ cup butter, softened
4 ounces thinly-sliced Swiss
 cheese

Combine crab meat, parsley, lemon juice, mayonnaise, sour cream, and garlic salt in bowl; mix well. Slice rolls into halves lengthwise; spread with butter. Place in shallow baking pan. Place Swiss cheese slices on rolls. Spread with crab meat mixture.

Bake at 350° for 25 minutes or until edges brown. Serve hot with salad and white wine. Yield: 8 servings.

Approx Per Serving: Cal 377; T Fat 26g; 62% Calories from Fat; Prot 24g; Carbo 12g; Chol 131mg; Sod 665mg.

Pioneer Pantry

Where's the Meat Veggie Burgers

1 large Spanish onion,
 chopped
2 tablespoons olive oil
1 cup red or green pepper,
 chopped
1¼ cups mushrooms, chopped
1⅓ cups carrots, shredded
1 cup eggplant, peeled and
 chopped

1½ cups quick cooking
 oatmeal
¼ teaspoon pepper
½ teaspoon salt
1 teaspoon tamari
1 teaspoon garlic powder
¼ teaspoon coriander powder
½ cup whole wheat flour

Sauté onion in olive oil until opaque. Add remainder of vegetables and cook until soft, adding more oil, if necessary. Remove from heat and stir in oats; allow to stand 5 minutes. Add remaining ingredients and form into 8 patties. Sauté in 12-inch skillet with small amount of oil; or brush each patty generously with oil and bake on oiled pan in a 375° oven, turning until crisp and brown. Serve on toasted buns with lettuce, tomato, and catsup.

Tradition in the Kitchen 2

The Blimpie Blast

Tailgreat is an annual extravaganza that takes "tailgating" to the limit. Illini fans enjoy a carnival-like atmosphere as they cruise a midway filled with displays, games, and activities by students, alumni and local businesses. Catch the "Illini Spirit!" Traditionally held prior to the first U of I home football game.

Often enjoyed by Illini "tailgaters" is the six-foot sandwich.

1 (6-foot) loaf bread, 6 inches wide, sliced lengthwise

2 pounds whole boneless ham, cut in ½-ounce slices

1 pound Genoa hard salami, cut in ½-ounce slices

1 pound prosciutto, cut in ½-ounce slices

1 pound Cappacola, cut in ½-ounce slices

1 pound provolone, cut in ½-ounce slices

Cover with tomato slices, shredded lettuce, onions, green pepper, and black olives. Garnish with oil and vinegar or mayonnaise and mustard. Serves up to 35 persons.

Cook Book: Favorite Recipes from Our Best Cooks

Pesto Linguine

5 large garlic cloves
1 packed cup fresh parsley, tough stems removed
1 packed cup basil leaves, tough stems removed
1 cup olive oil
½ cup grated, good quality domestic or imported Parmesan cheese
1 pound thin linguine
4–6 tablespoons butter

Place the garlic, parsley, and basil in a blender and mix until all the ingredients are finely chopped. Then add the oil and blend for 10–20 seconds. Add the grated cheese and blend for 10–15 seconds longer. Cook the linguine to the al dente stage in rapidly boiling, lightly salted water, according to package instructions. Drain. Add the butter to the hot linguine. Mix in 4–8 tablespoons pesto sauce. If too dry, add a few tablespoons of warm water and/or a few drops of olive oil. Top with additional grated cheese and serve immediately.

Caring is Sharing

Betty's Tomato, Basil and Brie Sauce

6–8 tomatoes, peeled and cubed in small pieces
½ pound Brie, cubed in small pieces
¼ cup olive oil
1 cup basil, chopped
3–4 cloves garlic, minced
½ teaspoon oregano
Salt and pepper to taste
1 tablespoon red wine vinegar

Put all ingredients in a large bowl and let stand in a warm place (outside on a warm day) for several hours. Serve over cooked pasta.

Jubilee

Lower-Fat Pesto

1 cup firmly packed fresh
  basil leaves
½ cup torn fresh spinach
  leaves
¼ cup grated Parmesan
  cheese

¼ cup pine nuts, walnuts
  or almonds
2 cloves garlic, quartered
2 tablespoons olive oil or
  cooking oil

In a blender container or food processor bowl, combine basil, spinach, cheese, nuts, garlic and ¼ teaspoon salt. Cover; blend or process with several on-off turns till paste forms, stopping the machine several times and scraping sides. With the machine running slowly, gradually add the oil and 2 tablespoons water and blend or process to the consistency of soft butter. Transfer to a storage container. Cover and refrigerate up to 2 days or freeze up to 1 month. Makes ¾ cup.
Spinach pesto: Prepare pesto as directed, except substitute fresh torn spinach for all the fresh basil and add 1 teaspoon dried crushed basil.

Favorite Herbal Recipes Vol. III

Green Tomato Mincemeat

3 pints apples, peeled and
  chopped
3 pints green tomatoes,
  chopped
3 cups raisins
4 cups brown sugar
1½ cups vinegar

3 teaspoons cinnamon
1 teaspoon cloves
¾ teaspoon allspice
¾ teaspoon mace
2 teaspoons salt
¾ cup butter

Combine apples and tomatoes in large kettle; drain. Add remaining ingredients except butter. Bring mixture to a boil; simmer 3 hours. Add butter; allow to melt. Can mixture and seal. Yield: 6 pints.

An Apple From The Teacher

In 1897, the Chicago Teachers Club and other groups met to protest the sale of cigarettes, saying they were "poison-laden, memory-destroying, and corrupting."

Gnocchi

4 pounds potatoes (must be
   Idaho)
2 tablespoons salt
½ cup butter (1 stick)
2 eggs, beaten

4 cups flour
Salt, to taste
2 tablespoons salt
Parmesan cheese, grated
Meat sauce

Cook potatoes with jackets on in salted water. Peel and mash while hot. Place butter in center of hot mashed potatoes. When butter has melted (about 15 minutes) mix potatoes thoroughly. Cover with dish towel and allow to cool.

Make small well in center of potatoes and pour eggs in and mix well. Gradually add flour and salt, to taste. Knead well to form dough. Separate mixture into 4 equal parts. Sprinkle each with flour. Roll each portion into a roll the thickness of a sausage. Slice in pieces slightly thicker than ½ inch. Gently roll each piece on flat grater, slightly curling each piece. Pieces should resemble macaroni shells.

Cook in 4 quarts boiling salted water (cook about ⅓ of total amount at one time) about 20–30 seconds. Gnocchi will rise to top of boiling water when done. Gently scoop out with slotted spoon as they rise to top. Sprinkle Parmesan cheese on top of cooked Gnocchi and top with generous amounts of meat sauce. Serves 8.

Herrin's Favorite Italian Recipes Cookbook

The 48-foot-tall concrete monolith of a Native American that towers over the Rock River in Lowden State Park near Oregon was created by Lorado Taft. The public has named it "Blackhawk" in honor of the great Sauk warrior who was noted for his struggle against the westward movement of the white men in Illinois.

Seafood

Blackhawk Statue in Lowden State Park. Oregon.

Rolled Sole with Broccoli

1 pound sole fillets (firm,
large fillets that you can
easily roll)
1 tablespoon margarine,
melted

1 package frozen chopped
broccoli, cooked
½ cup sliced fresh mushrooms
Wedge of fresh lemon
½ cup shredded Swiss cheese
1 tablespoon paprika

Brush sole fillets with melted margarine. Place cooked broccoli and mushrooms in center of fillet. Roll fish with filling
inside and stand in baking dish that you have already sprayed
with oil. Secure each fish roll-up with long toothpick or
wooden skewer. Bake 20–30 minutes and the last five minutes, top with lemon squeeze and shredded Swiss cheese, and
sprinkle with paprika.

The Fishlady's Cookbook

Salmon Patties

1 (16-ounce) can salmon
2 eggs
½ teaspoon salt
⅛ teaspoon pepper

1½ tablespoons grated onion
3 tablespoons sour cream
½ cup bread crumbs

Drain salmon, remove skin. Mash with fork. Add remaining
ingredients. Divide into 8 patties and fry until golden brown
in hot oil. Serves 6–8.

C-U in the Kitchen

Lincoln's New Salem, 20 miles northwest of Springfield, is a reconstruction of
the village in which Abraham Lincoln grew from a gangling youngster to a
man of purpose and destiny.

Salmon Grilled with Red Onion Butter

2 (6-ounce) salmon filets   Olive oil
Salt and pepper to taste

Season filets. Brush with olive oil. Grill to medium.

RED ONION BUTTER:
1 red onion, sliced   1 cup red wine
1 pound unsalted butter   2 tablespoons cream
Pinch of salt

Sweat the onions in a little butter with a pinch of salt, cover
the pan and cook for 5 minutes. The moisture will be drawn
out of the onions without caramelizing them. Add the red
wine. Reduce, then add the cream; reduce until thick. Whip
in the softened butter, one chunk at a time. Season with salt
and pepper. Place salmon on plate; put the red onion butter
on side. Garnish with fresh vegetables. Yield: 2 servings.

GARNISH:
Carrot curls   Daikon slices*
Zucchini and squash slices

*Japanese mild radish, available in most produce sections.
*From Melange Restaurant, 1515 Sheridan, Plaza del Lago,
Wilmette.*

Best Recipes of Illinois Inns and Restaurants

Brett's Dill Broiled Salmon

This is healthy, low in fat and tastes great!

CUCUMBER-DILL SAUCE:

1 cup sour cream
1 cucumber, peeled, grated
1 tablespoon grated onion
1 tablespoon lemon juice

1 teaspoon fresh dill or 2
  teaspoons dried dill
½ teaspoon salt (optional)
Pepper to taste

Combine sour cream, cucumber, onion, lemon juice, dill, salt and pepper to taste in bowl; mix well. Set aside and chill for 1 hour or longer.

1 teaspoon dried dillweed
2 tablespoons white vinegar
3 tablespoons oil
1 teaspoon lemon juice
1 teaspoon salt (optional)
Dash of pepper

6 salmon steaks
Chopped parsley or paprika,
  to taste
1 lemon, sliced or cut into
  wedges

Combine dillweed, vinegar, oil, lemon juice, salt, and dash of pepper in mixer bowl; mix well. Let stand for 1 hour.

Beat vinegar mixture again to mix well. Baste salmon with vinegar mixture; place on preheated greased rack in broiler pan. Broil 2 inches from heat source for 5–8 minutes on each side or until fish flakes easily, basting with remaining vinegar mixture.

Serve with chilled Cucumber-Dill Sauce. Top with parsley or paprika and lemon slices. Yield: 6 servings.

Recipe from Brett Fischer.

The Cubs 'R Cookin'

Red Snapper in Mayonnaise
(Psari Majoneza)

While waiting for a fishing boat to dock, we heard the woes heaped on those sly fishmongers who dripped blood on the eyes and gills of fish to make them appear fresher: they straightaway landed in jail! Against such deception, Greek people market with sharp eyes, looking for the characteristics of fresh fish: Pink eyes, pink gills, firm scales and back, and a fresh sea smell. After cooking, a fresh fish emerges tender and succulent, with white, flaky meat and white bones. And in the city of Chicago, people know and expect to buy "catch" fresh fish—period!

6 pounds whole fresh red
  snapper
Salt
Juice of 2 limes
2 tablespoons olive oil

3 bay leaves
½ teaspoon salt
6 small potatoes
Mayonnaise

Wash fish thoroughly in cold water; pat dry with a paper towel. Rub fish with salt and fresh lime juice, including the cavity. Set aside for ½ hour.

To cook fish, use a flat pot with a rack, or wrap the fish in a very porous, clean cheesecloth, and place fish flat in bottom of pot. Pour in enough hot water to barely cover the fish; add olive oil, bay leaves, and salt. Simmer 20–25 minutes, or until cooked. Carefully unwrap fish and gently place on a wide-lipped platter. Set aside to cool.

Boil potatoes, peel, and quarter. Place around fish in platter. Serve with mayonnaise. Makes 6–8 servings.

Garnish: 4 hard-boiled eggs, sliced and placed all over fish. Arrange and decorate fish platter with black olives, sliced gherkins, radishes, chopped parsley, and grated nutmeg.

Opaa! Greek Cooking Chicago Style

Swedish immigrants seeking religious freedom founded Bishop Hill in 1846. More than one thousand immigrants led by Erik Jansson sailed from Sweden to New York, then by way of the Great Lakes, arrived in Chicago from where they walked the final 160 miles to Bishop Hill.

Blackened Red Snapper

1 pound red snapper fillets
2 tablespoons light margarine
½ teaspoon garlic powder
½ cup Cajun spice

Use your outdoor grill and make sure your coals are very hot. Spray iron skillet with non-stick coating. Mix margarine, garlic powder and Cajun spice together. Brush thickly onto snapper fillets. Sear fillets in iron skillet until blackened on both sides. Reduce heat and grill until fish flakes easily when tested with a fork. Serves 2.

Serve with Brussels sprouts and a potato kabob.

Nutritional value (per serving): 270 calories, 9 grams fat.

The Fishlady's...Forever Dieter's Book

Fried Catfish

4 cups seasoned croutons
2 pounds catfish fillets
3 cups buttermilk
Salt
Freshly ground black pepper
Cayenne pepper
Oil for frying
Lemon wedges

Process croutons in food processor or blender to make fine crumbs. Place fillets in a non-metallic pan. Pour buttermilk over fillets; let set for 30 minutes.

Remove fillets; season with salt, pepper, and cayenne to taste. Coat fillets with crouton crumbs. Let set for 30 minutes. Fry fillets in 375° oil, turning once, until coating is dark golden brown. Serve immediately with lemon wedges. Makes 4–6 servings.

Honest to Goodness

In 1972, Chicago-born high school dropout Bobby Fischer became the first American to win the official world chess championship. He defeated defending champion Boris Spassky of the Soviet Union in the most publicized chess match in history.

Butter-Herbed Baked Fish

½ cup melted butter or
  margarine
⅔ cup finely crushed saltines
½ teaspoon each: basil, oregano,
  and salt

¼ teaspoon garlic powder
¼ cup Parmesan cheese
1 pound white fish fillets such
  as halibut or orange roughy

Preheat oven to 350°. Melt butter or margarine. Mix crumbs, herbs, and Parmesan cheese. Dip fish in butter or margarine, then in crumbs. Arrange in baking dish and bake 25–30 minutes. Serves 3–4.

Still Gathering

Oven-Fried Red Snapper

1 tablespoon oil
2 (8-ounce) fillets red snapper
½ cup seasoned bread crumbs

½ teaspoon paprika
½ teaspoon garlic powder
Fresh lemon

Preheat oven to 400°. Oil bottom of baking dish very lightly. Wet fillets. Roll in combined dry ingredients above. Place in baking dish. Squeeze on fresh lemon. Bake 20–30 minutes without turning. Fish is done when flaky. Serves 2.

Serve with whipped potatoes and broccoli. (Don't forget the tarter sauce.)

The Fishlady's Cookbook

Trout Meniere

2½ cups peanut oil
3 trout fillets, (2½ pounds)
  halved (smaller fillets
  equaling same weight
  will suffice)
1 cup flour

1 cup butter
2 tablespoons lemon juice
2 teaspoons Worcestershire
  sauce
1 teaspoon salt
¼ cup chopped parsley

In a frying pan, preheat the oil to 350°. Test the temperature by dropping a small amount of water in the oil; if it pops, the oil is hot enough. (Be careful when testing.) Dredge the trout evenly in the flour and fry it, 2 pieces at a time, over medium heat, for 5–7 minutes on each side. Transfer the fried fillets to a heated platter and keep them warm.

In a heavy saucepan, melt the butter and brown it lightly. Stir in the lemon juice, Worcestershire sauce, salt, and parsley; heat thoroughly. Pour some of the sauce over the fillets and serve the remaining portion in a sauceboat. Serves 6.

A Cause for Applause

Foil Wrapped Halibut Steaks

2 (8-ounce) halibut steaks
1 tablespoon margarine
¼ slice fresh lemon
½ teaspoon parsley flakes
½ teaspoon paprika
¼ teaspoon garlic powder
¼ teaspoon lemon pepper

4 slices fresh jumbo
  mushrooms
1 tablespoon green peppers
  (sliced)
1 tablespoon carrots
1 tablespoon green onion
  (chopped)

Cut foil large enough to hold each halibut steak individually (2 pieces foil for each steak). This can be cut in the shape of a fish, if you like.

Spray each piece of foil with a non-stick coating, or just oil each piece of foil lightly. Dot fish with margarine and squeeze of fresh lemon. Sprinkle with above seasonings. Arrange veggies on steak. Seal package tightly with second piece of foil. Bake 30 minutes at 400° or grill 10 minutes per side.

The Fishlady's Cookbook

Easy Stir-Fry

1 package frozen Chinese
   vegetables
1 tablespoon soy sauce

1 pound peeled and deveined
   raw shrimp
½ cup chunky pineapple

Sauté Chinese vegetables in soy sauce. Add raw shrimp and pineapple and simmer, stirring occasionally until shrimp are pink, not translucent. Serve over cooked rice. Serves 2.

Nutritional value (per serving): 350 calories, 4 grams fat.

The Fishlady's...Forever Dieters Book

Basil Shrimp

⅓ cup chopped onion or
   shallots
2 cloves garlic, chopped
1 tablespoon olive oil
1 tablespoon butter
1 tablespoon chopped fresh
   basil (or 1 teaspoon dried)
Freshly ground pepper

16 fresh or frozen shrimp,
   peeled and deveined
½ cup cream sherry
½ cup minced fresh tomatoes
2 tablespoons chopped
   parsley (fresh or dried)
Salt to taste

Sauté onion or shallots and garlic in oil and butter until transparent. Add basil, pepper, and shrimp. Increase heat to high and sauté about 1 minute or so. Add cream sherry, tomatoes, and parsley. Season to taste. When shrimp curl, the dish is ready. Serve with rice or pasta. Makes 2–3 servings.

First There Must Be Food

During the 1890s, two neighboring Congregational churches in Galesburg agreed to become Central Church together. To symbolize their union, their bells were melted down and recast as one, weighing 34,000 pounds. The church's Rose Window is one of the most beautiful historic treasures of Galesburg.

Baked Shrimp

Quite shrimply, the best. This is one of the easiest and most successful dinner parties to give. Figure at least ½ pound of shrimp per person. Cover your table with newspapers. Use paper plates. Have plenty of paper napkins—people eat so enthusiastically, the sauce runs down to their elbows. Make a simple tossed salad with dressing and chunks of blue cheese. Put the pan of shrimp in the middle of the table, flank it with loaves of crusty bread for dipping, and watch people wade in. The shrimp are tender and flavorful, and the sauce is a miracle. There's so much of it, you think it will go to waste. Instead it goes to waist, because the bread sopped in the sauce is phenomenal.

This can be expensive, but I watch the grocery ads for sales on shrimp. Sometimes you can find a truck on a corner selling fresh shrimp. Put these in clean milk containers, fill them with water and freeze them. When you use the shrimp, they'll taste as if they're only 2 minutes from the ocean.

2 pounds raw, frozen shrimp-in-the-shell
1 cup (½ pound) butter
1 cup (½ pound) margarine
¼ cup Worcestershire sauce

Run shrimp under cold water to remove the frost. Place shrimp and sauce (melted butter and margarine mixed with Worcestershire) in 9x13-inch pan. Bake uncovered at 350° for 30 minutes.

The Lucy Miele 6-5-4 Cookbook

Shrimp in Pernod Sauce

8 tablespoons butter
1¼ pounds shrimp or bay
  scallops
2 tablespoons shallots
¾ ounce Pernod
5 cloves garlic, minced

4 ounces dry white wine
4 ounces fish stock
1 cup whipping cream
1 tablespoon tarragon
Salt and pepper

Melt 3 tablespoons butter. Add the shrimp (or scallops) and shallots. Add Pernod and ignite. Add the garlic and wine; simmer 2 minutes. Remove the shrimp. Reduce the sauce by ⅓. Add the stock and reduce the sauce by ½. Add the cream and tarragon and cook until the sauce thickens. Add the shrimp and serve. Yield: 4 servings.

Holy Cow!

Shrimp Creole

4 tablespoons margarine
1 cup chopped green pepper
1 cup chopped celery
1 cup chopped green onion
1 clove garlic, bruised and
  minced

¼ teaspoon cayenne pepper
2 (14½-ounce) cans whole
  tomatoes
1 pound raw shrimp (peeled
  and deveined)
6 cups cooked rice

Melt margarine in skillet. Add green pepper, celery, green onion, and garlic and sauté until almost tender. Add cayenne pepper and tomatoes and cook over medium heat for 5 minutes. Add shrimp and simmer for five minutes or until shrimp are pink. Serve over cooked rice. Serves 4.

The Fishlady's Holiday Entertaining Cookbook

 The Mississippi River doubles in volume at Cairo, where it joins the Ohio River. This part of the state was once called "Little Egypt," because it resembled the fertile Nile River.

Herbed Shrimp De Jonghe

Great taste! Serve over rice or fettucini with crisp French bread.

½ cup butter, softened
3 cloves of garlic, crushed
2 teaspoons chopped chives
1 teaspoon tarragon
2 teaspoons chopped parsley
Mace, thyme, nutmeg, salt,
  black pepper, and cayenne
  pepper to taste

2 tablespoons sherry
¼ cup (about) fresh bread
  crumbs
12 ounces fresh shrimp,
  peeled, deveined

Combine the butter with the garlic, chives, tarragon, parsley, mace, thyme, nutmeg, salt, black pepper, and cayenne pepper in a bowl. Add the wine; mix well. Add enough bread crumbs to form a paste-like mixture. Chill for 2 hours or longer

Let butter mixture stand at room temperature for 1 hour. Cut the shrimp into halves lengthwise. Place in a shallow baking dish. Spread the herbed butter evenly over the shrimp. Bake at 400° for 15 minutes. Serves 4.

Generations

Crab Casserole

1 (7-ounce) package egg
  noodles
1 jar sliced mushrooms
1 can cream of mushroom soup
½ cup shredded Cheddar cheese

½ pound crab-seafood blend
½ cup breadcrumbs or
  potato chips

Cook noodles until tender, drain and pour into a casserole dish. Add mushrooms, soup, Cheddar cheese, and crab blend. Mix together. Sprinkle breadcrumbs or crushed potato chips over top. Bake in 350° oven for 30 minutes.

The Fishlady's Cookbook

The annual Great Cardboard Boat Regatta is held on SIU-Carbondale campus lake in April. Boats are created entirely of cardboard and powered by propellers, paddle wheels, or sails.

Scallop Sauté

1 pound fresh scallops,
  drained
3 tablespoons margarine,
  melted
1 small onion, sliced and
  separated into rings

1 cup sliced fresh mushrooms
¼ cup dry white wine
2 teaspoons seafood
  seasonings
1 tomato, diced

Sauté scallops in margarine in large skillet about 5 minutes or until tender. Drain and set aside. Reserve drippings in skillet. Sauté onion and mushrooms in drippings in skillet for 4 minutes or until tender; drain and set aside. Reserve drippings in skillet. Add wine and seafood seasonings to drippings in skillet; cook over high heat until mixture is reduced by about half. Add scallops, mushrooms, onion, and tomato to drippings in skillet. Cook over high heat for 1 minute or until heated. Serve immediately. Yield: 3–4 servings.

Our Favorite Recipes

Lobster Newburg

1 pound cooked lobster (cut into pieces)
2 tablespoons margarine
1 cup sherry

¼ teaspoon paprika
Salt and pepper
1 cup cream
6 pastry shells

Lightly simmer lobster in margarine. Add sherry, paprika, salt and pepper. Simmer 2 minutes. Add cream and simmer until slightly thickened. Serve over toast or in baked pastry shell. Serves 4–6.

The Fishlady's Holiday Entertaining Cookbook

Indian legend tells that the Rock River found the land in Grand Detour so beautiful that it turned around for a second look, thus creating the oxbow bend for which the settlement was later named by early French explorers. John Deere, who gained fame for his farm equipment, lived there (1837-1848). His home and museum are open for tours. The John Deere Company is headquartered in Moline.

Poultry

JOHN DEERE, PROP.

Editor Barbara Moseley visits John Deere's blacksmith shop, where he forged the first successful steel plow. Grand Detour.

Harry's Chicken Vesuvio

This recipe is a specialty of Chef Abraham Aguirre, chef at Harry Caray's restaurant, "Holy Cow!!!"

½ chicken cut into 4
   pieces
½ teaspoon salt
½ teaspoon pepper
2 teaspoons oregano
2 teaspoons granulated
   garlic
2 ounces frozen peas

1 teaspoon sugar
Boiling water
1 baking potato, peeled, cut
   into quarters
7 tablespoons olive oil
2 large cloves of garlic
½ cup dry white wine
2 teaspoons chopped parsley

Rinse chicken and pat dry. Season with salt, pepper, oregano and garlic.

Combine peas, sugar and enough boiling water to cover in bowl; mix well. Let stand for 1 minute; drain.

Sauté potato in 1 tablespoon olive oil in skillet until golden brown; drain.

Heat 6 tablespoons olive oil to 300° in 10-inch skillet. Add garlic cloves. Cook for 2 minutes, stirring occasionally. Add chicken. Sauté until brown on both sides. Add potato; mix well.

Deglaze skillet with white wine. Spoon into baking pan. Bake in 400° oven for 20–30 minutes or until chicken is tender. Transfer chicken to serving platter. Arrange potato and peas around chicken. Pour sauce over top. Sprinkle with parsley. Yield: 4 servings.

Recipe by Harry Caray.

The Cubs 'R Cookin'

Chicken Papaya

1 frying chicken, cut up	1 tablespoon cornstarch
1 cup papaya nectar	2 tablespoons water
½ cup brown sugar	1 papaya, cut into chunks
1 tablespoon soy sauce	(about ½ cup)
1 tablespoon lemon juice	

Bake chicken in lightly greased pan at 350° for 45 minutes. Combine nectar, brown sugar, soy sauce, and lemon juice. Heat until boiling, stirring well. Combine cornstarch with 2 tablespoons water and add to pan. Cook 4 minutes longer. Remove and add papaya. Pour sauce over chicken and bake 25 minutes. Makes 4 servings.

Tradition in the Kitchen 2

Skillet Chicken Risotta

1 (3-pound) chicken, cut up	1 small can mushroom pieces
2 tablespoons oil	3 carrots, peeled and bias
½ cup rice	sliced
½ cup onion, chopped	1 cup tomatoes, chopped
2 teaspoons salt (to taste)	1½ cups water
½ teaspoon poultry seasoning	

Brown chicken in oil. Remove chicken pieces from skillet. Drain all but 2 tablespoons fat from skillet. To skillet add rice, onion, salt, and poultry seasoning. Cook and stir until rice is lightly browned. Add mushrooms, carrots, tomatoes, and water. Place chicken atop rice mixture. Cover and simmer 45 minutes or until chicken and rice are done.

Herrin's Favorite Italian Recipes Cookbook

 All streets in Chicago are designated north or south, and east or west of State and Madison Streets, making it one of the easiest cities to find your way around in. After the 1871 fire, city planners did a good job of laying out a new city.

Chicken Morocco

This is a combination of 2 different recipes, and the sum is far superior than either of the 2 parts.

6 ounces boneless chicken breasts	1 medium white onion, sliced into strips
1 green pepper, cored, seeded and cut into julienne strips	8 medium figs, cut into small pieces
1 sweet red pepper, cored, seeded and cut into julienne strips	½ cup cream sherry
	¼ cup olive oil

Place all ingredients in large skillet and simmer covered until chicken is done, about 8 minutes. Add Sweet-Hot Sauce and bring back to a boil. Serve with rice. Serves 4.

SWEET-HOT SAUCE:

3 tablespoons olive oil	1 teaspoon cayenne
1 large onion, chopped coarsely, about 1 cup	1 teaspoon cumin
2 teaspoons finely minced garlic	4 tablespoons brown sugar
	3 cups tomato juice
1 teaspoon cinnamon	½ teaspoon salt
1 teaspoon ground ginger	½ teaspoon pepper

Sauté the onion in the hot oil for about 10 minutes; add garlic and continue to cook 3–4 minutes longer. Add spices, sugar, and tomato juice; season to taste. Simmer 30 minutes, until flavors are blended, and sauce is slightly thickened. Keep warm.

More to Love...from The Mansion of Golconda

Starved Rock State Park in Northern Illinois derived its name in the 1760s when the Illiniwek took refuse on top of the towering 125-foot sandstone butte and were surrounded by Ottawa-Potawatomi Tribes. After being trapped for many days, the Illiniwek starved to death. Today the park is one of Illinois' most visited attractions, with scenic river views and spectacular geological rock formations, and 18 canyons.

Chicken Marsala

4 chicken breasts, boned,
  skinned
½ cup flour
Salt and pepper to taste
¼ cup butter
1 (13-ounce) can beef broth
13 ounces dry Marsala

⅓ pound fresh mushrooms,
  sliced
¼ cup chopped fresh parsley
1 (9-ounce) package fresh egg
  fettucini
1 tablespoon cornstarch
1 tablespoon water

Rinse chicken; pat dry. Pound to ¼-inch thickness. Coat with mixture of flour, salt and pepper. Brown chicken in butter in heavy skillet over medium-high heat; do not over-cook. Remove to heated platter; keep warm.,

Add broth and wine to skillet. Simmer for 5 minutes. Add mushrooms. Simmer until reduced by ⅓. Return chicken to skillet. Sprinkle with parsley; reduce heat. Cook covered, for 2 minutes.

Cook pasta in boiling salted water for 3 minutes; drain and place on warm serving platter. Place chicken on pasta. Add desired amount of cornstarch dissolved in water to skillet. Cook until thickened just enough to cling to pasta. Pour over chicken and pasta. Garnish with parsley sprigs. Serve immediately with green salad and red wine. Yield: 4 servings.

Approx Per Serving: Cal 629; T Fat 18g; 26% Calories from Fat; Prot 39g; Carbo 61g; Fiber 1g; Chol 103mg; Sod 476mg.

Pioneer Pantry

Rey's Mexican Orange and Pineapple Chicken

1 (3–3½-pound) chicken,
  cut up
½ cup flour
1 teaspoon salt
½ teaspoon pepper
3 tablespoons oil
¾ cup orange juice
½ cup raisins

¼ cup dark rum
1 (8-ounce) can crushed
  pineapple
¼ teaspoon cinnamon
⅛ teaspoon ground cloves
¼ cup slivered almonds
1 tablespoon butter

Rinse chicken and pat dry. Coat with mixture of flour, salt and pepper. Brown on all sides in heated oil in skillet; remove to 9x13-inch baking dish.

Combine orange juice, raisins, rum, undrained pineapple, cinnamon, and cloves in bowl; mix well. Pour over chicken. Bake at 350° for 40–50 minutes or until chicken is cooked through.

Sauté almonds in butter in skillet until golden brown. Sprinkle over chicken. Serve over rice. Yield: 4 servings.
Recipe by Rey Sanchez.

The Cubs 'R Cookin'

Broiled Apricot Chicken

1 cup apricot nectar
3 tablespoons brown sugar
1 teaspoon grated orange
  peel
2 tablespoons catsup
2 tablespoons cornstarch

1 tablespoon horseradish
  mustard
½ teaspoon salt
6 chicken breasts
1 can apricot halves (drained)

Preheat broiler. Combine apricot nectar, brown sugar, orange peel, catsup, cornstarch, horseradish mustard, and salt. Stir until cornstarch is fully dissolved. Bring to a boil and hold for 1 minute. Remove from heat.

Broil chicken breasts 4–5 minutes on each side. Brush often with apricot sauce during broiling and before serving. Garnish with apricot halves. Makes 6 servings.

The French-Icarian Persimmon Tree Cookbook

Chicken Parmigiana

4 boneless, skinless, chicken breast halves
2 eggs, beaten
1 cup Progresso Italian Style Bread Crumbs
¼ cup olive oil

1 (15½-ounce) jar meat flavored spaghetti sauce
½ cup Parmesan cheese, grated
1 cup (4-ounce) shredded mozzarella cheese

Preheat oven to 400°. Dip chicken into eggs, then bread crumbs. Coat thoroughly. In medium skillet, heat olive oil. Cook chicken in oil until done and well browned. Pour spaghetti sauce in 11x7-inch pan. Place chicken on sauce and top with cheeses. Bake 15 minutes or until cheese is melted and lightly browned. Makes 4 servings.

Favorite Recipes of Collinsville Junior Service Club

Sweet and Sour Baked Chicken

1 (3-pound) broiler-fryer, cut up
½ cup chopped onion
½ cup coarsely chopped green pepper
½ cup coarsely chopped carrots
¼ cup butter or margarine
¾ cup ketchup
1 cup pineapple juice

2 tablespoons vinegar
¼ cup firmly packed brown sugar
1 tablespoon soy sauce
½ teaspoon garlic salt
1 teaspoon salt
¼ teaspoon pepper
Dash ground red pepper
Dash ground ginger
1 cup pineapple chunks

Preheat oven to 400°. In medium skillet, cook onion, green pepper, and carrots in butter for 5 minutes, stirring. Stir in ketchup, pineapple juice, vinegar, sugar, soy sauce, garlic salt, salt, peppers, and ginger. Cook, stirring constantly, until mixture boils. Add pineapple chunks. Arrange chicken pieces, skin-side-up in a 9x13-inch baking pan. Pour sweet and sour sauce over all. Bake covered for 45 minutes. Uncover and bake about 30 minutes longer, or until chicken tests done.

Our Favorite Recipes

Chicken Casserole

1 large package chicken
  Stove Top Dressing
1 stick oleo, melted
1 cup water
1 chicken, cooked and cubed
¼ cup chopped green onions
  (including tops)

1½ cups mayonnaise
¾ teaspoon salt
2 eggs
1½ cups milk
1 can cream of chicken soup
1 cup grated cheese

Mix dressing mix with oleo and water. Put ½ of mixture in greased 9x13-inch pan. Mix chicken with green onions, mayonnaise, and salt. Put over stuffing mix in pan. Top with remaining stuffing mixture. Beat eggs; add milk; pour over bread mixture. Cover with foil, refrigerate overnight.

Before baking, spread cream of chicken soup over top. Bake 30 minutes at 350°, uncovered. Sprinkle grated cheese over top. Bake 10 minutes more. Cut in squares and serve. Serves 10.

A Collection of Recipes From St. Matthew Lutheran Church

Hot Chicken Salad

4 cups cooked white meat
  chicken
4 cups chopped celery
1 cup toasted almonds
1 teaspoon salt
1 teaspoon Accent seasoning

4 teaspoons grated onion
2 cups Hellmann's mayonnaise
1 cup grated American or
  Cheddar cheese
1½ cups crushed potato chips

Mix all ingredients and pile high in Pyrex baking dish. Bake at 450° for 10 minutes or until heated through. This is good served with fruit. Makes 8 generous servings.

Inn-describably Delicious

Billy's Spicy Fried Chicken Breasts

4 whole chicken breasts,
  split, skinned
1–2 teaspoons black pepper
½ teaspoon poultry
  seasoning
½ teaspoon paprika
½ teaspoon cayenne pepper

¼ teaspoon dry mustard
⅔ cup flour
2¼ teaspoons garlic salt
¼ teaspoon salt
¼ teaspoon celery salt
¼ cup oil

Rinse chicken and pat dry. Sprinkle chicken with mixture of next 5 ingredients; press lightly. Combine flour and salts in bag. Add chicken 1 piece at a time, shaking to coat.

Heat oil in skillet over medium heat. Place chicken meaty side down in oil; sprinkle with remaining flour mixture. Fry for 30 minutes, turning every 10 minutes. Increase temperature to medium-high. Fry for 5 minutes or until chicken tests done; drain. Yield: 8 servings.
Recipe from Billy Williams.

The Cubs 'R Cookin'

Baked Chicken Soufflé

9 slices white bread, crusts
  removed
4 cups diced, cooked chicken
1 (4-ounce) can mushrooms
1 (8-ounce) can water
  chestnuts, drained and
  sliced
½ cup mayonnaise
½ pound Cheddar cheese

4 eggs, beaten
2 cups milk
1 teaspoon salt
1 can mushroom soup
1 can celery soup
1 (2-ounce) jar pimento,
  chopped
Bread crumbs from crusts
¼ cup melted butter

Line flat, buttered 9x13-inch pan with bread. Top with chicken and mushrooms. Spoon water chestnuts over chicken. Dot with mayonnaise. Top with cheese. Combine eggs, milk and salt and pour over chicken. Mix soups and pimento and spoon over all. Cover with foil and store in refrigerator overnight. Bake at 350° for 1½ hours. Sauté bread crumbs in butter and sprinkle over the top last 15 minutes. Remove from oven and set aside for 10 minutes before cutting to serve. Serves 12.

Five Loaves and Two Fishes II

Crab-Stuffed Chicken Breasts

May be prepared the night before serving.

**4 chicken breasts, boned,
  skinned, halved**
¼ cup butter
**½ cup thinly sliced green
  onion**
**¼ cup thinly sliced
  mushrooms**
6 tablespoons flour
½ teaspoon thyme

1 cup chicken broth
1 cup milk
1 cup dry white wine
Salt and pepper
8 ounces crabmeat
⅓ cup chopped parsley
⅓ cup dry bread crumbs
1 cup shredded Swiss cheese

Pound chicken between 2 sheets of plastic wrap until ¼-inch thick. Set aside.

Melt butter in large skillet; sauté onions and mushrooms; add flour and thyme. Blend in broth, milk, and wine; cook and stir until thickened; add salt and pepper to taste. Remove ¼ cup sauce.

Make stuffing of ¼ cup sauce, crabmeat, parsley, and dry bread crumbs. Spoon crab mixture evenly on 8 chicken breasts. Roll meat around filling and place seam-side-down in greased 8x12-inch baking dish.

Pour remaining sauce over chicken breasts. Sprinkle with cheese. Cover and bake at 400° for 35 minutes; uncover and bake 10 minutes more.

Brunch Basket

Swiss Chicken

4 whole chicken breasts,
split, boned, and skinned
8 sandwich slices Swiss
cheese
5 tablespoons butter
(divided use)
2 tablespoons flour

½ cup milk
½ cup chicken broth
Salt
Freshly ground black pepper
¼ cup white wine
1 cup dry stuffing mix

Place chicken breasts in buttered baking dish. Cover each breast with one slice of cheese. Melt 2 tablepoons butter over low heat. Add flour and blend over heat until smooth and bubbling. Slowly stir in milk and chicken broth. Season with salt and pepper to taste. Add white wine. Pour over chicken. Mix stuffing mix with 3 tablespoons melted butter. Spread over top of chicken. Bake at 350° for 45–60 minutes. Makes 8 servings.

Honest to Goodness

Spinach Stuffed Chicken Breasts

10 ounces frozen chopped
spinach, thawed, drained
4 ounces canned water
chestnuts, drained, finely
chopped
1 (8-ounce) package cream
cheese or low-calorie cream
cheese

¾ cup sour cream or sour
half-and-half
1⅝ ounces dry vegetable
soup mix
4 boneless chicken breasts,
split (skin on)

Combine all ingredients except chicken. Mix well. Divide mixture into eighths. At neck end of each piece of chicken, carefully lift skin. With long handled spoon, fill space between skin and meat with ⅛ spinach mixture, taking care not to break membrane connecting skin to meat. Tuck ends of chicken under and place in oven-proof baking dish. Repeat process with remaining chicken. Bake covered in preheated 350° oven 30 minutes. Uncover and bake additional 30 minutes.

May be served hot or cold. Cold chicken breasts are attractive sliced and arranged on platter. Serves 6–8.

Noteworthy

Aunt Hattie's Dressing

2 chickens, boiled
1½ loaves bread, torn up
1 stick margarine
1 large onion, chopped
1 cup celery, chopped
6 eggs, beaten
1 package crackers, crushed

Salt to taste
Pepper to taste
Sage to taste
1 can cream of mushroom soup
1 can cream of chicken soup
Broth
Oysters (if desired)

Boil chicken till tender; reserve broth. Tear bread in pieces the night before to let stale.

In margarine, sauté onion and celery. Mix celery, onion, bread, eggs, crackers, salt, pepper, and sage. Add soups, broth, and oysters (if desired). Be sure to add enough broth to make this thin, because it will be very dry if enough broth isn't added. Bake at 350° to 375° for 1 hour or until dressing is pulling away from pan.

Old-Fashioned Cooking

Parmesan Chicken

1 cup crushed herb-seasoned
   stuffing mix
⅔ cup grated Parmesan
   cheese
¼ cup chopped, fresh parsley

¾ cup butter
1 large clove garlic, crushed
1 (3-pound) frying chicken,
   cut up

Preheat oven to 375°. Mix crumbs, cheese, and parsley together in small bowl. Melt butter in small skillet. Add garlic while butter is melting, so flavors can blend. Dip chicken in butter. Roll in crumbs. Place in baking dish. Sprinkle remaining crumbs and butter over chicken. Bake at 375° for 45 minutes, or until chicken is done. May be refrigerated several hours before baking. Makes 4 servings.

Elsah Landing Heartland Cooking

Forbidden City Chicken

¼ cup soy sauce
2 tablespoons butter, melted
1 tablespoon curry powder
1 teaspoon cinnamon
1 teaspoon ground ginger
1 garlic clove, crushed

2 dashes hot red pepper
   sauce
2 small broiler chickens,
   split
Sesame seeds

In a bowl mix together all ingredients except chicken and sesame seeds. Spread mixture over chicken and chill for 1 hour.

Preheat oven to 325°. Sprinkle sesame seeds over chicken and bake for about 1 hour until chicken is golden. Yield: 4 servings.

One Magnificent Cookbook

 In March of 1911, the city of Zion put up a sign at its corporate limits proclaiming that it was a perfect city because it had no tobacco, whiskey, beer, theaters, doctors, drugs, pork or oysters.

Lincoln Logs

1½ cups diced, cooked chicken
1½ cups bread crumbs
1 cup walnuts, finely chopped

¼ cup celery, finely chopped
¼ cup onion, finely chopped
½ teaspoon salt
¼ teaspoon paprika
Bread crumbs

WHITE SAUCE:
½ cup chicken stock

½ cup cream

Mix chicken, bread crumbs, walnuts, celery, onion, salt and paprika. Moisten with sauce. Form mixture into logs 3-inches long. Roll in bread crumbs and fry in oil. Drain and serve with white sauce.

Cook Book: Favorite Recipes from Our Best Cooks

Garlic-Grilled Chicken

This is a low-fat, low-cholesterol recipe.

4 chicken breast halves, skinned and boned
1 cup picante sauce
2 tablespoons vegetable oil
1 tablespoon lime juice
2 cloves garlic, minced

½ teaspoon ground cumin
½ teaspoon dried whole oregano, crushed
¼ teaspoon salt
Additional picante sauce

Place each chicken breast between 2 pieces of plastic wrap. Flatten chicken to ¼-inch thickness, using a meat mallet or rolling pin; cut into 1-inch wide strips. Place chicken in a shallow container.

Combine next 7 ingredients, mixing well. Pour over chicken; cover and chill 1–2 hours.

Thread chicken onto skewers; cook over hot coals 6–8 minutes or until done, turning occasionally and basting with remaining marinade. Serve with picante sauce.

Home Cookin' is a Family Affair

Chicken With Red Pepper Salsa

2 cloves garlic, crushed
3–4 tablespoons olive oil
1 teaspoon salt
2 medium onions, chopped
1 large ripe tomato, chopped
½ teaspoon cumin
½ teaspoon crushed red
  pepper

2 bay leaves
3 tablespoons chopped fresh
  parsley
4 chicken breasts, skinned
  and boned
2 cups cooked white rice

In a 3-quart saucepan, sauté garlic in oil and salt. Add onions, tomato, cumin, crushed red pepper, bay leaves and parsley; stir to mix. This becomes a rich and thick sauce. Thin by adding ½ cup of water if necessary.

Cut chicken open to less than ½-inch thick and divide each piece in two. Add chicken to salsa mixture and mix well. Cover and cook at medium heat for 20–25 minutes. Remove bay leaves. Serve over white rice. Makes 2–3 servings.

Sugar Snips and Asparagus Tips

Orange Chicken

12 pieces chicken, cut up: 4
  breasts, 4 thighs, 4 drumsticks
Flour
Oil for frying
Salt and pepper to taste
2 large onions, sliced

1 cup orange juice
¼ cup orange marmalade
1 teaspoon celery seed
¼ cup orange liqueur
1 orange

Dust chicken pieces with flour. Put 2 tablespoons oil in a large frying pan on medium heat and brown the chicken pieces 4 at a time. Add salt and pepper and remove to a plate. Lower heat.

Put onions into pan and sauté gently without browning. Add orange juice, marmalade, and celery seed, and bring to a simmer. Add liqueur and ignite with a match. Place chicken and sauce in a Dutch oven or large covered casserole. Add 1 orange cut into wedges. Cover and bake at 325° for 1–1½ hours.

Note: Excellent party dish, as it tastes even better the second day. Serves 6.

C-U in the Kitchen

Ratatouille with Chicken and Pesto

The smell while this is cooking is almost as wonderful as the taste.

2 whole chicken breasts, boned, skinned
1 medium red onion, thinly sliced
1 medium green bell pepper, chopped
4 cloves of garlic, crushed
¼ cup olive oil
1 small eggplant, chopped
Salt and black pepper to taste
2 small zucchini, cut into bite-sized pieces
3 tablespoons chopped fresh basil or 1 tablespoon dried basil
2 teaspoons oregano
1 teaspoon thyme
4 medium tomatoes, peeled, seeded, chopped
8 ounces mushrooms, sliced
1 (8-ounce) can tomato sauce
Cayenne pepper to taste
½ cup orzo, cooked, drained

Rinse the chicken and pat dry. Cut into thin slices. Sauté the red onion, green pepper, and garlic in the olive oil in a skillet for 2 minutes. Stir in the eggplant. Sauté for several minutes. Season with salt and black pepper. Stir in the zucchini. Sauté for 2 minutes.

Add the chicken, basil, oregano, thyme, and additional black pepper; mix well. Cook over high heat until the chicken is tender, stirring constantly. Stir in the tomatoes, mushrooms, tomato sauce, and cayenne pepper. Adjust the seasonings. Simmer, covered, until of desired consistency. Stir in the orzo. May be prepared in advance, chilled until serving time and reheated on the stove or in the oven. Serves 6.

Generations

Chicken Jambalaya

This easy one-dish is great outdoors.

3 medium onions, chopped
4 chopped celery stalks
2 cloves garlic, minced
2 green peppers, chopped
¼ cup vegetable oil
1 (3-ounce) can tomato paste
1 (29-ounce) can stewed
  tomatoes
1 pound smoked sausage,
  thinly sliced
4 cups cooked, cubed chicken

½ teaspoon cayenne pepper
1 teaspoon chili powder
1 tablespoon chopped parsley
1 tablespoon Worcestershire
  sauce
2 drops hot pepper sauce
2 teaspoons salt
½ teaspoon pepper
2½ cups chicken broth
1 cup rice

In large skillet, sauté onions, celery, garlic, and peppers in oil. Add tomato paste, tomatoes, sausage, chicken, and seasonings. Cook over low heat 30–35 minutes; add chicken broth and uncooked rice. Bring to a boil; cover and cook until tender, about 20 minutes. Serves 6.

Brunch Basket

Chicken with Rice

1 envelope dehydrated onion
  soup mix
¾ cup rice (½ white, ½ wild)
2½ pounds chicken parts
  (thighs, legs and breasts)

Salt to taste
1 (10½-ounce) can cream
  of chicken soup
½ soup can of milk
½ soup can of water

Sprinkle dry soup in the bottom of an ungreased 9x13-inch ovenproof glass baking dish. Wash rice and place in a layer on top of soup. Salt chicken lightly and place in a single layer on top of rice. Mix chicken soup with milk and water. Pour over chicken and bake uncovered, 325° for 2 hours. Watch carefully toward the end and add water, if needed. If chicken is getting too brown, cover pan with foil. Makes 6-8 servings. **Note:** All breasts may be used instead of chicken parts. This is a good dinner for parties. Very little work with just a salad, rolls, and dessert to complete the meal.

Cookbook 25 Years

Pheasant Jubilee

4 pheasants, quartered
Flour
½ cup butter
1 onion, chopped
¾ cup seedless raisins
1 cup chili sauce
½ cup water

½ cup brown sugar
2 tablespoons Worcestershire
 sauce
¼ teaspoon garlic powder
1 cup sherry
1 (1-pound) can pitted dark
 sweet cherries, drained

Shake pheasants in flour; remove excess. Brown in butter. Place birds in a deep casserole. In the same skillet, combine onion, raisins, chili sauce, water, brown sugar, Worcestershire, and garlic powder. Bring to a boil. Pour over pheasants; cover and bake at 325° for 1 hour. Add sherry and cherries; bake another 20 minutes, uncovered, or until pheasants are tender. Makes 6 servings.

Soupçon I

Bonnie Blair, champion speed skater, is the holder of six Olympic medals—more than any other American woman, winter or summer—in Olympic history. She won gold and bronze medals in Calgary, Alberta, in 1988; two golds in Albertville, France, in 1992; and two more golds in Lillehammer, Norway, in 1994. Bonnie has a street named after her in her hometown of Champaign; has had a song written about her; has been on the Kelloggs Corn Flakes box; and was featured in *Sports Illustrated* as 1994's "Sports Woman of the Year." Her spirit, determination, and patriotism make her a favorite daughter not only of Champaign, but of the entire nation.

Meats

The Lincoln Tomb. Springfield.

Italian Beef

1 (6-pound) rump roast
3 large onions
1 teaspoon salt

¼ teaspoon coarse ground
   black pepper

Place beef in roaster, half filled with water. Add onions, salt, and pepper. Bake in moderate oven, covered, 350°. Roast until tender. Take from oven. Remove from roaster, transferring to a container in which meat and seasoning can stand overnight. Next day remove fat. Slice beef very, very thin. Almost shave it. Strain liquid and add:

½ teaspoon garlic salt
½ teaspoon oregano
¼ teaspoon basil

½ teaspoon seasoned salt
1 teaspoon Accent
½ teaspoon Italian seasoning

Bring all ingredients to a boil. Remove from stove. Place thinly sliced beef in layers in pan, sprinkle each with seasoning (salt and pepper). Pour remaining liquid over to cover beef. Place in 350° oven for 1 hour. Serve warm on buns or hard bread and serve with small hot peppers.

Cookbook 25 Years

Easy Italian Beef

1 (3–4-pound) roast beef
   (rump roast or sirloin tip)
1 jar pepperochini peppers
   (juice and all)

1 can beer
1 (10¾-ounce) can beef
   bouillon

Combine all ingredients in a large crockpot. Cook on high for 30 minutes, reduce heat to low. Cook till beef is tender. Remove meat from juices, slice and return to pot. Serve on hoagie buns. Dip sandwiches in juices.

For supper, start cooking before leaving for work. It's ready to eat when you get home. For a luncheon, start cooking before you go to bed, allowing it to cook while you sleep!

Carol's Kitchen

Italian Beef

3½ pounds rump roast
4 cups hot water
4 beef bouillon cubes
1½ teaspoons salt
1 teaspoon pepper

2 dashes garlic salt
1½ teaspoons oregano
2 green peppers, cut into
  strips
2 tablespoons butter

Brown roast at 450° for 30 minutes. Mix remaining ingredients except peppers and butter. Pour mixture over browned meat. Cover and bake 3 hours at 350°. Refrigerate in pan overnight.

Brown green peppers in butter. After browning, cover and steam for about 20 minutes. Pour green peppers into juice around meat and slice meat very thinly and put into juice. Reheat and serve on buns. Makes about 15 sandwiches. If there are leftovers, you may have to add 1 cup beef bouillon when reheating.

Five Loaves and Two Fishes II

Italian Steak

2 eggs
2 cups bread crumbs
½ cup Parmesan or Romano
  cheese, grated
2 cloves garlic, chopped fine

2 tablespoons parsley
Salt and pepper to taste
2 packages sandwich steak,
  cut in serving pieces

Beat eggs. In a separate container, combine the bread crumbs, cheese, garlic, parsley, salt and pepper. Dip meat in eggs and then in bread crumb mixture. Fry in hot oil until brown, about 2 minutes on each side. Don't overcook. Drain steaks on paper towels. Serve hot with pasta or cold in a sandwich.

Cooking with Daisy's Descendants

 Illinois has several nicknames: Land of Lincoln, Prairie State, and Inland Empire.

Thelma's Roast Beef

5 pound arm or chuck roast	1 envelope onion soup mix
1 cup water	1 envelope Au Jus gravy mix

Place roast in roaster without rack. Combine water, onion soup mix and Au Jus gravy mix. Pour over roast and bake at 350° for 3 hours. Slice. Pour some of the broth over the slices to keep hot in a baking dish until serving time. Make gravy with the rest of the broth, thinned with potato water and thickened with 1 tablespoon cornstarch to each cup of broth.

Our Cherished Recipes

Peppery Brisket Roast

1 teaspoon garlic salt	1 (3–4-pound) well-trimmed
1 teaspoon onion salt	boneless brisket
2 teaspoons celery salt	3 tablespoons brown sugar
2 teaspoons Worcestershire	1 tablespoon dry mustard
sauce	1 tablespoon soy sauce
1½ teaspoons salt	1 tablespoon lemon juice
2 teaspoons black pepper	3 drops Tabasco
1 tablespoon liquid smoke	½ cup catsup
	Dash nutmeg

Combine garlic salt, onion salt, celery salt, Worcestershire sauce, salt, pepper, and liquid smoke.

Spread brisket evenly with above mixture. Place in greased roasting pan or baking dish. Cover and chill overnight. Allow brisket to come to room temperature. Preheat oven to 300°. Cover brisket and bake 30 minutes.

Combine brown sugar, dry mustard, soy sauce, lemon juice, Tabasco, catsup, and nutmeg. Mix well. Pour over brisket. Cover and bake 1–1½ hours, or until tender. Makes 6–8 servings.

Elsah Landing Heartland Cooking

Orange-Wine Brisket

5–6 pound brisket of beef
Salt, pepper, and paprika to
   taste
3 onions
1 teaspoon sugar

1 cup orange juice
½ cup red wine
2 tablespoons catsup
6 potatoes (optional)

The night before cooking, rub meat with salt, pepper, and paprika. Cover and refrigerate overnight. Place sliced onions on bottom of roasting pan, reserving some slices for top. Place meat, fat-side-up, on top of onions. Make sauce of sugar, juice, wine, and catsup. Pour over roast. Top with remaining onions. Bake 3–4 hours at 325°, covered. About 1 hour before done, place pared potatoes in pan and baste with juices, if desired. Take roast out of oven to rest ½ hour before slicing against the grain. Serves 10–12.

Note: If desired, prepare potatoes separately. Either parboil or not, slice lengthwise in 6ths or 8ths, depending on size of potatoes, roll them in oil and lay them in a row in a shallow pan, sprinkle with a little salt and paprika, and bake for about ½ hour.

C-U in the Kitchen

No Peek Stew

2 pounds chuck roast (cut up
   in chunks)
1 package dry onion soup mix
1 can cream of mushroom soup

1 (2½-ounce) can
   mushrooms, drained
1 cup ginger ale

Throw all ingredients into a pot with a tight fitting lid and bake at 350° for 2½–3 hours. Do not peek. Makes 6 servings.

Home Cookin' is a Family Affair

 The world's largest livestock exposition is held at the Illinois State Fair in Springfield.

Country Fried Steak

¾ cup flour
½ teaspoon salt
½ teaspoon pepper
4 (5-ounce) beef cube steaks

¼ cup plus 1 tablespoon
  vegetable oil
1 cup chopped onion
1 cup water
1 cup milk

Combine flour, salt and pepper; measure out and reserve ¼ cup flour mixture. Place remaining ½ cup flour mixture in a shallow dish. Pound steaks to ¼-inch thickness; dredge in flour mixture, coating well on both sides and pressing flour into meat.

Heat 3 tablepoons oil in a large heavy skillet over medium-high heat. Dredge steaks again in any remaining flour mixture and fry until browned on both sides, adding 1 or 2 tablespoons additional oil to skillet if needed. Remove steaks and set aside. Add onion to skillet and sauté until lightly browned. Add water, stirring to loosen clinging particles.

Return steaks to skillet; cover and simmer 30 minutes or until tender. Remove steaks, reserving drippings in skillet. Add reserved ¼ cup flour mixture, stirring until smooth. Cook until lightly browned, stirring constantly. Stir in milk with a wire whisk. Cook, stirring constantly, until thickened.

Return steaks to skillet, turning to coat with sauce; simmer until hot.

Thank Heaven for Home Made Cooks

Tempel Farms in Wadsworth, the largest such stable outside of Austria, is home to the famous Lipizzans. Here these beautiful, rare horses perform their intricate "ballet of the white stallions."

Salisbury Steak Deluxe

1 can condensed cream of
  mushroom soup, undiluted
1 tablespoon prepared mustard
2 teaspoons Worcestershire
  sauce
1 teaspoon prepared
  horseradish
1 egg
¼ cup dry bread crumbs

¼ cup finely chopped onion
½ teaspoon salt
Dash of pepper
1½ pounds ground beef
1–2 tablespoons cooking oil
½ cup water
2 tablespoons chopped fresh
  parsley

In a bowl, combine the soup, mustard, Worcestershire sauce
and horseradish. Blend well, set aside. In another bowl,
lightly beat egg. Add bread crumbs, onion, salt, pepper, and ¼
of the soup mixture. Add beef; mix well. Shape into 6 patties.

In large skillet, brown patties in oil. Drain. Combine
remaining soup mixture with water, pour over patties, cover.
Cook over low heat 10–15 minutes or until meat is done.
Remove patties to serving platter; spoon sauce over meat.
Sprinkle with parsley.

Decades of Recipes

Ground Beef and Rice Casserole

1 pound hamburger
2 small onions, chopped
1 can chicken noodle soup

1 can mushroom soup
1 soup can of water
½ cup uncooked rice

Brown meat and onions; add soups, water, and rice. Mix well. Pour in greased casserole. Bake 1½ hours at 350°

Cookbook 25 Years

Beef and Wild Rice Casserole

4 cups boiling water
1 cup uncooked wild rice
1 can cream of celery soup
1 can cream of mushroom soup
1 can beef bouillon
2 teaspoons salt
¼ teaspoon each of celery salt,
  garlic salt, pepper, and paprika

1 pound fresh mushrooms
3 tablespoons butter
½ cup celery, chopped
½ cup onion, chopped
2 pounds lean ground beef
½ cup slivered almonds

Preheat oven to 325°. Pour boiling water over rice. Cover and let stand 15 minutes. Drain; place rice in casserole. Add soups and seasonings. Mix gently.

Slice and sauté mushrooms in 2 tablespoons butter. Mix into rice.

Sauté celery and onion in 1 tablespoon butter until limp. Mix into rice.

Brown meat; add to rice and mix. Sprinkle with almonds. Cover and bake 1½ hours. May be refrigerated up to 24 hours before baking. Yield: 10 servings.

An Apple From The Teacher

Lumpies

1 pound ground beef (raw)
½ cup onions, if desired
Salt and pepper to taste

Won ton skins (found in
    produce department)
Taco sauce

Mix beef, onions, salt and pepper in bowl. Lay a square of dough down (if you use "large" squares cut into 4 squares) and place small amount of meat mixture in center. Roll up like a cigarette. Roll all Lumpies before cooking. You may have to wet side of dough to keep together. Drop each roll into hot oil. Cook for 2–3 minutes or until golden brown. Serve hot. Dip in taco sauce.

Franklin County Homemakers Extension Cookbook

Italian Spaghetti and Meatballs

1½ pounds ground beef
½ cup fine dry bread
    crumbs
¼ cup Parmesan cheese,
    grated
¼ cup warm water
3 eggs, slightly beaten
1½ teaspoons salt
½ teaspoon basil
¼ teaspoon pepper

3½ cups (#2½ can) tomatoes
1 (6-ounce) can tomato paste
¼ cup onion, chopped
2 cloves garlic, minced
1 teaspoon basil
2 tablespoons parsley, chopped
1 teaspoon salt
1 teaspoon crushed oregano
1 (8-ounce) package spaghetti

Combine meat with next 7 ingredients; form in about 36 (1-inch) balls. In large skillet, brown meat slowly in small amount of hot oil. Add remaining ingredients, except spaghetti. Simmer, uncovered, (don't boil) stirring occasionally for 1½–2 hours, until thick. Cook spaghetti. Serve.

Cooking with Daisy's Descendants

The Ernest Hemingway Museum collection focuses on his first 20 years in Oak Park. The town is internationally recognized for the architectural masterpieces of Frank Lloyd Wright and several of his Prairie School disciples. Edgar Rice Burroughs is also a native son of Oak Park.

German Meatballs with Red Cabbage

1 egg, beaten	¾ cup sauerkraut
½ cup bread crumbs	1 pound apples, sliced
1½ pounds lean ground chuck	½ teaspoon marjoram
¼ cup sauerkraut	1½ pounds red cabbage,
¾ cup finely chopped apple	chopped
2 tablespoons grated onion	½ cup chopped onion
1 teaspoon salt	½ teaspoon caraway seed
Pepper to taste	1 cup chicken broth
½ teaspoon marjoram	2 tablespoons red wine vinegar
4 slices bacon, chopped	1 tablespoon sugar

Mix first 9 ingredients in bowl. Shape into meatballs. Sauté bacon in skillet until crisp. Remove with slotted spoon; drain. Set aside.

Brown meatballs in bacon drippings in skillet; drain. Remove to warm platter. Add remaining ingredients to skillet. Bring to a boil, stirring frequently. Add meatballs. Simmer, covered, for 30 minutes. Spoon into serving bowl; sprinkle with reserved bacon. Yield: 8 servings.

Approx Per Serving: Cal 308; T Fat 15g: 45% Calories from Fat; Prot 21g; Carbo 24g; Fiber 5g; Chol 85mg; Sod 723mg.

Pioneer Pantry

Gingery Meat Balls

3 (12-ounce) cans gingery ginger ale (or regular ginger ale with ¼ teaspoon ginger)	1 (14-ounce) bottle catsup 2½ pounds ground beef ¾ cup bread crumbs

Pour ginger ale and catsup into large pot. Shape meat and crumbs into balls and add to sauce. Cook, covered, on top of stove for 1½ hours. Uncover for last ½ hour to thicken sauce.

Tradition in the Kitchen 2

 The Chicago River was the first river in the world to be altered to flow "backward" (in 1900), away from its natural mouth (Lake Michigan), to carry away sewage and become part of a canal system.

Beef Stroganoff

1¾ pounds ground chuck
1 teaspoon salt
¼ teaspoon pepper
4 teaspoons steak sauce
⅓ cup packaged dry bread
  crumbs
1 egg

4 tablespoons butter
½ pound sliced mushrooms
2 tablespoons flour
1 teaspoon catsup
1 can beef broth
½ package dry onion soup mix
1 cup sour cream

Make beef balls: In large bowl lightly toss ground chuck, salt, pepper, steak sauce, bread crumbs, and egg; mix well. Make meat into balls ½-inch in diameter. Brown beef balls in 2 tablespoons butter in large skillet on all sides. Reduce heat and cook 10 minutes. Remove.

To drippings in skillet add 2 tablespoons butter. Sauté mushrooms 5 minutes, stirring. Remove from heat; stir in flour and catsup. Gradually stir in broth. Add onion soup mix; bring to a boil. Simmer for 2 minutes. Add beef balls; simmer 5 minutes. Stir in sour cream; heat. Serve over noodles or rice.

Old-Fashioned Cooking

Shish Kabobs

½ cup oil
¼ cup vinegar
¼ cup chopped onion
1 teaspoon salt
Dash of pepper
2 teaspoons Worcestershire
  sauce
2 pounds sirloin tip, cut
  into 1-inch cubes

Onion, zucchini, cucumber,
  and green bell pepper chunks
Cherry tomatoes
Mushrooms
Bacon slices
Cheez Whiz
Rolls

Combine oil, vinegar, chopped onion, salt, pepper, and Worcestershire sauce in bowl. Add steak. Marinate for 3 hours to overnight. Thread vegetables and steak onto skewer intertwining with bacon slices. Cook over hot coals. Spread Cheez Whiz on rolls. Serve shish kabobs on rolls. Yields 8 servings.

River Valley Recipes

Tenderloin Chasseur

16 filet mignons, 6 or 8
  ounces each
3 cloves garlic, divided and
  crushed
1 tablespoon seasoned salt
1 teaspoon freshly ground
  pepper
9 tablespoons butter,
  divided
4 tablespoons brandy

6 tablespoons flour
4 teaspoons tomato paste
1½ cups dry red wine
2 cups chicken broth
1 cup beef broth
½ teaspoon Worcestershire
  sauce
4 tablespoons currant jelly
1 pound mushrooms, sliced

One day ahead: Mix 2 cloves garlic, seasoned salt and pepper and rub both sides of steaks. In a large heavy skillet melt 3 tablespoons butter and sauté steaks over high heat until brown on each side. Do not crowd in skillet; add more butter if needed. Put steaks in two 9x13-inch baking dishes leaving ½ inch between steaks.

Add brandy to frying pan and stir well to scrape browned bits left in pan. Add 6 tablespoons butter. When foamy stir in flour and reduce heat. Whisk constantly until golden brown. Add 1 crushed clove garlic and tomato paste; stir in wine, chicken and beef broth. Bring to a boil over moderate heat, stirring constantly for 10 minutes. Add Worcestershire sauce, jelly, and mushrooms, stirring to coat with sauce. If sauce is too thick, add more wine; if too thin, cook longer to thicken. Taste to adjust seasonings. Pour cooled sauce over steaks, until the sauce is halfway to top of dishes. Cover dishes with plastic wrap and refrigerate overnight. Reserve remaining sauce.

Next day: Two hours before serving, remove from refrigerator so steaks will return to room temperature. Preheat oven to 400°. Put uncovered baking dishes in oven and bake: 16–20 minutes for medium rare; 20–25 minutes for medium well.

Serve meat, spooning mushrooms and sauce over steak. Heat remaining sauce and pass. Makes 16 servings.

Note: Recipe may be cut in half to serve 8.

Sugar Snips and Asparagus Tips

Beef and Potato Casserole

1½ pounds ground beef
1 (32-ounce) jar spaghetti
  sauce
⅔ cup water

3 or 4 medium potatoes,
  peeled and thinly sliced
Mozzarella cheese

Cook ground beef. Drain off grease. Add spaghetti sauce and water. Stir and cook for 1 minute. Put half of this mixture in a 13x9x2-inch pan. Layer potatoes over the meat. Put rest of meat mixture over the potatoes. Cover with foil. Bake at 350° for about 1 hour. Remove foil. Arrange thin slices of mozzarella cheese over casserole or use 8 ounces shredded cheese. Bake until cheese melts.

Decades of Recipes

Illini Pork Medallions

2 large pork tenderloins
  (1¼ pounds each)
2 tablespoons oil
¼ cup butter, melted
1 medium onion, sliced
½ cup thinly sliced celery
¼ pound fresh mushrooms,
  sliced
1 tablespoon flour

½ cup beef stock or 1 beef
  bouillon cube dissloved in
  ½ cup hot water
½ cup white wine
1 teaspoon salt
¼ teaspoon freshly ground
  black pepper
Cooked rice

GARNISH:
Spiced crab apples

Orange slices

In hot skillet, brown meat in oil and set aside. Sauté onion, celery, and mushrooms in butter until tender. Combine flour and stock and stir into vegetables. Stir in wine. Arrange tenderloins in a 9x13-inch pan and sprinkle with salt and pepper. Pour vegetable mixture over all. Cover and bake for 1½ hours at 325°. Cook to internal temperature of 180° for fresh pork. Remove pork from pan and cut into ½-inch thick slices. Arrange on platter; garnish with spiced crab apples and orange slices. Serve with rice. Makes 6 servings.

Honest to Goodness

Pork Medallions in Tarragon Sauce

1¼ pounds pork tenderloin,
  cut into 1-inch slices
2 tablespoons butter
½ cup beef broth

½ teaspoon dried tarragon
½ cup half-and-half
1 tablespoon Dijon mustard
Pepper to taste

Brown pork in the butter and reduce heat and cook until no longer pink (5 minutes). Remove to heated platter. Add beef broth and tarragon to drippings, stirring to scrape brown bits loose. Simmer until ½ has evaporated. Add half-and-half, Dijon mustard, and pepper, and simmer and stir until slightly thick.

Serve with buttered spinach noodles and pour sauce over pork. May also use lamb chops.

Jubilee

Wild Rice and Pork Chop Casserole

5–8 pork chops or pork loin
Flour
1 can Campbell's golden
  mushroom soup
1 can water

1 can Campbell's beef bouillon
  soup
1 box Uncle Ben's long grain and
  wild rice

Roll pork chops in flour and brown. Mix remaining ingredients together and put in casserole. Place browned pork chops on top and cover with lid or aluminum foil. Bake at 350° for 1 hour.

Seasoned with Love

In Southern Illinois, barbecue is king. A September competition in Murphysboro draws crowds of 10,000 or more. Award-winning world famous barbecue can be found there at the 17th Street Bar and Grill. Dixie Bar-B-Que in Jonesboro is also on the top of the taste list, with scores of others in small towns on "the barbecue trail" throughout Southern Illinois.

Stuffed Pork Chops

4 thick pork chops

FILLING:

2 apples, cored and chopped
½ cup raisins
¾ cup bread crumbs
1 tablespoon brown sugar
½ teaspoon black pepper
½ teaspoon salt

½ teaspoon cloves
2 tablespoons melted butter
2 tablespoons chopped chives
  or parsley
2 tablespoons butter
1 cup beef broth

Trim fat off chops. Make a slit in thick end of chop. In bowl, combine apples, raisins, bread crumbs, brown sugar, pepper, salt, and cloves. Add melted butter and chives or parsley; mix well. Stuff each chop with filling. Skewer with toothpick to close.

Heat butter in skillet. Brown chops slowly over medium heat on both sides. Add beef broth; bring to a simmer over low heat for about 30 minutes or until tender. Remove toothpicks, put on platter, pour pan juice over chops, and serve with a green salad and steamed broccoli.

A Collection of Recipes From St. Matthew Lutheran Church

Pork Chops with Stuffing and Apples

1 tablespoon minced onion
Few sprigs parsley, chopped
1 tablespoon fat
1 cup dry bread crumbs

⅛ teaspoon savory seasoning
Salt and pepper to taste
6 pork chops
3 tart apples (red)

Cook the onion and parsley in the fat for a few minutes; add the bread crumbs and seasonings and stir until well mixed. Sprinkle the chops with salt and pepper, rub lightly with flour and brown in a skillet. Lay the chops on a rack in a baking dish with cover. Cover each chop with the bread crumb mixture and then with half an apple, cored but not pared, cut-side-down. Cover, and bake in a moderate oven (350°) for about 30 minutes, or until the meat and apples are done. Lift the chops onto a hot platter and serve.

What's Cooking "Down Home"

Apple-Glazed Pork Kebabs

1 pound boneless pork loin, cut into 1-inch cubes

**2 tablespoons lemon juice
Salt to taste**

APPLE GLAZE:
1 cup apple jelly
2 tablespoons lemon juice

1 teaspoon cinnamon
2 tablespoons butter

Sprinkle lemon juice and salt evenly over pork cubes. In small saucepan, make glaze by mixing together the jelly, lemon juice, cinnamon, and butter. Simmer until well blended (makes 1¼ cups).

Thread pork onto skewers and spoon glaze over all. Grill over hot coals, 10–12 minutes, turning frequently. Baste frequently. Serves 4.

Cook Book: Favorite Recipes from Our Best Cooks

The Jackpot

4–8 (2-inch) pork chops (about 6 ounces each)

MARINADE:

1½ cups vegetable oil	⅓ cup chopped parsley
1 celery rib, sliced	8 whole peppercorns
1 carrot, sliced	⅛ teaspoon thyme
1 bay leaf	¼ cup wine
½ cup chopped onion	1 teaspoon rosemary
1 teaspoon finely minced fresh garlic	3½ cups red wine

Combine all and bring to a boil. Cool to room temperature and add 2-inch portions of boneless pork loin. Turn to coat with marinade and refrigerate overnight.

APPLEJACK SAUCE:

1 (21-ounce) can apple pie filling	½ cup applejack or apple brandy
2 tablespoons cinnamon "red-hots"	1 tablespoon chicken base or bouillon granules
2 tablespoons Jackpot marinade	2 cups water
	12 ounces butter (¾ pound)

Process apple pie filling in food processor until smooth. Place in heavy-bottomed saucepan with remaining ingredients. Simmer until thick and syrupy. Whisk in butter.

Broil 1 (2-inch) pork loin per person, until tender, about 8 minutes on each side. Nap with hot sauce.

More to Love...from The Mansion of Golconda

Born in Kentucky, later a resident of Indiana, Lincoln moved to Illinois in 1830. Lincoln loved Springfield. When he left, he said, "For more than a quarter of a century, I have lived among you and...have received nothing but kindness at your hands."

Italian Pork Chops

4 pork chops
Garlic powder, oregano, celery
  salt, and pepper to taste

1 (8-ounce) can tomato sauce
4 slices mozzarella cheese

Sprinkle pork chops on both sides with seasonings. Place in 8x8-inch baking dish. Cover with tomato sauce. Bake at 350° for 1 hour. Top with cheese. Bake for 5 minutes longer or until cheese is melted. Yield: 4 servings.

Approx Per Serving: Cal 326; T Fat 15g; 43% Calories from Fat; Prot 40g; Carbo 5g; Fiber 1 g; Chol 113mg; Sod 570mg.

Pioneer Pantry

Dan's Sweet and Sour Pork

1½ pounds boneless pork,
  cut into strips
1 teaspoon paprika
2 tablespoons shortening
1 medium onion, chopped
1 medium green bell pepper,
  chopped
3 tablespoons brown sugar
¼ cup dry milk powder

2 tablespoons cornstarch
½ teaspoon salt
1 (15-ounce) can pineapple
  tidbits
⅓ cup vinegar
1 tablespoon soy sauce
1 tablespoon Worcestershire
  sauce

Sprinkle pork with paprika. Sauté pork in shortening in skillet. Combine pork with onion and green pepper in slow cooker.

Mix brown sugar, milk powder, cornstarch, and salt in bowl. Drain pineapple, reserving juice. Add enough water to reserved juice to measure ⅔ cup. Combine pineapple juice with vinegar, soy sauce and Worcestershire sauce in small bowl. Add to brown sugar mixture; mix well. Stir into slow cooker. Cook on low for 6–7 hours.

Add pineapple. Cook for 2 hours longer. Serve over rice. Yield: 4 servings.

Recipe by Dan Plesac.

The Cubs 'R Cookin'

Bean Chalupa

Great after a football game or day of Christmas shopping.

1 pound pinto beans
3 pounds pork roast
7 cups water
½ cup chopped onion
2 cloves garlic
1 tablepoon salt
2 tablespoons chili powder

1 tablespoon cumin
1 teaspoon oregano
1 (4-ounce) can chopped
  green chiles
1 (2-ounce) jar pimientos, diced
Frito corn chips

TOPPINGS:
Shredded Cheddar cheese
Diced avocado
Sliced green onions

Diced tomatoes
Hot sauce

Place uncooked beans, roast, water, onion, garlic, seasonings, chiles, and pimientos in a heavy kettle. Cover and simmer on top of the range about 5 hours or until roast is fork tender. Remove roast and break up with a fork. Return meat to the pot and continue to cook until mixture thickens, about ½ hour.

Place a handful of corn chips in a soup bowl or mug. Serve meat mixture over the chips. Garnish individually to taste. Serves 8–10.

Jubilee

Casuia

1 stick butter or oleo
3 medium onions, chopped
2 garlic cloves
2 pounds lean pork, cubed
1 bunch carrots, sliced

1 can tomatoes
1 small head cabbage (thick
  part of leaves removed),
  cut-up
Salt and pepper

Simmer first 4 ingredients together 20 minutes. Add carrots and tomatoes. Cook 20 minutes; add cabbage. Cook until all ingredients are done. Season to taste with salt and pepper. Serve over polenta or with Italian bread.

Herrin's Favorite Italian Recipes Cookbook

Ham Pastries

2 eggs
⅓ cup milk
1½ cups soft whole wheat
  bread crumbs (2-3 slices)
1 cup finely chopped celery
1 cup peeled, shredded, and
  drained butternut squash
½ cup finely chopped onion

1 teaspoon prepared horseradish
1 teaspoon soy sauce
¼ teaspoon pepper
¾ pound ground fully cooked
  ham
1 (10-ounce) package of 6
  frozen patty shells, thawed*
Milk or beaten egg

Combine the 2 eggs and milk; stir in crumbs, celery, squash, onion, horseradish, soy sauce, and pepper. Add the ham; mix well. Divide meat mixture into 6 portions. Shape into patties about 3½ inches in diameter. Place on greased baking sheet.

On floured surface roll each patty shell into 6-inch circle. Drape each pastry circle over a ham patty. Flute edges. Using a sharp knife, lightly score a design in top of pastry, if desired. Brush each with milk.

Bake in 400° oven about 20 minutes or till golden brown. Serve immediately. Makes 6 servings.

*Pie dough cut in 6-inch circles works well.

Family Celebrations Cookbook

Lamb in Gingered Cranberry Sauce

2 pounds cubed lean lamb
½ cup diced onion
2 teaspoons seasoned salt
¼ teaspoon pepper
¼ teaspoon garlic powder
¼ teaspoon ground oregano

¼ teaspoon ground ginger
1 (6-ounce) can tomato paste
1 cup red burgundy
½ cup water
1 (16-ounce) can whole
  cranberry sauce

In a large skillet, brown lamb; pour off fat. Add onion, seasonings, tomato paste, wine, and water; cover and simmer 45 minutes. Add cranberry sauce and simmer an additional 45 minutes more. Serve hot over rice. Yield: 4–6 servings.

Holy Cow!

Roast Lamb

1 leg of lamb, half shank (4 pounds)
2 large onions, thinly sliced
1 cup dry white wine (cheap Chablis works well)
1 cup water

2 teaspoon salt
1 teaspoon rosemary
½ teaspoon cracked pepper
6 large carrots, quartered lengthwise
1½ cups fresh mushrooms, sliced

Put everything except the carrots and mushrooms in a small roasting pan with lid. Cover and bake at 325° for 1 hour. Add carrots and mushrooms and re-cover and return to oven for another hour, or until lamb and carrots are tender. Let meat rest 10 minutes before carving.

Note: If you don't have fresh mushrooms, used canned mushrooms. If you don't have canned mushrooms, skip them. I once thought lamb cried for garlic. Baa. This lamb is delicious.

The Lucy Miele 6-5-4 Cookbook

Polenta and Rabbit

Polenta, instead of bread, is to be eaten with rabbit.

POLENTA:

¾ box of yellow cornmeal
2 quarts water (warm)

1 tablespoon salt
½ stick butter

Mix cornmeal with warm water and salt; stir until smooth. Stir over medium heat, stirring constantly until it comes to a boil. Cover, simmer for about 45 minutes. Uncover and stir about every 10 minutes. Add butter before removing from heat, stir. Serve hot in individual plates. Place polenta on each plate and rabbit over it.

RABBIT COOKED IN WINE:

1 rabbit
Water to cover
Salt
Baking soda
½ stick butter
1 small onion

Small piece salt pork (cubed)
½ can tomatoes
1 cup red, dry wine
Salt and pepper to taste
½ teaspoon ground allspice
1 cup warm water

Soak rabbit in water with a little baking soda and salt. Take rabbit out of water, cut into serving pieces. Fry butter, sliced onion, and salt pork until brown. Place rabbit in saucepan and cook slowly. Cook about 10 minutes and add tomatoes. When rabbit is half done, add wine, salt, pepper, allspice, and warm water and cook. To thicken gravy, add flour and cold water paste. Stir, in order to keep gravy smooth.

Herrin's Favorite Italian Recipes Cookbook

 Southern Illinois is considered one of the best hunting areas in the Midwest, where pheasant, goose, duck, squirrel, quail, rabbit, dove, and deer are prevalent. This region also boasts that it has some of the best crappie fishing to be found.

Cakes

The three-room cottage where Carl Sandburg was born. Galesburg.

Blueberry Pound Cake

1 cup butter or margarine,
  softened
2 cups sugar
4 eggs
2½ teaspoons vanilla
3 cups flour, divided

½ teaspoon salt
1 teaspoon baking powder
1 pint fresh blueberries or
  2 cups canned, drained and
  rinsed

Cream butter or margarine and sugar. Add eggs, one at a time, beating until light and fluffy. Add vanilla. Sift 2 cups flour with salt and baking powder and mix into creamed mixture. Mix well. Use remaining flour to dredge blueberries and gently fold these into mixture. Prepare greased 10-inch tube pan and coat with sugar. Bake cake at 325° for 1 hour 15 minutes. Allow cake to cool in pan 10 minutes, then turn out onto rack. Makes 15 servings.

Tradition in the Kitchen 2

Buttery Pound Cake

¾ cup light margarine
  (Promise)
3 cups sugar
1⅓ cups egg substitute
1½ cups low-fat sour cream

1 teaspoon baking soda
4½ cups sifted cake flour
¼ teaspoon salt
1 teaspoon liquid Butter Buds
1 teaspoon vanilla

Preheat oven to 350°. Pam a 10-inch tube pan. Cream together on medium speed in mixer the margarine and sugar until well combined. Gradually add egg substitute, beating well after each addition. In small bowl, combine sour cream and baking soda and set aside. Sift together flour and salt. Put mixer on slow speed and (beginning and ending with flour mixture) alternately add the sour cream and the flour to the mixer bowl. Stir in butter buds and vanilla. Spoon batter into tube pan and bake at 350° for 1 hour and 35 minutes, or until tooth pick inserted in the center comes out clean. Cool in pan 10 minutes. Remove cake from pan and cool on a wire rack.

18 servings; 7g fat; 0mg cholesterol; 250 calories

The Lucy Miele Too Good To Be Low-Fat Cookbook

Apple Dapple Cake

2 cups sugar
1 cup vegetable oil
3 eggs
3 cups flour
1 teaspoon soda
1 teaspoon salt
1 teaspoon ground cinnamon

2 teaspoons vanilla
3 cups apples, peeled and
  chopped
2 cups flaked coconut
1 cup dates, chopped
1 cup pecans, chopped

Mix together sugar and oil. Add eggs and beat well. Blend in flour, soda, salt, cinnamon, and vanilla. Stir in apples, coconut, dates, and pecans. Spoon batter into prepared 9- or 10-inch tube pan.

Bake 1½ hours at 350° or until wooden pick inserted in cake comes out clean. Remove immediately.

CARAMEL TOPPING:
1 cup brown sugar, firmly
  packed

½ cup milk
½ cup butter

Combine ingredients in saucepan; heat and stir until blended. Boil 2 minutes. Pour hot topping over hot cake and allow to soak in.

Old-Fashioned Cooking

Fresh Apple Cake with Penuche Frosting

2 medium eggs, slightly
    beaten
2 cups sugar
2 teaspoons vanilla extract
¼ cup vegetable oil
1 cup butter
1 teaspoon salt
1½ teaspoons baking soda
3 cups flour

1½ teaspoons cinnamon
1 teaspoon mace
1 teaspoon freshly grated
    nutmeg
3 cups Granny Smith or other
    tart apples, peeled, seeded
    and chopped
1 cup pecans, chopped

TOPPING:
½ cup flour
1 teaspoon cinnamon
¼ cup sugar

¼ cup chopped pecans
3 tablespoons butter at room
    temperature

Preheat oven to 375°. In a large bowl thoroughly mix together eggs and sugar. Add vanilla, oil, and butter and mix well.

In a separate bowl sift together salt, baking soda, flour, cinnamon, mace, and nutmeg. Add to egg mixture and combine well. Stir in apples and pecans. Mixture will be stiff and heavy. Pour into greased and floured 12-cup tube pan.

Combine topping ingredients. Crumble on top of batter in tube pan. Bake for 1 hour. Cool and serve with Penuche Frosting. Yield: 12 servings.

PENUCHE FROSTING:
½ cup butter
1 cup firmly packed brown
    sugar
¼ cup whole milk, heated

3½ cups confectioners'
    sugar
¼ cup chopped walnuts

Melt butter in saucepan. Add brown sugar. Bring to a boil. Cook 1 minute, stirring constantly or until slightly thickened. Cool 15 minutes.

Add hot milk and beat until smooth. Beat in confectioners' sugar until mixture achieves spreading consistency. Use frosting immediately. Top with a sprinkle of chopped nuts.

One Magnificent Cookbook

Pumpkin Pie Cake

1 (29-ounce) can solid pack
   pumpkin
4 eggs
1 (12-ounce) can evaporated
   milk
1½ cups sugar
2 teaspoons cinnamon
1 teaspoon ginger

½ teaspoon nutmeg
½ teaspoon ground cloves
1 package yellow cake mix
   without pudding
1 cup margarine (2 sticks),
   melted
1 cup chopped nuts

Beat first 8 ingredients and put in 9x13-inch ungreased cake pan. Sprinkle dry cake mix over mixture. Pour melted margarine over cake mix and sprinkle with nuts. Bake at 350° for 1 hour. Top with whipped cream if desired.

Franklin County Homemakers Extension Cookbook

West Salem Moravian Sugar Cake

2 cups granulated sugar
2 cups hot mashed potatoes
3 packages yeast, dissolved
   in 2 cups lukewarm potato
   water

2 teaspoons salt
1½ cups melted Crisco
   (can use ½ margarine)
4 eggs, beaten
8 cups flour

Stir sugar into hot potatoes, add dissolved yeast, salt, melted shortening, and eggs. Stir after each addition. Add flour, stirring until worked in. Cover and let rise in warm place until doubled in size. Have 7 (9-inch) pans greased and floured. Spoon batter ½-inch deep into pans. Let rise until puffy, about 1 hour (covered with a towel).

TOPPING:
1 pound box brown sugar
Sprinkle of cinnamon

1 stick oleo, melted

Put brown sugar and cinnamon on top of cakes. Poke holes and drizzle butter in them. Bake at 350° for 20 minutes.

Our Cherished Recipes

Kahlua White Russian Cake

CAKE:

3 tablespoons Kahlua
2 tablespoons vodka
½ cup (3-ounces) white chocolate
2 cups sifted cake flour
¾ teaspoon baking soda
¼ teaspoon baking powder

½ cup butter
1¼ cups sugar
2 tablespoons shortening
3 eggs
¾ cup buttermilk
⅓ cup apricot jam

Grease well and flour lightly two 9-inch cake pans. Combine Kahlua, vodka, and chocolate in medium saucepan and put on low heat until chocolate melts, stirring to blend. Cool slightly. Re-sift cake flour, baking soda, and baking powder into medium bowl and set aside.

In large mixing bowl, cream together butter, sugar, and shortening until light and fluffy. Beat in eggs 1 at a time. Blend in Kahlua-chocolate mixture. Then blend in flour mixture alternately with buttermilk. Divide batter between two pans and bake at 350° for 25–30 minutes or until toothpick inserted in center comes out clean.

Cool in pans 10 minutes, then turn out onto wire racks until completely cool. Spread bottom surface of one cake layer with half the jam and ⅖ cup frosting. Spread bottom surface of second layer with remaining jam. Place on top of first layer. Swirl remaining frosting on top and sides. Refrigerate. Remove 30 minutes before serving.

FROSTING:

2 cups heavy cream
⅓ cup sifted powdered sugar

⅓ cup Kahlua
2 teaspoons vodka

Beat heavy cream and sugar with an electric mixer until thickened. Gradually beat in Kahlua and vodka and continue beating until stiff. Yield: 10 servings.

Holy Cow!

In 1896, Peoria had a medal-winner in the first modern Olympic Games in Athens. By that time, Peoria had already been credited with being the oldest continuously inhabited American community west of the Allegheny Mountains.

Aunt Judy's Italian Cake

1 fudge marble cake mix
  (Duncan Hines)
2 pounds ricotta cheese

4 eggs
1 cup sugar
1 teaspoon vanilla

Mix cake mix per instructions on the box. Put into 13x9-inch pan, but do not bake this yet. Mix ricotta cheese, eggs, sugar, and vanilla together. With large spoon, spoon the cheese mixture over the top of cake. It should cover the entire surface. Bake at 350° for 1 hour and 5 minutes. Let cool well!

TOPPING:

1 (3-ounce) package instant
  chocolate fudge pudding
1 cup milk

1 (12-ounce) container Cool
  Whip

Mix pudding with 1 cup milk and add this to the Cool Whip. Spread on the cake as frosting. This cake is best when baked the day before needed. Refrigerate.

Cookin' With Friends

Mrs. Lincoln's White Cake

1 cup butter
2 cups sugar
3 cups cake flour
2 teaspoons baking powder
1 cup milk
1 teaspoon vanilla

1 teaspoon almond extract
1 cup chopped blanched
  almonds
6 egg whites
¼ teaspoon salt

Cream butter and sugar until light and fluffy. Sift together flour and baking powder; remove 2 tablespoons and set aside. Add sifted ingredients, alternating with milk, to creamed mixture. Stir in vanilla and almond extract. Combine almonds with reserved flour and add to batter.

Beat egg whites until stiff; add in salt. Fold into batter. Pour into 3 greased and floured 8- or 9-inch cake pans. Bake at 350° until a cake tester comes out clean, 20–25 minutes. Cool 5–10 minutes; remove from pans and cool on racks. Frost.

FROSTING:
2 cups sugar
1 cup water
2 egg whites
½ cup chopped candied
  cherries

½ cup chopped candied
  pineapple
Few drops vanilla or almond
  extract

Combine sugar and water in a saucepan, stirring until sugar is dissolved. Bring to a boil; cover and cook about 3 minutes until the steam has washed down any sugar crystals that may have formed on side of pan. Uncover and cook until syrup reaches 238–240°.

Whip egg whites until frothy; pour in syrup in thin stream, whipping egg whites constantly until frosting is spreading consistency. Add cherries, pineapple and flavoring.

Honest to Goodness

 Lincoln Log Cabin in Lerna is the last home of Thomas and Sarah Bush Lincoln, parents of Illinois' favorite son, Abraham Lincoln. It shares the site with Sargents Farm, an 1840s living-history farm.

Threshers' Spice Cake

1½ cups sugar	2 teaspoons cinnamon
½ cup butter	¼ teaspoon cloves
1 or 2 eggs	¼ teaspoon allspice
1 cup sour milk	¼ teaspoon nutmeg
1 teaspoon baking soda	1 cup raisins
2 cups flour	1 cup chopped nuts

Preheat oven to 375°. Grease and flour a 9x13x2-inch pan. Cream sugar and butter. Add eggs. Stir soda into milk and add to mixture. Stir in remaining ingredients. Bake for 25 minutes, or until a toothpick inserted in center comes out clean. Yield: 24 servings.

An Apple from the Teacher

Red Velvet Cake

4 (½-ounce) bottles red food coloring	1 teaspoon vanilla
3 tablespoons cocoa	2¼ cups sifted cake flour
½ cup vegetable shortening	1 teaspoon salt
1½ cups granulated sugar	1 cup buttermilk
2 eggs	1 tablespoon vinegar
	1 teaspoon soda

Mix food coloring with cocoa and set aside. Beat shortening with sugar. Add eggs one at a time, beating after each addition. Add food coloring mixture and vanilla. Alternately add flour, salt, and buttermilk. Beat well. Stir in vinegar and baking soda. Bake in a 350° oven for 30 minutes.

FROSTING:

1 stick butter or margarine	3 tablespoons flour
8 tablespoons vegetable shortening	2–3 teaspoons milk
2 cups powdered sugar	1 teaspoon vanilla

Mix butter until fluffy. Add shortening, 1 tablespoon at a time and beat until fluffy. Add sugar, flour, milk, and vanilla; beat well. Do not cook. Ice cooled cake.

Good Cookin' Cookbook

Country Line Dance
White Chocolate Cake

1 white chocolate cake mix
1 (6-ounce) bar white baking
  chocolate, divided
1 package frozen raspberries
1 jar seedless red raspberry
  preserves

2 packages fresh raspberries
1 carton whipped topping
2 cartons white chocolate
  frosting
Confectioners' sugar

Prepare white chocolate box cake mix according to package directions, substituting ½ required oil or butter for 3 ounces melted white chocolate. Bake in 2 round cake pans. Cool and divide layers into 4 round layers and set aside.

Prepare white chocolate curls from remaining baking bar that is slightly warm, around 80°, using a vegetable peeler. Refrigerate curls in a container in a single layer on waxed paper until ready to use.

Prepare filling by combining defrosted raspberries and ¼ cup preserves into a medium paste. Set aside.

Wash, dry and set aside fresh berries for top of cake.

Combine whipped topping and both containers of white chocolate frosting until blended.

To assemble, place first layer on cake plate and frost top, follow with ⅓ of filling. Repeat cake, frosting and filling until all 4 cake layers are used. Frost top and sides with remaining frosting. Gently add white chocolate curls to the top and sides and garnish top with fresh well drained raspberries. Dust top with confectioners' sugar. Refrigerate until served.

Note: Yellow cake mix and strawberries may be substituted.

Five Loaves and Two Fishes II

Cherry Delight

1 can cherry pie mix
1 small box white cake
   mix (Jiffy)

½ pound melted butter (1 cup)
½ cup chopped nuts
½ cup coconut

Spread cherry pie mix into 8x8-inch pan. Sprinkle dry cake mix over it. Pour melted butter over cake mix. Sprinkle nuts and coconut on top. Bake at 350° for 55 minutes. Serve with whipped cream.

Our Favorite Recipes

Plum Kuchen

¼ pound plus 4 tablespoons
   butter, divided
1¼ cups sifted flour,
   divided
Pinch baking powder

¾ cup plus 1 tablespoon
   sugar, divided
1 tablespoon whipping cream
20–24 blue Italian plums,
   pitted, quartered
½ teaspoon cinnamon

Combine ¼ pound butter, 1 cup flour, baking powder, 1 table-spoon sugar, and cream. Mix well. Spread mixture on bottom and sides of 9-inch tart pan with removable sides.

Starting at edge of pan, place plum quarters evenly in over-lapping circles, covering entire crust. Using 2 knives mix together remaining ¾ cup sugar, ¼ cup flour, 4 tablespoons butter, and cinnamon. Mixture should resemble small peas. Sprinkle over plums. Bake in preheated 350° oven 1 hour 20 minutes.

To freeze kuchen, bake 1 hour only. Cool. Freeze. Remove directly from freezer to preheated 350° oven. Bake 30 min-utes or until filling bubbles.

If desired, buy extra plums in season. Clean, pit, halve and freeze. Prepare kuchen using frozen plums. Serves 8.

Noteworthy

Athens Pecan Cake

This recipe is a big hit at the Taverna Anna Restaurant in North Filotheh, a suburb of Athens. If you like pecans, you'll enjoy this cake.

½ pound butter
1 cup sugar
6 eggs, well beaten
Rind of 1 orange

1 cup chopped pecans
½ ounce brandy
2 cups flour
4 teaspoons baking powder

Cream butter and sugar. Fold in beaten eggs and blend well. Add orange rind, nuts, and brandy and mix well. Add flour and baking powder, blending thoroughly. Pour into a greased 9x13-inch baking pan. Bake in a 350° oven for 40 minutes, or until done. Makes 24 servings.

Opaa! Greek Cooking Chicago Style

White Turtle Cake

1 (2-layer) package yellow
  cake mix
1 cup water
1 (14-ounce) can sweetened
  condensed milk

1 cup vegetable oil
3 eggs
1 (14-ounce) package caramels
1 cup chopped pecans

Preheat oven to 350°. Combine cake mix, water, ½ of condensed milk, oil, and eggs; beat well. Spread ½ the batter into greased 9x13-inch pan. Bake 30 minutes. Melt caramels with remaining condensed milk, stirring often. Stir in pecans. Pour over hot cake. Spread remaining batter over caramel layer. Bake for 20 minutes. Spread White Turtle Frosting over warm cake.

WHITE TURTLE FROSTING:
½ cup melted margarine
1 pound powdered sugar

6 tablespoons milk
1 teaspoon vanilla extract

Combine margarine, sugar, and milk; beat well. Add vanilla; mix well.

Seasoned with Love

Turtle Cake

1 box German chocolate cake
  mix
14 ounces caramels
⅓ cup milk

10 ounces pecans, chopped
6 ounces chocolate chips
1 carton Cool Whip

Mix German chocolate cake mix following box directions. Pour ½ of batter into greased 9x13-inch pan and bake at 350° for 15 minutes. Melt caramels and milk together; pour over baked cake. Pour 8 ounces pecans over caramels; add chocolate chips over pecans. Top with remaining batter and bake for 20 minutes. Let cake cool and top with Cool Whip and remaining chopped pecans.

Favorite Recipes of Collinsville Junior Service Club

Earthquake Cake

1 box German chocolate cake
  mix
1 cup coconut
1 cup chopped pecans

1 stick margarine, softened
1 (8-ounce) package cream
  cheese, softened
2 cups powdered sugar

Grease and flour a 9x13-inch cake pan. Put coconut and pecans in bottom of pan; spread evenly. Mix cake mix as directed on box (with eggs, water, etc.). Pour cake mix over coconut and nuts. Mix margarine, cream cheese, and powdered sugar. Spoon on top of cake mix (in dollops). Bake at 350° for 50 minutes.

College Avenue Presbyterian Church Cookbook

The large "Old Order Amish" settlement surrounding Arthur is Illinois' only Amish colony. More than 3,500 members of this religious faith, most living within a buggy-ride of Arthur, have shunned the fast-paced life of modern society and continue to farm with horse-drawn implements, and operate their small businesses without the aid of modern conveniences.

Pecan Praline Cake

Topping cooks fast, so watch carefully.

1 cup buttermilk
½ cup butter
2 cups light brown sugar
2 eggs
2 cups flour

1 teaspoon baking soda
½ teaspoon salt
3 tablespoons unsweetened
  cocoa
1 tablespoon vanilla

In a small saucepan, warm buttermilk and butter just until barely warm. Pour into a large bowl; add brown sugar and eggs; beat well. Combine dry ingredients and sift into bowl. Mix until smooth. Stir in vanilla. Pour batter into a greased and floured 9x13-inch pan. Bake at 350° for 25 minutes.

TOPPING:
½ cup butter
1 cup pecans, chopped
1 cup brown sugar

⅓ cup light cream or
  evaporated milk

Combine all topping ingredients in a saucepan. Heat until butter melts. Spread mixture over hot cake in oven; put under broiler and cook until icing bubbles and turns golden, 1–2 minutes. Serves 16.

Brunch Basket

Ice Cream Torte

3 cups crushed Oreo cookies
½ cup melted margarine
2 (3¾-ounce) packages
  instant vanilla pudding mix
1½ cups milk

1 quart butter pecan ice cream,
  softened
2 (5-ounce) Heath bars, crushed
1 (9-ounce) carton whipped
  cream

Mix crumbs and margarine. Remove ⅓ cup for topping. Press remaining crumbs into 9x13-inch pan. Set aside.

  Combine pudding mixes and milk. Beat 3 minutes. Stir in softened ice cream until well blended. Spread over crust; chill to harden while preparing topping. Fold crushed candy into whipped cream and spread over filling. Top with reserved ⅓ cup crumbs. Cover and freeze.

A Collection of Recipes From St. Matthew Lutheran Church

Ice Cream Cake

2 cups Captain Crunch
  cereal, crushed
½ cup flaked coconut
½ cup nuts

½ cup brown sugar
½ cup melted margarine
½ gallon ice cream,
  softened

Mix together first 5 ingredients and put ½ in bottom of 9x13-inch pan. Then spread with soft ice cream. Put rest of mixture on top and freeze.

Franklin County Homemakers Extension Cookbook

Tunnelfudge Muffins

This recipe will have many fans—kids, chocolate lovers, and the chef!

½ cup butter
⅓ cup water
5 squares semi-sweet
  chocolate
5 tablespoons cocoa
⅔ cup granulated sugar
2 cups all-purpose flour

1 tablespoon baking powder
¼ teaspoon salt
1 egg
½ cup milk
½ cup sour cream
2 teaspoons vanilla extract
12 Hershey Kisses candies

Heat oven to 375°. In a small saucepan, melt the butter over low heat. Add the water and semi-sweet chocolate squares and stir until the chocolate is melted. Add the cocoa and sugar and cook 5 minutes until the sugar is melted. Cool.

In a large bowl, sift together the flour, baking powder, and salt. In another bowl, combine the egg, milk, sour cream, and vanilla extract and blend on low speed with an electric mixer. Make a well in the center of the dry ingredients, and pour in the egg mixture and the cooled chocolate mixture. Blend at medium speed.

Fill greased muffin tins. Take one Hershey Kisses candy and push it down into the center of each cup of batter. Bake for 20 minutes or until a tester inserted into a muffin comes out clean. (Insert the tester off center to avoid the candy.) Cool. Makes one dozen muffins.

Muffins—104 Recipes from A to Z

White Chocolate Cheesecake

CRUST:

1 cup crushed chocolate
   cookie wafers

2 tablespoons melted
   margarine

Combine crust ingredients. Mix well. Press in the bottom of springform pan. Set aside.

FILLING:

1 envelope unflavored
   gelatin
½ cup water
½ cup sugar
1 (8-ounce) package cream
   cheese, softened

1 cup sour cream
6 ounces white baking
   chocolate, melted
1 cup whipping cream
½ teaspoon vanilla

TOPPING:

1 cup sliced fresh strawberries   1 kiwi fruit peeled and sliced

In small saucepan combine gelatin and water. Let stand 1 minute. Add sugar; stir over medium heat until mixture is dissolved. In large bowl, beat cream cheese and sour cream until creamy. Gradually add melted chocolate, gelatin mixture, whipping cream and vanilla. Beat until smooth. Pour into crust. Cover and refrigerate 1½–2½ hours or until firm.

Shortly before serving, run a knife around edge of pan to loosen cheesecake. Carefully remove form sides of pan. Arrange fruit over cheesecake. Store in refrigerator. Makes 16 servings.

Inn-describably Delicious

Cheesecake

This is my family's very favorite cheesecake and a favorite of any friends I serve it to. I sometimes serve it with a can of cherry or blueberry pie filling on top.

CRUST:

1 package cinnamon graham crackers
¼ cup sugar
¼ cup melted margarine

Mix together crushed graham crackers, sugar, and melted butter. Line bottom of spring-form pan.

FILLING:

3 (8-ounce) packages cream cheese
1 cup sugar
3 eggs
Vanilla (1½-2 teaspoons)

Mix the filling ingredients and beat 4 minutes with mixer. Pour over crust and bake at 350° for 30 minutes.

TOPPING:

1 pint sour cream
⅓ cup sugar
1 teaspoon vanilla

Mix ingredients and pour over cake. Turn oven up to 425°, return cake to oven and bake for 10 minutes. Refrigerate.

Our Best Home Cooking

Creamy Baked Cheesecake

⅓ cup margarine, melted
1¼ cups graham cracker crumbs
¼ cup sugar
2 (8-ounce) packages cream cheese
1 (14-ounce) can Eagle Brand Sweetened Condensed Milk
3 eggs
¼ cup ReaLemon Lemon Juice
1 (8-ounce) container sour cream

Preheat oven to 300°. Combine margarine, crumbs, and sugar; press firmly on buttom of 9-inch spring-form pan. In larger mixer bowl, beat cheese until fluffy. Gradually beat in sweetened condensed milk until smooth. Add eggs and ReaLemon; mix well. Pour into prepared pan. Bake 50–55 minutes or until set. Cool. Chill thoroughly. Spread sour cream on top.

A Collection of Recipes From St. Matthew Lutheran Church

Moon Cake

1 cup water
1 stick oleo or butter
1 cup flour
4 eggs
2 boxes vanilla instant
    pudding, 1 large and 1 small

3 cups milk
1 (8-ounce) package cream
    cheese, softened
1 large carton Cool Whip
Chocolate syrup
Chopped nuts

In 2-quart saucepan, boil water, add oleo or butter; stir until butter melts and comes to a bubble. Remove from heat. Mix in flour (all at once), then eggs (unbeaten, one at a time). Spread on lightly greased cookie sheet. Batter will be hard to spread and seem very thin in places, but spread to edges. Bake at 400° for 30-35 minutes until golden.

Let cool. Mix puddings with milk. Beat in cream cheese. Spread over crust. Top with Cool Whip. Drizzle cold chocolate syrup over that and sprinkle with nuts.

Note: While crust is baking, it tends to bubble. Prick with fork to remove bubbles!

Favorite Recipes of Collinsville Junior Service Club

Dirt Cups

1 (16-ounce) package
    chocolate sandwich cookies
2 cups cold milk
1 (4-serving) package
    chocolate instant pudding
1 (8-ounce) tub Cool Whip

8–10 (7-ounce) paper or plastic
    cups
Decorations (gummy worms and
    frogs, candy flowers, chopped
    peanuts or granola)

Crush cookies in zipper-style plastic bag with rolling pin or in food processor. Pour milk into large bowl; add pudding mix. Beat with wire whisk 2 minutes; let stand 5 minutes. Stir in Cool Whip and ½ of the crushed cookies.

Place about 1 tablespoon crushed cookies in each cup. Fill cups about ¾ full with pudding mixture. Top with remaining crushed cookies. Refrigerate 1 hour or until ready to serve. Decorate as desired.

Thank Heaven for Home Made Cooks

Cookies and Candies

Skyline of downtown Peoria.

Creme De Menthe Bars

1¼ cups butter or oleo
½ cup cocoa
3½ cups sifted powdered
  sugar
1 beaten egg

1 teaspoon vanilla
2 cups graham cracker crumbs
⅓ cup green creme de menthe
1½ cups semi-sweet
  chocolate chips

Bottom Layer: In saucepan combine ½ cup oleo and cocoa. Heat and stir until well blended. Add ½ cup powdered sugar, egg, and vanilla. Stir in crackers; mix well. Press into ungreased 13x9x2-inch pan.

Middle Layer: Melt ½ cup oleo. Mix in creme de menthe at low speed of mixer. Beat in remaining 3 cups powdered sugar until smooth. Spread over chocolate layer. Chill 1 hour.

Layer: Combine ¼ cup oleo and chocolate pieces. Cook and stir over low heat until melted. Spread over mint layer. Chill 1–2 hours. Store in refrigerator. Freezes well.

A Collection of Recipes From St. Matthew Lutheran Church

Meringue Raspberry Bars

¾ cup softened butter or
  margarine
¼ cup sugar
2 eggs, separated
1½ cups all-purpose flour
1 tablespoon milk

1 (10-ounce) jar raspberry
  preserves
¾ cup chopped pecans
½ cup sugar
½ cup flaked coconut

Cream margarine and ¼ cup sugar until light and fluffy. Beat in egg yolks. Stir in flour and milk. Spread evenly in ungreased 13x9x2-inch pan. Bake at 350° for 15-18 minutes. Remove from oven. Place on rack while preparing meringue.

Beat egg whites in small bowl until foamy. Add ¾ cup sugar gradually until meringue forms stiff peaks. Stir in coconut. Spread preserves on baked layer. Sprinkle with nuts. Dot meringue on raspberry-nut layer. Spread evenly. Bake at 350° for 25 minutes. Cool in pan on rack. Cut into bars. Makes 24 bars.

Home Cookin' is a Family Affair

Chocolate Marshmallow Bar

¾ cup margarine
1½ cups sugar
3 eggs
1 teaspoon vanilla
1⅓ cups flour
1 teaspoon baking powder
½ teaspoon salt

3 tablespoons cocoa
½ cup chopped nuts
4 cups miniature marshmallows
1⅓ cups chocolate chips
3 tablespoons margarine
1 cup peanut butter
2 cups Rice Krispies cereal

Cream margarine and sugar. Add eggs and vanilla; beat until fluffy. Combine flour, baking powder, salt, and cocoa; add to creamed mixture. Stir in nuts. Spread in greased jelly roll pan. Bake at 350° for 15–18 minutes. Sprinkle marshmallows evenly over cake. Return to oven 2–3 minutes. Using a knife dipped in water, spread melted marshmallows evenly over cake.

Combine chocolate chips, 3 tablespoons margarine, and peanut butter in small pan (in double boiler for better results); cook over heat, stirring constantly, until melted. Stir in cereal. Mix. Spread over bar.

Old-Fashioned Cooking

Oh' Henry Bars

1 cup brown sugar	½ cup white syrup
1 cup soft margarine	6 ounces chocolate chips
4 cups quick oatmeal	¾ cup peanut butter.

Mix first 4 ingredients together like a pie crust. Pat in ungreased 10x15-inch cookie sheet. Bake 15 minutes at 350°. Melt chocolate chips and peanut butter in microwave on HIGH for 2 minutes. Spread over slightly cooled oatmeal mixture, refrigerate.

Decades of Recipes

Rich Mint Brownies

BROWNIES:

1 cup sugar	¼ cup butter, melted
1 cup flour	4 eggs
16 ounces chocolate syrup	

Mix together ingredients. Pour into greased 11x16-inch baking pan or jelly roll pan. Bake at 350° for 20 minutes. Cool completely.

MINT FROSTING:

½ cup butter, softened	2 teaspoons peppermint
1 pound powdered sugar	extract
¼ cup milk	10 drops green food coloring

Beat together ingredients. Spread mixture evenly over cooled Brownies. Refrigerate for at least 20 minutes.

CHOCOLATE GLAZE:

12 ounces semi-sweet	½ cup butter or margarine
chocolate chips	

Melt together ingredients. Spread on top of Mint Frosting. Refrigerate until firm. Cut into small squares, cleaning knife after each cut. Makes 8 dozen cookies.

Honest to Goodness

Frosterrific Brownies

These are sinfully rich and yummy!

2 cups sugar
1 cup butter or margarine,
  softened
4 eggs, beaten slightly
½ cup half-and-half
1½ cups sifted all-purpose flour

½ teaspoon salt
3 (1-ounce) squares unsweetened
  chocolate, melted
1 cup chopped pecans or
  walnuts, optional

Preheat oven to 325°. Grease and flour 9x13-inch baking pan. Cream sugar and butter, add eggs and mix well. Add half-and-half. Mix flour and salt; add to sugar mixture. Blend in chocolate and nuts. Mix well. Pour into prepared pan. Bake for 25–30 minutes. Cool.

FROSTING:
6 tablespoons butter or
  margarine, softened
1 teaspoon vanilla extract
2 cups powdered sugar

3–4 tablespoons half-and-half
1 (1-ounce) square semi-sweet
  chocolate, melted

Cream butter and vanilla. Gradually add powdered sugar, beating thoroughly after each addition. Stir in half-and-half and beat until the frosting is of spreading consistency.

Frost the cooled brownies in pan and drizzle melted chocolate over frosting. Cut into bars. Makes 2 dozen bars.

Sugar Snips and Asparagus Tips

Pecan Squares

These freeze beautifully.

PASTRY:

2 sticks unsalted butter	¼ teaspoon salt
½ cup sugar	Grated rind of a lemon
1 egg	3 cups sifted flour

Preheat oven to 375°. Butter a jelly roll pan and chill. Cream butter and sugar. Beat in egg, salt and rind. Gradually add flour and mix until smooth and the dough holds together. Press into the bottom of the pan and place in freezer for 10 minutes. Prick bottom of the pan and bake for 20 minutes. Prepare topping while shell is baking.

TOPPING:

2 sticks butter	5 cups pecan halves or large
½ cup honey	pieces
¼ cup granulated sugar	¼ cup heavy cream
1 cup dark brown sugar + 2	
tablespoons	

Cut butter into pieces and place in a saucepan with honey, and heat until melted. Add sugars and stir to dissolve. Bring to a boil and let boil for 2 minutes. Immediately add the pecans and cream; stir well. Pour into the shell while still warm and bake for 25 minutes. Remove from oven and let cool to room temperature. Release sides. Cover with a cookie sheet and invert. Cover with a large rack and invert again. Slide onto a cutting board and cut into squares. Makes 24–48 pieces.

A Cause for Applause

Cherry Bars

1 cup margarine, softened
1¾ cups granulated sugar
4 eggs
3 cups flour

½ teaspoon salt
1½ teaspoons baking powder
1 can cherry pie filling

Cream margarine and sugar together. Add eggs, one at a time, beating well. Add flour, salt, and baking powder and mix all. Save out 1 cup of this batter. Spread out the rest on a well greased 11x17-inch pan. Spread 1 can cherry pie filling over this. Dot with remaining cup of batter and lightly swirl. Bake at 350° for 40 minutes or till lightly brown. Glaze while hot.

GLAZE:
1 tablespoon butter
1½ tablespoons milk

1 cup powdered sugar
¼ teaspoon vanilla

Heat butter and milk till butter melts. Add powdered sugar and vanilla. Mix well. Drizzle over cooled bars.

Carol's Kitchen

Chocolate Cherry Bars

This tastes like the Black Forest Cake.

1 chocolate cake mix
1 can cherry pie filling

1 teaspoon almond extract
2 eggs, beaten

Grease and flour jelly roll pan. In large bowl, combine all ingredients. Stir by hand until well mixed. Pour into prepared pan. Bake at 350° for 25–30 minutes, or until cake tester comes out clean.

Frost with chocolate frosting. Or put mixture into greased and floured 9x13-inch pan; bake for about 35 minutes. Frost with sweetened whipped cream and chocolate curls.

Our Best Home Cooking

 The Art Institute of Chicago is one of the world's leading art museums. It has one of the largest collections of French Impressionist masterpieces.

Peach Meringue Bars

1 cup shortening	1 pint peach preserves
½ cup sugar	1 cup sugar
¼ teaspoon salt	1 teaspoon vanilla
4 egg yolks (save whites for top)	¾ cup chopped pecans or
2½ cups flour	coconut

Cream together first 5 ingredients and spread on 2½x13x10-inch cookie sheet. Cover with peach preserves. Beat egg whites until stiff. Add sugar and vanilla to whites. Spread on top of preserves. Sprinkle chopped pecans on top, or coconut, or both. Bake at 350° for 35–40 minutes.

Franklin County Homemakers Extension Cookbook

Peanut Butter Cookies

¾ cup shortening	1¼ cups peanut butter,
¾ cup butter or margarine	creamy or crunchy
1½ cups sugar	3 cups flour
(granulated)	1¼ teaspoons baking soda
1¼ cups brown sugar	1 teaspoon baking powder
1¼ teaspoons vanilla	1 teaspoon salt
3 eggs, beaten	

Cream shortening, butter, and sugars until light and fluffy. Add vanilla and mix. Add beaten eggs and peanut butter to creamed mixture. Mix and sift dry ingredients. Add to above. Form dough into balls. Put on baking sheet, flatten and criss-cross with fork dipped in cold water. Bake at 350° about 8 minutes. Remove while warm. Don't wait for cookies to brown!

Caring is Sharing

Illinois is bordered by the Mississippi, Ohio, and Wabash rivers and Lake Michigan. These borders shape Illinois like a giant arrowhead.

Cherry Chip Cookies

¾ cup margarine
1 cup brown sugar
1 egg
1 teaspoon vanilla
2¼ cups flour
1 teaspoon baking powder
½ teaspoon salt
½ cup maraschino cherries,
  cut small
1 cup minature chocolate chips
½ cup coconut

Using mixer, cream together margarine and brown sugar. Add egg and vanilla; mix well. Mix flour, baking powder, and salt; add gradually to creamed mixture. Mixture will be stiff. Using spoon, stir in cherries, chocolate chips, and coconut. Chill in refrigerator about 2 hours. Roll chilled dough between hands into ½-inch small balls. Place balls on greased cookie sheets. Bake at 350° for 8 minutes or until light brown. Makes 85 small cookies.

College Avenue Presbyterian Church Cookbook

Lemon Drop Cookies

COOKIE:
½ pound butter
½ cup confectioners' sugar
2 cups flour

Combine butter, confectioners' sugar, and flour. Mix well. Roll into small balls. Flatten and dent centers. Place on greased cookie sheets. Bake in preheated 350° oven 10–12 minutes. Remove to rack and cool.

LEMON CURD:
1 egg, beaten
¾ cup sugar
1½ tablespoons butter
3 tablespoons lemon juice
Rind of 1 lemon, grated
Confectioners' sugar

In saucepan combine all curd ingredients. Cook, stirring, until thick. Cool. Spoon curd into dent of each cookie. Sprinkle with confectioners' sugar.

This curd may also be used as ice cream topping, spread for toast, or combined with fresh pineapple, oranges, and coconut. Yield: 50–60 cookies.

Noteworthy

Cashew Drops

½ cup butter
1 cup brown sugar
1 egg
½ teaspoon vanilla
2 cups flour
¾ teaspoon baking powder
¾ teaspoon baking soda
¼ teaspoon salt
⅓ cup sour cream
1 (6-ounce) can cashews, chopped

Cream butter and sugar. Add egg and vanilla. Add rest of ingredients with sour cream. Fold in nuts.

Drop by teaspoonful onto cookie sheet. Bake at 400°, for 8–10 minutes. Cool cookies before frosting.

FROSTING:
½ cup butter
3 cups powdered sugar
2 teaspoon vanilla
Hot water

Mix with just enough hot water to make a nice spreading consistency.

Grand Detour Holiday Sampler

Crunchy Cookies

2 cups soft margarine
2 cups sugar
2 teaspoons vanilla
3 cups all-purpose flour
2 teaspoons cream of tartar
2 teaspoons baking soda
2½ cups cornflakes
1 (7-ounce) can coconut
8 ounces white chocolate, cut into small chunks, (optional)
1½ cups macadamia nuts, coarsely chopped, (optional)

Cream together margarine, sugar, and vanilla. Add flour, cream of tartar and baking soda to creamed mixture. By hand, add 2½ cups cornflakes (do not crush) and coconut. If desired, fold in white chocolate and nuts. Drop by teaspoonful onto an ungreased cookie sheet. Bake at 350° for 10–12 minutes. Yield: 5 dozen.

Holy Cow!

French Macaroons

Macaroons are believed to have become popular in the city of Nancy during the French Revolution when the local convents were closed during the troubles.

Two Carmelite sisters were given refuge in a private home in Nancy. To repay their benefactor, they recalled a convent recipe for the macaroons and began making up batches and selling them in the neighborhood. Macaroons are now made all over the world.

8 egg whites	½ pound almonds (grated)
1 pound granulated sugar	¼ cup candied orange peel
½ teaspoon vanilla extract	½ pound candied cherries

Beat egg whites until foamy. Add sugar, 2 tablespoons at a time, beating between additions. Add the vanilla, grated nuts, and orange peel. Put in the refrigerator for 4–5 hours, then drop by tablespoon onto unglazed paper on cookie sheets. Press a candied cherry into center of each cookie.

Bake in preheated 300° oven for about 1 hour or until cookies can be lifted from paper. Makes about 80 cookies.

The French-Icarian Persimmon Tree Cookbook

Mary Lincoln's Sugar Cookies for Grand Levee

2 sticks oleo or butter	2 teaspoons vanilla
1 cup vegetable oil	4½ cups flour
1 cup sugar	1 teaspoon soda
1 cup powdered sugar	1 teaspoon cream of tartar
2 eggs	1 teaspoon salt

Beat butter, oil, and sugars until creamy. Add 2 eggs, one at a time. Beat in remaining ingredients.

Roll into little balls (1 inch); drop balls in granulated sugar; dip glass or cookie press in sugar and press out on cookie sheet.

Bake at 350°, on a lightly greased cookie sheet, for 12 minutes, or until edges are lightly browned. Makes 3 dozen.

Cook Book: Favorite Recipes from Our Best Cooks

Mother's Icebox Cookies

2 sticks oleo
1 pound brown sugar
2 eggs
1 teaspoon vanilla

3½ cups flour
1 teaspoon soda
½ teaspoon salt
1 cup chopped nuts

Cream oleo, sugar, and eggs. Add vanilla. Blend in dry ingredients and nuts. Roll into 4 rolls and wrap in waxed paper; chill overnight. Slice and bake about 8 minutes at 375°. One of my favorites.

Dawdy Family Cookbook

Lebkuchen

⅔ cup honey
⅔ cup brown sugar, firmly
  packed
1 egg
1 teaspoon grated lemon rind
1 tablespoon lemon juice
2⅔ cups sifted
  all-purpose flour
½ teaspoon soda
1 teaspoon cinnamon

1 teaspoon ginger
1 teaspoon ground cloves
½ cup chopped candied citron
½ cup chopped nuts
Candied cherries
Whole, blanched almonds
1 cup sugar
½ cup water
¼ cup sifted confectioners'
  sugar

Heat honey to boiling; cool. Add brown sugar, egg, lemon rind, and juice, flour, soda, and spices; blend well. Stir in citron and ½ cup chopped nuts; chill dough several hours. Roll out on floured board ¼-inch thick. Cut in rectangles 2x3 inches; place on greased cookie sheets; decorate with cherries and almonds. Bake in hot oven (400°) 10–12 minutes.

While cookies are baking, bring sugar and water to boil in small saucepan; boil three minutes; stir in confectioners' sugar. Brush hot cookies with hot glaze; cool on wire racks. If glaze becomes stiff, add a few drops of water; heat until clear again. Store in a tightly covered container to mellow. Makes about 3 dozen.

Jubilee

Scottish Shortbread

1 pound butter, softened
1 cup confectioners' sugar, sifted

3 cups flour, sifted
¾ cup cornstarch, sifted

Preheat oven to 350°. Blend butter and sugar. Add flour and cornstarch, a little at a time. Dough will be stiff as pie crust dough. Divide dough in half. Pat each half into an oval, ½–¾-inch thick, on a foil-lined cookie sheet.

Pinch edges pie-crust fashion. Pierce surface with fork. Bake 5 minutes at 350°, then reduce heat to 300°. Bake until lightly golden and firm, 25–30 minutes. Remove from oven and immediately cut into squares or diamond shapes with sharp knife. Yield: 5 dozen.

An Apple From The Teacher

Swedish Cream Wafers

1 cup butter (or margarine with butter flavor)
2 cups flour

⅓ cup thick cream (or evaporated milk)

Mix ingredients and chill dough. Roll dough thinly; cut with 1½-inch cookie cutter. Sprinkle with granulated sugar; prick with a fork. Bake on ungreased cookie sheet in a 375° oven for 7–9 minutes. Cool. Put 2 cookies together with cream filling.

FILLING:
¼ cup butter or margarine
¾ cup confectioners' sugar

1 teaspoon vanilla
1 egg yolk

Blend ingredients until light and fluffy.

Cooking with Daisy's Descendants

Freeport's founder, William "Tutty" Baker, offered travelers free ferry rides, meals and lodging, hence the name "free port." The second of the famous Lincoln-Douglas debates was held there and is marked by a life-size statue.

Meltaways

1 cup butter, softened
1¼ cups confectioners'
  sugar
1 teaspoon vanilla
1 cup sifted flour

2 tablespoons cornstarch
¼ teaspoon salt
1 cup chopped nuts
10 ounces milk chocolate,
  melted, cooled

Cream butter and sugar; add vanilla. Sift together flour, cornstarch, and salt. Add to butter. Fold in nuts and chocolate. Shape into small balls, 1 rounded teaspoon each. Place on ungreased cookie sheets, allowing room for spreading. Bake on middle rack at 250° for 40 minutes. Store in airtight container. Makes 10 dozen.

Soupçon II

Chocolate Delicious

24 chocolate sandwich
  cookies
¼ cup butter or margarine,
  melted

1 (14-ounce) can sweetened
  condensed milk
12 ounces chocolate chips
4 ounces chopped nuts

Crush cookies and combine with butter. Press into 9x13-inch greased Pyrex pan. In a saucepan, combine milk and ½ of chips. Heat until melted. Spread evenly over cookie crust. Sprinkle with remaining chips and chopped nuts. Bake at 350° for 20 minutes. Do not overbake. Makes 1 dozen.

Tradition in the Kitchen 2

One of America's best-preserved nineteenth-century towns, Galena has 60 antique shops and 40 bed and breakfast houses. It was once a major river port and commercial hub, famous for producing 85% of the nation's lead.

Whoopee Cookies with Filling

OATMEAL SANDWICH COOKIES:

8 cups brown sugar
3 cups oleo
8 eggs
2 teaspoons salt
9 cups flour
8 cups oatmeal

4 teaspoons cinnamon
4 teaspoons baking powder
8 teaspoons soda dissolved
in ¾ cup boiling water,
(put in last)

Mix all ingredients. Drop by teaspoonfuls onto cookie sheet. Bake at 350° for 20–25 minutes.

FILLING: (OPTIONAL)

3 egg whites, beaten
1½ cups Crisco
3 tablespoons flour
3 teaspoons vanilla

3 tablespoons milk
4 cups powdered sugar, or as
needed

These oatmeal cookies are good individually, but when the filling is put between two cookies, they are extra-special!

Cook Book: Favorite Recipes from Our Best Cooks

Cuckoo Cookies

1¾ cups cake flour
½ teaspoon baking soda
½ teaspoon salt
½ cup cocoa
½ cup shortening
1 cup sugar

1 egg
½ cup milk
1 teaspoon vanilla
½ cup chopped walnuts
24 marshmallows, halved

Sift together flour, baking soda, salt, and cocoa. Cream shortening with sugar until fluffy. Beat in egg. Add flour, alternately with milk, beating until smooth. Add vanilla and nuts. Drop by teaspoonfuls on greased baking sheet. Bake in a 375° oven for 8 minutes.

Remove and top each cookie with a marshmallow half, placing cut-side-down and pressing gently into cookie. Bake for 4 minutes more. Cool and frost with cocoa glaze. Makes 48.

COCOA GLAZE:
2 tablespoons butter
2 tablespoons water

2 tablespoons cocoa
Powdered sugar

Melt butter and water together. Add cocoa and enough powdered sugar to make a glaze.

Our Best Home Cooking

S'Morsels

1 cup all-purpose flour
¾ cup graham cracker
  crumbs
⅔ cup butter or margarine,
  softened
¼ cup sugar

¼ cup packed brown sugar
¼ teaspoon salt
1 cup marshmallow cream
1½ cups semi-sweet
  chocolate morsels

Preheat oven to 325°. In mixer bowl blend flour, cracker crumbs, butter, sugar, brown sugar, and salt until crumbly. Press into greased 9x13-inch pan. Bake for 15 minutes. Spread marshmallow cream over base; sprinkle with chocolate morsels. Bake for 5 minutes longer. Cool. Cut into squares.

Our Favorite Recipes

Chocolate Cashew Fudge

2¼ cups sugar
½ cup margarine
¾ cup evaporated milk

6 ounces chocolate chips
1 teaspoon vanilla extract
1 cup chopped cashews

Combine sugar, margarine, and milk in saucepan. Bring to a boil. Cook for 10 minutes; remove from heat. Stir in chocolate chips and vanilla. Beat with electric mixer until creamy. Add cashews. Pour into buttered dish. Let stand until firm. Cut into squares. Yields 36 ounces.

Approx. Per Ounce: Cal 124; Prot 1.3gr; T Fat 6.4gr; Chol 1.6mg; Carbo 16.8gr; Sod 38.1mg; Potas 50.4mg.

River Valley Recipes

Foolproof Chocolate Fudge

18 ounces semi-sweet
 chocolate morsels
14 ounces sweetened
 condensed milk

1½ teaspoons vanilla
Dash of salt

In heavy saucepan, on low heat, melt morsels with condensed milk. Remove from heat and stir in vanilla and salt.

Spread evenly into wax paper-lined 8-inch square pan. Chill 2–3 hours. Peel off paper and cut. Store in covered dish. Makes 1¾ pounds.

Thank Heaven for Home Made Cooks

Holiday Jiffy Fudge

1⅔ cups sugar	1½ cups chocolate chips
2 tablespoons butter	2½ cups small marshmallows
½ teaspoon salt	¾ cup chopped pecans
⅔ cup evaporated milk	1 teaspoon vanilla

Combine sugar, butter, salt, and milk in electric skillet. Set dial at 280°. Bring to a boil, stirring constantly with a wooden spoon. Boil for 5 minutes. Turn dial to off position and add remaining ingredients. Beat until marshmallows melt and are blended into mixture. Pour into greased pan. Cool. Cut into squares.

Our Cherished Recipes

Old Fashioned Fudge

Candy has to be made with feeling or it just won't do.

3 cups sugar	½ stick butter
3 tablespoons cocoa	⅛ teaspoon salt
¼ cup dark Karo syrup	1 teaspoon vanilla
1½ cups half-and-half	1 cup pecan pieces

Combine sugar and cocoa and syrup, then half-and-half and stir. Place lid on saucepan and heat to boiling. Allow to boil 1 minute. Remove the lid and lower heat and cook to a medium-soft ball stage when dropped by a teaspoon into cold water.

Remove candy from heat. Add butter, salt, vanilla, and nut pieces. Place saucepan in cold water and stir as it cools. Do not beat the candy. When mixture begins to be creamy, pour into a buttered pan.

Family Celebrations Cookbook

Irene's Divinity

2 egg whites, room
   temperature
2 cups sugar
½ cup white corn syrup

½ cup water
Salt
Vanilla
1 cup chopped pecans

Beat egg whites until stiff, set aside. In saucepan boil together the sugar, corn syrup, and water and boil to soft-ball stage, (use a candy thermometer). Pour ½ of syrup over beaten egg whites, beating it. Boil the remaining syrup to hard-ball stage; add slowly to mixture. Beat until the right consistency for candy. Add a pinch of salt and flavor with vanilla. Stir in nuts. Drop by teaspoon on greased sheet. Store in covered tin.

Favorite Recipes of Collinsville Junior Service Club

When the Mississippi River changed its course in the late 1800s, the town of Kaskaskia was wiped out. Kaskaskia Bell Memorial, (at Ellis Grove), is located on the 14,000-acre Kaskaskia Island, the only community in Illinois west of the Mississippi River (the only entrance is from St. Mary's, Missouri). The old church bell is known as the Liberty Bell of the West.

Chocolate Truffles

Easy and just the right touch to end a special dinner.

¼ cup strong coffee (or 1
   tablespoon instant coffee
   dissolved in ¼ cup boiling
   water)
7 ounces semi-sweet baking
   chocolate

2 ounces unsweetened
   chocolate
¾ cup chilled unsalted
   butter, cut into thin slices
¼ cup brandy or orange liqueur
¾ cup unsweetened cocoa

Break up chocolates and stir into the hot coffee. Soften in top of double boiler. Beat with electric mixer until smooth and creamy. Remove from hot water and beat another minute to cool. Gradually beat chilled butter into chocolate with mixer. When smooth, beat in liqueur by dribbles. Chill for 2 hours or until firm. When firm, roll into small balls. Then roll in unsweetened cocoa. Makes about 3 dozen.

Soupçon II

Creamed Pecan Nuts

Most delicious!

½ **cup brown sugar, packed**
¼ **cup white sugar**
¼ **cup sour cream**

1½ **teaspoons vanilla**
1½ **cups pecan halves**

Combine sugars and sour cream in pan. Cook over low heat, stirring constantly, until sugars are dissolved. Cook until soft ball forms in cold water. Remove from heat. Add vanilla and pecans. Stir until light sugar coating begins to form on nuts. Turn out on wax paper. Separate nuts by hand; let cool.

Seasoned with Love

The Town of Pullman, one of America's first planned industrial communities, was built in the early 1880s fourteen miles south of downtown Chicago by industrialist George M. Pullman. Designed to provide a living environment superior to that available to the working class in any other city, the town included parks, shops, recreational and cultural facilities, a church, school, bank, and a variety of housing, from row houses to executive mansions. Now a city, state and national historic landmark, Pullman remains a viable community of people preserving the past, living in the present, and strongly committed to the future.

Pomona General Store sits in the heart of the Shawnee National Forest in Southern Illinois. Open since 1876, it has an old ice cream soda fountain—a favorite for everyone with a real thirst.

Pies and Desserts

The Pomona General Store in the Shawnee National Forest.

Buttermilk Pie Crust

Makes enough for 2 crusts. A favorite for fresh fruit pies. The combination of buttermilk and the vegetable shortening causes a flaky, puffy finish.

3 cups flour
2 tablespoons sugar
1 teaspoon salt
½ cup butter, chilled (1 stick)

½ cup chilled butter-flavored vegetable shortening
¼ cup, plus 2 tablespoons buttermilk

Combine flour, sugar, and salt in large bowl. Add butter and shortening. Cut in, using pastry blender until mixture resembles coarse meal. Add buttermilk and stir with fork until moist clumps form. You can also make this in food processor by combining all ingredients, and using on-off turns, process until ball forms.

Gather dough together, and form into ball. Divide into 2 pieces and wrap each in plastic wrap and flatten into disk. Chill 30 minutes. Can be refrigerated up to 1 week or frozen up to 1 month. Let dough stand at room temperature to soften slightly before using.

More to Love...from The Mansion of Golconda

Strawberry-Rhubarb Pie

1 recipe Buttermilk Pie Crust
3 cups fresh strawberries, stemmed and sliced
3 cups fresh rhubarb, cut into ¾-inch dice

1½ cups sugar
2 tablespoons cornstarch
2 tablespoons flour
⅓ cup raspberry liqueur (or you may substitute orange juice)

Combine strawberries, rhubarb, sugar, cornstarch, flour, and liqueur. Place in large saucepan and bring to a boil. Cook until juices thicken. Roll out half of the pie crust and fit into deep-dish pie plate. Spoon in hot filling. Roll out remaining pie crust and fit top crust; flute and cut steam vent. Bake in preheated oven about 45 minutes. Since filling is hot, this will not take as long as pies with raw fruit filling. Serve warm with ice cream.

More to Love...from The Mansion of Golconda

No Roll Pie Crust

1½ cups flour
1½ teaspoons sugar
1 teaspoon salt
½ cup oil
2 tablespoons milk

Put first 3 ingredients in pie pan. Combine oil and milk in shaker and pour over flour mixture; use fork to mix and shape in pan. Prick with fork and bake at 425° for 12–15 minutes.

Cookbook 25 Years

Frozen Strawberry Margarita Pie

GRAHAM CRACKER CRUST:
1⅓ cups graham-cracker
  crumbs
¼ cup sugar
¼ cup (½ stick) butter,
  melted

Combine crumbs, sugar and butter in a small bowl; press into bottom and sides of a 9-inch pie plate.

1 (14-ounce) can sweetened
  condensed milk
¼ cup freshly squeezed lime
  juice
3 tablespoons tequila
3 tablespoons Triple Sec
½ cup frozen strawberries
  with syrup, thawed
2 cups heavy cream, whipped

Beat condensed milk, lime juice, tequila and Triple Sec in a large bowl with electric mixer at medium speed for 3 minutes until smooth. Lower speed; beat in strawberries with syrup for 1 minute. Fold whipped cream into strawberry mixture until no streaks of white remain. Pour into prepared graham-cracker pie shell, mounding in center. Freeze overnight.

Transfer to refrigerator 30 minutes before serving. Garnish with additional whipped cream around edge, strawberries and lime slices, if you wish. Makes 8 servings.

Carol's Kitchen

When a political campaign has appeal to middle-class citizens, the expression goes, "It'll play in Peoria."

Fresh Gooseberry Pie

3 cups fresh gooseberries
1½ cups sugar
3 tablespoons quick cooking
  tapioca

⅛ teaspoon salt
Almond pastry for 2-crust pie
2 tablespoons butter or
  margarine

Crush ¾ cup gooseberries and add to sugar, tapioca and salt. Stir in remainder of berries. Cook and stir until mixture thickens. Turn into pastry-lined 9-inch pie pan. Dot with butter. Adjust top crust and flute edges; cut vents. Brush with milk. Bake in hot oven (425°) 35–45 minutes, or until crust is golden. Serve slightly warm.

ALMOND PASTRY:
Before adding water to blended flour and shortening in making pastry for 2-crust pie, add 1 teaspoon almond extract. Also excellent for peach and cherry pies.

What's Cooking "Down Home"

Cream Cheese Pecan Pie

1 (8-ounce) package cream
  cheese
½ cup sugar
1 egg, beaten

½ teaspoon salt
1 teaspoon vanilla
1 (10-inch) unbaked pie shell
1¼ cups chopped pecans

TOPPING:
3 eggs
1 cup light corn syrup

¼ cup sugar
1 teaspoon vanilla

Cream together softened cream cheese, sugar, beaten egg, salt, and vanilla. Spread over bottom of unbaked pie shell. Sprinkle pecans evenly over cream cheese layer.

Combine topping ingredients and beat until smooth. Pour over pecans. Bake 45–50 minutes at 350° or until firm in center. Cool. May be served with whipped cream.

Our Best Home Cooking

Honey Crunch Pecan Pie

4 eggs, slightly beaten
1 cup light corn syrup
¼ cup brown sugar
¼ cup white sugar
2 tablespoons melted butter
1 teaspoon vanilla
½ teaspoon salt

1 cup chopped pecans
Unbaked pie shell
⅓ cup brown sugar
3 tablespoons butter
3 tablespoons honey
1½ cups pecan halves

In large bowl, combine eggs and next 6 ingredients. Mix well. Fold in chopped pecans. Pour into unbaked pie shell. Bake at 350° for 50–55 minutes. On stove over medium heat, cook remaining ingredients, except pecans, until sugar dissolves. Stir in pecans. Add to top of pie. Bake for 10 minutes more.

Five Loaves and Two Fishes II

Topsy Turvy Pecan Apple Pie

½ stick butter, softened
Pecan halves
⅔ cup brown sugar, packed
2-crust pastry

6 cups apples, sliced, mixed with ½ cup sugar, and sprinkles of apple pie seasonings (flour, cinnamon, nutmeg)

Smooth butter around sides and bottom of pie pan. Stick pecans in butter, then press brown sugar evenly over pecans. Then put on 1 layer of crust extending about an inch beyond edge of pan. Add apple mixture next, and then top crust. Lap extended crust over top crust and flute edges.

Prick top with fork. Bake 10 minutes at 450° then reduce heat to 350° and continue baking 30–45 minutes or until done. Flip upside down to serve.

Home Cookin' is a Family Affair

When the *Chicago Tribune* called Henry Ford an anarchist in 1919, he sued the paper and won: six cents then, and a letter of apology from the publisher, Robert R. McCormick, on July 30, 1941, their mutual birthday.

Butterscotch Pie

1 cup brown sugar	2 egg yolks
3 tablespoons butter	2 cups milk
4 tablespoons cream	1 baked pie crust
6 tablespoons flour	

Cook and stir first 3 ingredients until thick and brown—the browner it is, the more butterscotch taste it has. Add remaining ingredients, stirring constantly until thick. Cool. Pour into baked pie crust. Refrigerate until set.

Our Favorite Recipes

Frost-on-the-Pumpkin Pie

1½ cups confectioners' sugar, divided	⅓ cup granulated sugar
½ teaspoon vanilla extract	1¼ cups pumpkin
½ teaspoon cinnamon	½ cup milk
1 cup heavy cream, whipped	½ teaspoon cinnamon
1 tablespoon unflavored gelatin	½ teaspoon allspice
¼ cup cold water	¼ teaspoon ginger
3 eggs, separated	¼ teaspoon nutmeg
	1 (9-inch) baked pie shell

Fold 1¼ cups confectioners' sugar, vanilla extract, and cinnamon into whipped cream; chill.

Soften gelatin in cold water. Mix well beaten egg yolks with granulated sugar, pumpkin, milk, and spices. Cook in a heavy pan, stirring constantly, until thick (about 5 minutes). Add gelatin and stir until dissolved. Chill thoroughly.

Beat remaining ¼ cup confectioners' sugar into 3 egg whites; beat until stiff; fold into pumpkin mixture. Turn half of pumpkin mixture into pie shell; cover with half of whipped cream mixture. Repeat layers. Chill for several hours or overnight. Serves 8.

First There Must Be Food

Marvelous Mocha Pie

20 chocolate Oreo cookies,
  crushed

¼ cup butter, melted
1 quart coffee ice cream

Melt butter. Mix well with crushed cookies and press into pie plate. Spread 1 full quart ice cream over crust and freeze.

CHOCOLATE SAUCE:

3 (3-ounce) squares
  unsweetened chocolate,
  melted
¼ cup butter

⅔ cup sugar
⅔ cup evaporated milk
1 teaspoon vanilla

Bring chocolate, butter, and sugar to a boil. Gradually add evaporated milk. Cook until thickened. Let cool; add vanilla. Spread over ice cream and return to freezer until sauce sets.

TOPPING:

1 cup whipping cream,
  whipped

Almonds (toasted, sliced or
  slivered)

Before serving, top with whipped cream; garnish with nuts. A small amount of Kahlua may be spooned over whipped cream before serving.

Soupçon II

Chocolate Turtle Pie

1 chocolate or graham
  cracker pie crust
¼ cup caramel dessert
  topping
½ cup chopped pecans

2 (3-ounce) packages
  chocolate cook-and-serve
  pudding
3 cups milk
Whipped topping

Spread topping on bottom of crust. Sprinkle with pecans. Refrigerate. Stir pudding mixes into milk in medium saucepan. Stirring constantly, cook on medium heat until mixture comes to full boil. Remove from heat. Cool 5 minutes, stirring twice. Pour into crust. Place plastic wrap on surface of filling. Refrigerate 3 hours or until set. Garnish with whipped topping.

Thank Heaven for Home Made Cooks

Grasshopper Pie

24 cream-filled chocolate cookies, finely crushed
¼ cup butter or margarine, melted
¼ cup milk

Few drops peppermint extract
Few drops green food coloring
1 jar marshmallow cream
2 cups heavy cream, whipped

Combine cookie crumbs and butter or margarine. Press into 9-inch spring-form pan, reserving ½ cup mixture for topping. Gradually add milk, extract and food coloring to marshmallow cream, mixing until well blended. Fold in whipped cream; pour into pan. Sprinkle with remaining crumbs; freeze.

If desired, substitute ¼ cup green creme de menthe for milk; omit peppermint extract and coloring. Makes 8–10 servings.

Family Celebrations Cookbook

Mud Pie

1 cup granulated sugar
½ cup margarine or butter, melted
1 teaspoon vanilla
¼ teaspoon salt
2 eggs
⅓ cup Gold Medal all-purpose flour

⅓ cup cocoa
1 cup chopped nuts, optional
¼ cup fudge sauce or fudge ice cream topping
1 cup chilled whipping cream
2 tablespoons powdered sugar

Heat the oven to 325°. Grease a round pan, 8x1½-inches, or a pie plate, 8x1¼-inches, with shortening. Mix granulated sugar, margarine, vanilla, salt, eggs, flour, and cocoa in a medium bowl with wooden spoon; stir in nuts. Pour into pan. Bake until wooden pick inserted halfway between center and edge comes out clean, about 25 minutes.

Immediately prick holes in pie with a wooden pick; spread fudge sauce over top. Cool completely.

Beat whipping cream and powdered sugar in a chilled small bowl until stiff; spread over fudge sauce. Drizzle with additional fudge sauce or topping if you like. Store pie in refrigerator. Makes 6–8 servings.

Cookin' With Friends

Scintillating Lemon Pie

Customers always ask if this is Lemon Meringue, the only lemon pie most people know. This is not like any other lemon pie. They also wonder what "scintillating" means. You'll know after you taste it. It's one of our all-time favorite desserts.

Pastry for a 2-crust
  (9-inch) pie, divided
1½ tablespoons sugar
1 teaspoon nutmeg
3 lemons

1½ cups sugar
⅓ cup butter
3 tablespoons flour
3 eggs
½ cup water

Preheat oven to 400°. Roll out ½ of the dough into 9-inch circle. Cut into 6 wedges. Place wedges on cookie sheet. Mix sugar and nutmeg together in small bowl. Sprinkle over pastry wedges. Bake at 400° for no longer than 5 minutes, or until set. Remove from cookie sheet and set aside.

Grate yellow part of 1 lemon rind. Peel and slice lemons very thinly. Set aside.

Cream sugar, butter, and flour in mixer bowl. Beat in eggs. Beat in water. Stir in reserved lemon slices and grated rind. Roll out remaining pastry to form 9-inch pie shell. Pour lemon mixture into prepared pie shell. Bake at 400° for 25 minutes. Arrange baked pastry wedges on top of filling and bake for an additional 5 minutes, or until filling is firm. Makes 1 (9-inch) pie.

The Elsah Landing Restaurant Cookbook

Partridge-in-a-Pear Tree Pie

1¼ cups sugar
2 tablespoons cornstarch
¼ teaspoon salt
1¼ cups water
1 cup seedless raisins
2 cups cranberries

1 tablespoon butter
Pastry for 2-crust pie
1 tablespoon melted butter
1 (8-ounce) can pear halves
  drained, sliced
Sugar

Blend 1¼ cups sugar, cornstarch, and salt. Add water slowly. Cook until mixture thickens, stirring constantly. Add raisins, cranberries, and butter; cook 5 minutes.

Line a 9-inch pie plate with half of pastry; brush with melted butter. Add cranberry-raisin filling. Gently press pear slices into filling in a spoke-like design. Roll out remaining pastry; make partridge and tree designs to top pie. Sprinkle cut-outs with sugar. Bake at 450° for 20 minutes. Makes 6–8 servings.

Soupçon I

Cherries in Snow

12 graham crackers
½ stick oleo
1 (8-ounce) package
  Philadelphia Cream Cheese
1 cup powdered sugar

1 teaspoon milk
1 cup pecans
1 package Dream Whip
1 can red cherry pie filling

Make graham cracker crust first by mixing crackers and oleo. Put in 8x8-inch pan; press on bottom and sides.

Let Philadelphia Cream Cheese get soft. Mix cream cheese, powdered sugar, and milk together. Set aside chopped pecans. Set aside Dream Whip made according to directions on package.

Take Philadelphia Cream Cheese mixture and put with Dream Whip. Stir by spoon. Add chopped pecans; stir all together. Put on top of graham cracker crust.

Put red cherry pie filling on top. Cool for 3–4 hours in refrigerator.

Old-Fashioned Cooking

Apple Strudel

1 cup butter
2 cups sifted flour
1 cup sour cream
½ cup melted butter
2 cups bread crumbs

4 cups sliced apples
2 cups sugar
2 teaspoons cinnamon
½ cup chopped pecans
1 cup golden raisins

Cut butter into sifted flour in bowl until crumbly. Add sour cream; mix well. Divide dough into 3 portions. Shape into balls. Chill, covered, in freezer for 2 hours or in refrigerator overnight.

Roll each portion to ⅛-inch thickness on floured surface. Combine melted butter and bread crumbs in bowl; toss to mix. Add apples, sugar, cinnamon, pecans, and raisins; mix well. Spread filling equally over each portion. Roll as for jelly roll to enclose filling. Place on baking sheet. Bake at 350° for 1 hour or until golden brown. Yield: 27 servings.

Approx Per Serving: Cal 253; T Fat 12g; 43% Calories from Fat; Prot 3g; Carbo 35g; Fiber 2g; Chol 27mg; Sod 132mg.

Pioneer Pantry

Peaches and Cream

¾ cup flour
½ teaspoon salt
1 egg
1 small package vanilla
   pudding (not instant)

1 teaspoon baking powder
3 tablespoons butter, softened
1 cup milk
1 (15-ounce) can sliced peaches,
   drained (reserve juice)

Mix all ingredients except peaches and pour into greased 9x9-inch pan. Arrange peaches on top of batter.
   Cream the following:

1 (8-ounce) package cream
   cheese, softened

3 tablespoons peach juice
1 cup sugar

Pour over top of peaches. Bake at 350° for 30 minutes. Serves 6–8.

Seasoned with Love

Toffee Meringue Dessert

Sinfully rich.

4 egg whites
1 cup sugar
1 teaspoon vanilla
1 teaspoon vinegar

10 large (or 20 small) Heath
   bars, frozen
1 pint whipping cream, whipped

Beat egg whites until stiff but not dry. Gradually beat in sugar, then vanilla and vinegar. Pour into 2 greased 8-inch layer cake pans which have been lined with greased brown paper. Bake in 275° oven for 2 hours. Remove and quickly peel off paper. Cool.
   Put frozen Heath bars into blender, 1 at a time; chop finely and set aside. Whip cream; combine with chopped Heath bars, reserving ⅓ cup candy for topping. Spread between and on top of meringues. Sprinkle top with reserved candy. Chill for 24 hours. Serve in small wedge-shaped portions. Makes 8–10 servings.

Soupçon I

Peach Crisp with Maple Sauce

Wonderful taste.

PEACH CRISP:

1 cup flour
½ cup packed brown sugar
½ cup granulated sugar
½ teaspoon cinnamon
¼ teaspoon nutmeg
¼ teaspoon salt

½ cup butter
8 medium, fresh peaches, peeled, sliced (5–6 cups)
2 tablespoons maple syrup
Juice and rind of ½ lemon

For peach crisp, combine flour, sugars, cinnamon, nutmeg, and salt. Cut into butter with pastry blender or fork until crumbly. Combine peaches with maple syrup, lemon juice, and rind. Place in 9-inch square baking pan. Sprinkle with crumb mixture. Cover with foil. Bake at 375° for 30 minutes. Remove foil. Bake 15 minutes more, or until crisp on top. Serve warm or cold with Creamy Maple Sauce.

CREAMY MAPLE SAUCE:

1½ cups whipping cream
⅓ cup maple syrup

3 tablespoons light corn syrup

Combine ingredients and simmer about 30 minutes or until thickened and reduced. Chill. Makes 6–8 servings.

Soupçon II

Cherry Clafoutis

| 1 pound fresh cherries, | ½ cup Kirsch |
| pitted | 1 tablespoon sugar |

Put cherries into a large bowl. Add the Kirsch and sugar. Let marinate for 2 hours, stirring occasionally.

Make pastry and filling.

Drain marinated cherries, remove the pan with dough from the refrigerator. Arrange cherries carefully in the tart pan. Carefully pour the egg cream mixture over the cherries.

Bake for 40-45 minutes until knife inserted 1 inch from edge and withdrawn is clean. Do not overbake. Cool on wire rack, serve warm. Yield: 8 servings.

PASTRY:

1 cup flour	1 egg yolk
2 tablespoons sugar	½ teaspoon vanilla
¼ teaspoon salt	1 tablespoon fresh lemon juice
6 tablespoons unsalted butter	

Mix flour, sugar, and salt in a large bowl. Cut in butter until mixture resembles coarse crumbs. Make a well in the center of the flour, add the egg yolk, vanilla, and lemon juice. Mix with a fork just until dough gathers into a ball. Wrap and refrigerate for 30 minutes.

Preheat oven to 325°. Roll out the dough on a lightly floured surface. Fit into a 10-inch tart pan with removable bottom. Refrigerate for 5 minutes.

FILLING:

4 eggs	1 teaspoon vanilla
1 cup heavy cream	2 tablespoons cake flour
½ cup sugar	2 tablespoons Kirsch

Mix the eggs, cream, sugar, vanilla, flour, and Kirsch together.
From Le Francais, 269 South Milwaukee Street, Wheeling.

Best Recipes of Illinois Inns and Restaurants

Chuck's Crim Puffs

These are melt-in-your-mouth dessert treats that are easier to make than they sound. The puff shells are great filled with meats, veggies or seafood for appetizers.

1 cup water
½ cup butter or margarine
1 cup flour
4 eggs
1 (6-ounce) package vanilla
  or chocolate instant pudding

1½ cups milk
1 cup whipping cream, whipped
1 cup chocolate chips
1 tablespoon oil

Bring water and butter to a boil in saucepan. Stir in flour all at once. Cook until mixture leaves side of pan and forms a ball, stirring constantly; remove from heat. Beat in eggs 1 at a time. Drop by spoonfuls onto ungreased baking sheet. Bake at 400° for 15–20 minutes or until puffed and golden brown. Cool on wire rack. Slice off tops of puffs and discard uncooked filaments inside.

Combine pudding mix and milk in bowl; mix well. Fold in whipped cream. Spoon mixture into puffs; replace tops of puffs. Melt chocolate chips with oil in saucepan over low heat, stirring to blend well. Drizzle over filled puffs. Yield: 2 dozen.

Recipe by Chuck Crim.

The Cubs 'R Cookin'

Blueberry Dessert

BUTTER CRUNCH CRUST:

1 cup butter
½ cup brown sugar, packed
2 cups flour

1 cup pecans or walnuts,
chopped (or coconut)

Heat oven to 400°. Mix all ingredients with hands. Dump onto a cookie sheet. Bake 12–15 minutes. Stir once or twice during baking to prevent edges from burning. Press hot crumbs into a jelly roll pan. Cool.

FILLING:

1 (8-ounce) package cream
cheese (room temperature)
2 packages Dream Whip
topping mix

1 cup powdered sugar
½ cup cold milk
1 can blueberry pie filling

Beat all except pie filling until creamy. Spread on top of cooled crumb crust. Top with blueberry pie filling or fruit filling of your choice.

Cooking with Daisy's Descendants

Spumoni
(Luxurious Ice Cream Whip)

1 quart strawberries or
raspberries
Juice of 1 lemon
3 tablespoons sugar

1 cup chopped walnuts
1 cup chopped pistachio nuts
½ cup powdered sugar
3 cups whipped cream

Mash berries with lemon juice and sugar. Let them marinate ½ hour. Add nuts and powdered sugar, and stir vigorously. Fold into whipped cream. Pour into loaf pans or round ice cream mold, and freeze. Cut into inch slices to serve.

Herrin's Favorite Italian Recipes Cookbook

Sweetheart Pizza

CRUST:
1 cup flour
¼ cup powdered sugar

1 stick oleo, room temperature

Mix together and press into heart shape on a 12-inch pizza pan that has been sprayed with Pam or oiled. Bake at 325° 15–20 minutes. Cool completely.

CREAM CHEESE:
1 (8-ounce) package cream
    cheese

½ cup sugar

Blend together and spread on cooled crust.

STRAWBERRY GLAZE:
1 cup sugar
1 cup water
3 tablespoons cornstarch

3 tablespoons strawberry
    Jello (dry mix)
1 pint strawberries, sliced

Combine sugar, water, cornstarch and Jello in saucepan and cook, stirring constantly, until thick and clear. When cool, add sliced strawberries and pour on top of cream cheese layer. Chill before serving. If using a 16-inch pan, double crust, cream cheese and strawberry glaze recipes.

Family Celebrations Cookbook

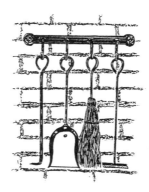

Chocolate Dumplings

SAUCE:

¾ cup brown sugar
¼ cup cocoa
1 tablespoon cornstarch

Dash of salt
2 cups water
2 tablespoons butter

Mix sauce in a large skillet and heat until it comes to a boil and thickens slightly. Remove from heat.

DUMPLINGS:

1 cup flour
½ cup sugar
2 teaspoons baking powder
1 teaspoon salt
2 tablespoons cocoa

1 egg, beaten
⅓ cup milk
3 tablespoons butter (soft)
1 teaspoon vanilla

Stir dumpling batter and beat 1 minute. Return sauce skillet to stove and bring to a simmer. Drop dumplings by tablespoons into sauce. Cover and simmer gently about 20 minutes. Peek just once to make sure sauce is simmering. Serve hot with whipped cream. Yields 6 servings.

Franklin County Homemakers Extension Cookbook

"Do Not Cook the Noodles" Kugel

½ pound medium noodles, raw
6 eggs, beaten
1 (15-ounce) can crushed pineapple, drained
½ cup butter or margarine, melted

2 cups cottage cheese
1 teaspoon vanilla
3 cups milk
Dash salt
½ teaspoon cinnamon
½ cup raisins

Grease a 9x13-inch pan with part of butter. Spread uncooked noodles on bottom of pan. Combine remaining ingredients and pour over noodles. Bake at 300° for 2 hours. Makes 15 servings.

Tradition in the Kitchen 2

Angel Food Orange Delight

1 (6-ounce) package orange
  Jello
2 cups boiling water
1 pint orange sherbet
1 small container Cool Whip

2 (11-ounce) cans mandarin
  oranges, drained
1 small can crushed pineapple,
  drained
1 angel food cake, baked

Mix Jello with boiling water; cool. Add orange sherbet and then add Cool Whip. Cut oranges into small pieces. Add drained oranges and drained pineapple. Trim brown off the cake and cut into cubes.

Line 11x13-inch dish with cake cubes, and pour ½ of mixture over cake. Add another layer of cake and add rest of Jello mix. Refrigerate overnight before serving.

Cook Book: Favorite Recipes from Our Best Cooks

Luscious Lady

A family tradition to prepare on Christmas Eve, but out of this world any day of the year.

4 squares unsweetened
  chocolate
¾ cup sugar
⅓ cup milk
6 eggs, separated
1½ cups unsalted butter
1½ cups confectioners' sugar
⅛ teaspoon salt

1½ teaspoons vanilla
1 cup maraschino cherries,
  halved
3½ dozen ladyfingers, split
Garnish: whipped cream,
  nuts, cherries, shaved
  chocolate

Melt chocolate. Combine sugar, milk, and egg yolks. Add to chocolate and cook until smooth and thickened, stirring constantly. Cool to room temperature.

Cream butter well. Add ¾ cup confectioners' sugar and cream thoroughly. Add chocolate mixture and mix well. Beat egg whites with salt until stiff and gradually beat in remaining ¾ cup confectioners' sugar. Fold in chocolate mixture. Add vanilla and cherries.

Line a deep 9-inch spring-form pan with split ladyfingers (bottom and sides). Chill overnight. Spoon mixture into pan, alternating layers using ⅓ of chocolate mixture with remaining ladyfingers. Garnish with whipped cream, nuts, cherries, and shaved chocolate. Serves 16.

Still Gathering

Million Dollar Dessert

1 box Jiffy Yellow Cake Mix
1 (8-ounce) package cream
  cheese
2 cups milk (divided)

1 package instant vanilla
  pudding
1 can pie filling (any flavor)
1 container Cool Whip

Mix cake mix as directed. Put into 9x13-inch pan. Bake for 12–15 minutes at 350°. Let cool. Combine cream cheese with ½ cup milk. Mix pudding with remaining 1½ cups milk, then mix together with cream cheese mixture. Spread on cake and let set. Cover with pie filling. Serve topped with Cool Whip. Makes 12–15 servings.

Inn-describably Delicious

Coffee Mallow

A light, elegant, easy dessert. Few people can guess the secret ingredient—marshmallows.

16 marshmallows	**1 cup heavy cream**
½ cup hot double-strength coffee	**½ teaspoon vanilla**

With wet scissors, cut marshmallows into quarters. Put in the top of a double boiler with coffee. When melted, take from heat and cool until it begins to thicken.

Beat cream until thick; fold together with marshmallow mixture and vanilla. Chill in pretty dishes until set.

Jubilee

Persimmon Pudding

2 cups persimmon pulp	**½ cup melted butter**
3 eggs	**2½ cups rich milk**
1¼ cups sugar	**2 teaspoons cinnamon**
1 cup all-purpose flour	**1 teaspoon ginger**
1 teaspoon baking powder	**½ teaspoon freshly grated nutmeg**
1 teaspoon soda	
½ teaspoon salt	

Mix ingredients together and pour pudding into a greased 9x9-inch baking dish. Raisins or nutmeats may be added, if desired. Bake at 325° until firm, about 1 hour. Serve with sauce.

SAUCE:

½ cup cream	**½ teaspoon vanilla**
¾ cup butter	**1 cup brown sugar**

Cook until sugar is dissolved and butter melts.

The French-Icarian Persimmon Tree Cookbook

Layered Banana Pudding

⅔ cup sugar
¼ cup cornstarch
¼ teaspoon salt
2 cups milk, scalded
3 egg yolks, slightly beaten
2 tablespoons butter

½ teaspoon vanilla
2–3 ripe bananas, sliced
1 (11-ounce) box vanilla wafers
½ cup heavy cream, whipped
Vanilla wafer crumbs

Mix sugar, cornstarch, and salt together in top of double boiler. Gradually add milk to sugar mixture. Stir constantly over boiling water for 10 minutes, or until mixture thickens and forms a pudding. Remove from heat.

Stir small amount of pudding into egg yolks. Stir egg yolk mixture into remaining pudding. Cook, stirring constantly, for an additional 5 minutes. Remove from heat. Stir in butter and vanilla. Cool. Fold in bananas.

Line bottom and sides of serving dish with vanilla wafers. Pour in pudding. Chill. Garnish with whipped cream and a sprinkle of crumbs. Makes 6 servings.

The Elsah Landing Restaurant Cooking

Chocolate Dessert Baskets

8 (1-ounce) squares
  semi-sweet chocolate
1 tablespoon butter

½ teaspoon vegetable oil
Pleated foil baking cups

Melt chocolate, butter, and oil in the top of a double boiler over hot, not boiling water. Beat thoroughly when completely melted. Pour the warm mixture into the baking cups, swirling to cover the inside. Chill the coated cups in a muffin pan until hard. To serve, peel off the foil carefully and fill with ice cream, sherbet, or mousse. Top each basket with a teaspoon of liqueur.

Brunch Basket

Baked Pineapple

1 (#2) can crushed
  pineapple, drained
2 eggs, beaten well
2 cups white sugar

½ cup butter, softened
½ cup milk or cream
32 crackers, crushed

Stir pineapple, eggs, sugar, butter, and cream together. Top with cracker crumbs. Bake for 1 hour at 350°.

Home Cookin' is a Family Affair

Banana Boats

12 bananas
4 (1½-ounce) Hershey
  bars, cut in thirds

2 cups miniature marshmallows
½ cup pecans

Peel back narrow strip in inside curve of bananas. Scoop out a small amount of banana. Add chocolate, marshmallows and pecans. Cover with banana skin. Wrap in foil. Place in coals. Cook until banana is hot. Yields 12 servings.

Approx. Per Serving: Cal 233; Prot 3.0gr; T Fat 8.3gr; Chol 2.9mg; Carbo 41.4gr; Sod 17.5mg; Potas 524.8mg.

River Valley Recipes

Lindsay's Frosty White Grapes

1 quart seedless grapes,
   washed, stemmed and chilled
1 pint sour cream
¼ cup granulated sugar

2 teaspoons vanilla
⅓ cup butter or margarine
1 cup brown sugar

Combine sour cream, granulated sugar and vanilla. Add chilled grapes. Pour into serving dishes. In saucepan or in microwave dish or 2-cup glass measuring cup, melt butter and stir in brown sugar, stirring until mixture is syrupy. Drizzle syrup over grapes, chill and serve with butter cookies. Or simply serve your grapes and "white sauce" with a sprinkle of brown sugar.

What's Cooking "Down Home"

Creamy Caramel Apples

1 bag caramels
1 can Eagle Brand milk
1 (8-ounce) carton Cool Whip

Sliced apples
Chopped nuts

In fondue pot, melt peeled caramels and Eagle Brand milk. Then add container of Cool Whip and stir mixture. Slice apples in bowl, pour some caramel mixture over them and sprinkle nuts on top.

Good Cookin' Cookbook

Villa Katherine was built in 1900 for Quincy native and world traveler, George Metz, based on his sketches and photos of villas in various ports of the Islamic world. It sits on a bluff with a breathtaking view of the Mississippi River. The only example of Mediterranean architecture in the Midwest, it now serves as Quincy's Tourist Information Center.

Index

Villa Katherine. Quincy.

INDEX

Catalog of
Contributing
Cookbooks

Civil War Memorial in Fairview Park. Decatur.

CATALOG
of
CONTRIBUTING COOKBOOKS

All recipes in this book have been selected from the Illinois cookbooks shown on the following pages. Individuals who wish to obtain a copy of any particular book may do so by sending a check or money order to the address listed. Prices are subject to change. Please note the postage and handling charges that are required. State residents add tax only when requested. Retailers are invited to call or write to same address for discount information.

AN APPLE FROM THE TEACHER

Illinois Retired Teachers Association
Springfield, IL

A handsome compendium of 247 pages with concise, easy-to-follow recipes. Seventy-five years of Illinois teacher anecdotal memories intersperse the drawings and the 250 recipes. Currently out of print.

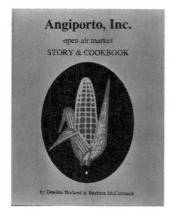

ANGIPORTO, INC.

by Barbara McCormack and Deedee Borland
Lake Forest, IL

Angiporto, Inc. was an open air market located in an alley off historic Market Square in Lake Forest, Illinois. Created there were muffins, jams pestos, salad dressings, and soups from locally grown produce. The book contains 125 recipes, and highlights the pleasures and pitfalls of starting and running a small business.

ISBN 0-9630876-0-6

BEST RECIPES OF ILLINOIS INNS AND RESTAURANTS

by Margaret Guthrie
Amherst, WI

The variety and diversity of Illinois food and cooking extends far beyond its famous big cities. A certain sophistication has come to the small, out-of-the-way restaurants, too. This collection, part of a 5-state series, proves it. Illustrated, 7x10-inch, laminated soft cover with 128 pages. Currently out of print.

BRUNCH BASKET

Junior League of Rockford, Inc.
4118 Pinecrest Road
Rockford, IL 61107   815-399-4518

Brunch Basket is a hardbound book with a hidden spiral binding, permitting it to lie flat, with a full color washable cover. A wonderful collection of recipes for meals, whether you are planning a brunch, lunch, dinner or any special dining experience. Truly a collector's item and the perfect gift for every occasion.

$16.95 Retail price
$ 1.06 Tax for Illinois residents
$ 2.50 Postage and handling
Make check payable to Junior League of Rockford, Inc.
ISBN 0-961356308

C-U IN THE KITCHEN

Champaign-Urbana Hadassah
c/o Sinai Temple
3104 W. Windsor Road
Champaign, IL 61821

Included among the more than 700 gourmet and cherished family recipes are special sections on Jewish holiday and Israeli foods. Recipes in the 310-page book are easy to understand and prepare, with the diverse ethnic and cultural backgrounds of the contributors combined in 14 chapters—with a distinctive flair.

$14.95 Retail price
$ 1.50 Postage and handling
Make check payable to C-U Hadassah

CARING IS SHARING

Nurses of Highland Park Hospital
Highland Park, IL

Caring is Sharing is a 170-page wonderful collection of recipes tested and tried by the nurses of Highland Park Hospital. It is in remembrance of the early days of the hospital when most of the produce and poultry was grown locally or by the hospital. It also offers cooking and buying tips, as well as equivalence charts and suggestions for serving large quantities. Currently out of print.

CAROL'S KITCHEN

Carol J. Moore
1032 Westshore Drive
Galesburg, IL 61401   309-342-6328

A hefty 420-page spiral bound book containing about 1,000 recipes. Compiled during 27 years of marriage; recipes are original, or were obtained from family, friends, or local bakeries and restaurants. Recipes range from simple basic to the demanding gourmet—something to please every cook!

$27.00 Retail price
$ 1.89 Tax for Illinois residents
$ 3.50 Postage and handling
Make check payable to Carol Moore
ISBN 0-9645003-0-2

A CAUSE FOR APPLAUSE

Elgin Symphony League
Elgin, IL

A Cause for Applause will perk up your appetites with a tasty spread of more than 650 recipes from musical cooks all over the country. This 241-page, tab divided, double indexed cookbook is easy to use and features everything from Preludes (appetizers) to Finales (desserts). It's great for every day, or for entertaining special guests. Currently out of print.

A Collection of Recipes
From St. Matthew Lutheran Church

A COLLECTION OF RECIPES FROM ST. MATTHEW LUTHERAN CHURCH

Rebecca Quilters
Galena, IL

A very good assortment of home-tested recipes by members of St. Matthew Lutheran Church. In 269 pages, there are about 700 recipes. Currently out of print.

COLLEGE AVENUE PRESBYTERIAN CHURCH COOKBOOK

Presbyterian Women of College Avenue Church
501 South College Avenue
Aledo, IL 61231   309-582-2182

The Presbyterian Women of College Avenue Church had not published a cookbook for about 95 years. Their new cookbook contains 187 pages and around 565 recipes of the church ladies past and present. Aledo is a farming community in Northwestern Illinois of less than 4,000 people—and we have very good cooks.

$10.00 Retail price
$ 1.00 Postage and handling
Make check payable to PW of College Avenue Presbyterian Church

COOK BOOK: FAVORITE RECIPES FROM OUR BEST COOKS

Central Illinois Tourism Council
Springfield, IL

A collection of almost 300 recipes from the Prairie State's rich bounty which has been feeding the world for generations. Sample our splendid local specialties, delightful delicacies, and outstanding main dishes, with contributions from the Governor's mansion and our most popular restaurants and hotels. Currently out of print.

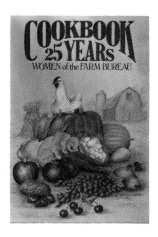

COOKBOOK 25 YEARS

Madison County Farm Bureau Women's Committee
P. O. Box 10
Edwardsville, IL 62025   618-656-5191

From the grassroots of Illinois farmland comes *Cookbook 25 Years*, a collection of recipes from today's families for today's families. The women of the Madison County Farm Bureau give a glimpse into the homes (and the dinner tables) of America's farmers, and offer a harvest of time-tested recipes straight from their own pantries.

$14.00 Paperback or $16.00 Hardcover
$ 3.00 Postage and handling
Make check payable to Madison County Farm Bureau
ISBN 0-9644914-0-0

COOKIN' WITH FRIENDS

Friends of the Graves-Hume Library
1401 W. Main Street
Mendota, IL 61342   815-538-3314

A collection of 682 home-tested favorites from the kitchens of F.O.L. members, their relatives, friends and neighbors. Features 57 sweet corn recipes of every kind imaginable in recognition of Mendota's Annual Sweet Corn Festival. 330 pages, from appealing appetizers to versatile veggies, sprinkled with humorous anecdotes, quips and quotes.

$ 8.50 Retail price
$ 2.00 Postage and handling
Make check payable to Friends of the Graves-Hume Public Library

COOKING WITH DAISY'S DESCENDANTS

by Elaine Gilbert Davis
101 Oak Street
Fairmount, IL 61841   217-733-2595

From my heart to yours, a mouth-watering, memory-provoking collection of 300 recipes, plus helpful hints. Spanning six generations of time-tested, family recipes; from old-fashioned puddings and dumplings to low-fat recipes for today's health conscious. Country rose vinyl, 3-ring binder allows easy additions. "The key to the heart of a family is a wooden spoon."

$10.00 Retail price
$ 2.50 Postage and handling
Make check payable to Elaine Davis

THE CUBS 'R COOKIN'

Cubs' Wives for Family Rescue
c/o The Chicago Cubs
1060 W. Addison Street
Chicago, IL 60613   773-404-2827

The wives of the Chicago Cubs' baseball players present a collection of favorite recipes, family photos and personal information from the players, coaches, broadcasters, executives and more. Proceeds benefit Family Rescue, an organization on Chicago's South Side that offers shelter, counseling, legal and social services and more to abused women and their children.

$10.00 Retail price
$ 3.00 Postage and handling
Make check payable to Cubs' Wives for Family Rescue
ISBN 0-87197-403-7

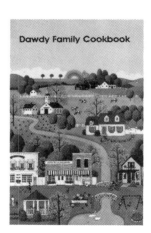

DAWDY FAMILY COOKBOOK

by Kae Dawdy Coates
Roodhouse, IL

The Dawdy Family Cookbook is an 80-page collection of 250 recipes printed in loving memory of a mother and grandmother who not only taught her family to love good food, but also to love life and one another. The book includes memories of a family with seven children growing up in the aftermath of the Great Depression in Greene County, Illinois. Currently out of print.

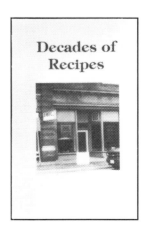

DECADES OF RECIPES

Fairmount Jamaica Historical Society
116 South Main Street
Fairmount, IL 61841

Decades of Recipes is a collection of recipes ranging from the 1930s thru 1994, from people who live or have lived in our area. The book contains a brief history of the area, 206 pages and 500 recipes.

$ 8.00 Retail price
$ 2.00 Postage and handling
Make check payable to Fairmount Jamaica Historical Society

ELSAH LANDING HEARTLAND COOKING

by Helen Crafton and Dorothy Lindgren
Grafton, IL

Two hundred pages of more soup, breads, desserts and menu recipes from the award winning Elsah Landing Restaurant. Currently out of print.

THE ELSAH LANDING RESTAURANT COOKBOOK

by Helen Crafton and Dorothy Lindgren
Grafton, IL

Over 200 pages of recipes printed at the request of customers. Three sections contain recipes of the restaurants' specialties: breads, soups, and desserts. The fourth section is a collection of favorites from the authors' files. Not all of the recipes are simple, but the instructions are clear, precise, and easy to follow. Currently out of print.

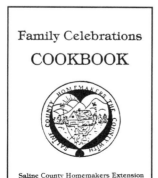

Family Celebrations

COOKBOOK

Saline County Homemakers Extension Association

FAMILY CELEBRATIONS COOKBOOK

Saline County Homemakers Extension Assn.
1025 Lewis Road
Harrisburg, IL 62946   618-253-4401

A book of favorite recipes by our members—family favorites used on special holidays and occasions. The sections are done by holidays with poems, etc., for that holiday interspersed among the recipes. They are all "tried and true." The divider pages are copies of antique postcards which belonged to our members.

$ 6.00 Retail price
$ .08 Tax for Illinois residents
$ 1.50 Postage and handling
Make check payable to Saline County Homemakers Ext. Assn.

FAVORITE HERBAL RECIPES

Herbs for Health and Fun Club
127 Washington
Centralia, IL 62801   618-532-2583

Our cookbook has some unique ways to use herbs as well as old favorites. In 72 pages, there are 200 recipes plus herb and cooking tips. All recipes are member tested.

$ 6.00 Retail price
$ 2.00 Postage and handling
Make check payable to Herbs for Health and Fun Club

FAVORITE RECIPES OF COLLINSVILLE JUNIOR SERVICE CLUB

Collinsville Junior Service Club
P. O. Box 373
Collinsville, IL 62234   618-344-4054

The Collinsville Junior Service Club Cookbook is a collection of everyone's favorite recipes. There are 296 pages of recipes with 9 different food sections. Many recipes are tried-and-true handed-down-through-family-and-friends favorites.

$ 7.00 Retail price
$ 3.00 Postage and handling
Make check payable to Collinsville Junior Service Club

FIRST THERE MUST BE FOOD

Volunteer Services
251 E. Huron • Feinberg Room 504
Chicago, IL 60611   312-908-2070

This cookbook is comprised of recipes compiled from hospital staff and volunteers. The book is divided into original recipes and the healthy version of the same recipe. The cookbook has 422 pages of recipes.

$15.95 Retail price
$ 1.40 Tax for Illinois residents
$ 2.00 Postage and handling
Make check payable to First Food
ISBN 0-9605996-2-2

THE FISHLADY'S COOKBOOK
The Fishlady
P. O. Box 1823
Springfield, IL 62702   217-528-3297

The Fishlady's Cookbook was written with *you* in mind—everyone who's ever been afraid to cook fish. After reading this 55-page book cover to cover, you will know how to cook fish. Humorously written with cartoons throughout, fish is becoming more and more popular with a little help from "The Fishlady."

$ 7.95 Retail price
$ .58 Tax for Illinois residents
$ 1.00 Postage and handling
Make check payable to The Fishlady

THE FISHLADY'S FOREVER DIETER'S COOKBOOK
The Fishlady
P. O. Box 1823
Springfield, IL 62705-1823   217-528-3297

"Don't let fish intimidate you" is the Fishlady's message. Her dieting book is filled with low-cal seafood recipes. And with the help of "Flip the Fish," they motivate you to eat right. With cartoons throughout, the book takes a fun approach to eating healthier. "If you want to stay *fit and trim*, eat healthy foods...that swim!" This book has been merged into *The Fishlady's Cookbook* (see above).

THE FISHLADY'S HOLIDAY ENTERTAINING COOKBOOK
The Fishlady
P. O. Box 1823
Springfield, IL 62705-1823   217-528-3297

The Fishlady and "Flip" bring you 60 pages of easy holiday recipes, such as a "Shrimp Tree" or a "Lobster Pizza." With cartoons throughout and a festive cover, this book is the perfect gift for seafood lovers and cookbook collectors alike. This book has been merged into *The Fishlady's Cookbook* (see above).

FIVE LOAVES AND TWO FISHES II

First United Methodist Church/United Methodist Women
501 E. Capital Avenue
Springfield, IL 62701   217-787-2693

There is a special bond among those who break bread together. The women of First United Methodist Church in Mr. Lincoln's hometown lovingly share family favorites. We serve up everything from appetizers to desserts. Included among the 500 recipes are regional favorites, microwave and Heart Smart dishes. Soft cover, 184 pages.

$ 5.00 Retail price
$ 2.00 Postage and handling
Make check payable to First United Methodist Church

FRANKLIN COUNTY HOMEMAKERS EXTENSION COOKBOOK

Franklin County Homemakers Extension
Benton, IL

Our cookbook is filled with many exciting, different and delicious recipes. A big book, 276 pages and 791 recipes, it is spiral bound for easy use in the kitchen. Currently out of print.

THE FRENCH-ICARIAN PERSIMMON TREE COOKBOOK

by Louise Lum
Icarian Living History Museum
2205 Parsley Street
Nauvoo, IL 62354   217-453-2281

This book is a tapestry of treasured home-style recipes from early French immigrant families. It is dedicated to the memory and spirit of the men, women, and children who established the Society of Icaria in America. 189 pages, more than 300 recipes.

$ 9.95 Retail price
$ .65 Tax for Illinois residents
$ 1.50 Postage and handling
Make check payable to The National Icarian Heritage Society
ISBN 0-924704-06-3

GENERATIONS

Junior League of Rockford, Inc.
4118 Pinecrest Road
Rockford, IL 61107   815-399-4518

Captured within this book are the aromas and tastes from generations of area cooks. *Generations* is a timeless tradition with over 300 recipes doubly-tested. A beautifully photographed and tastefully designed 8½x11-inch volume which is easy on the eye and on the cook. Withstanding the test of time, these recipes will become the favorites of a new generation.

$19.95 Retail price
$ 1.25 Tax for Illinois residents
$ 2.50 Postage and handling
Make check payable to Junior League of Rockford, Inc.
ISBN 0-87197-408-8

GOOD COOKIN' COOKBOOK

New Life Class
P. O. Box 70
Benton, IL 62812   618-439-6584

Recipes are from members of First Baptist Church, Benton, IL. In these 104 pages, there are delicious recipes to satisfy even the pickiest pallets.

$ 5.00 Retail price
$ 3.00 Postage and handling
Make check payable to New Life Class

GRAND DETOUR HOLIDAY SAMPLER

by Karen Stransky
8190 S. Pine Street/Grand Detour
Dixon, IL 61021-9432   815-652-4445

The recipes in this sampler were donated by the friendly residents of Grand Detour, where John Deere invented his first steel plow. Proceeds are donated to St. Peter's Preservation Committee, to restore Illinois' second oldest Episcopal church, located in the village.

$ 5.00 Retail price
$ 2.00 Postage and handling
Make check payable to Karen Stransky

HERRIN'S FAVORITE ITALIAN RECIPES COOKBOOK

Herrin Hospital Auxiliary/Attn: Wilma Miriani
201 South 14th Street
Herrin, IL 62948   618-942-2171

Approximately 400 recipes within 225 pages, all from collections of first, second, and third generations of Italian immigrants to Herrin from the early 1900s. They were mostly from the Lombardy area in Northern Italy. This book features some of our earliest settlers and lists all the family names up to the present time.

$10.00 Retail price
$ 3.00 Postage and handling
Make check payable to Herrin Hospital Auxiliary

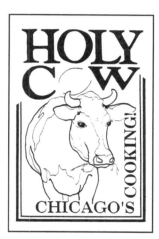

HOLY COW, CHICAGO'S COOKING!

Kenilworth, IL

With the Great Chicago Fire as its theme, 360 imaginative and delicious recipes are found within 254 pages. The hardcover and comb spine allows the book to lie flat. Sales directly help those in need in the metropolitan Chicago area. Currently out of print.

HOME COOKIN' IS A FAMILY AFFAIR

Aldersgate United Methodist Women
1201 North Fair Street
Marion, IL 62959   618-997-6065

Home Cookin' is a Family Affair contains 407 family tested recipes. The cookbook features a cover that can be cleaned and a label on the spiral binding to help you find it on the shelf. Aldersgate Church is known for its good cooks! I'm sure you will agree after trying these family favorites.

$ 7.00 Retail price
$ 3.00 Postage and handling
Make check payable to Aldersgate United Methodist Women

HONEST TO GOODNESS: HONESTLY GOOD FOOD FROM MR. LINCOLN'S HOMETOWN

Junior League Publications
1018½ W. Lawrence
Springfield, IL 62704   800-369-0178

Honest to Goodness contains over 350 triple-tested recipes. It is divided into eight sections and includes a "Hometown Favorites" section. Hardbound, with a cover that features a beautiful food mosaic of Lincoln, the book offers color photographs of Lincoln-era artifacts along with historical vignettes highlighting Lincoln's humor and lifestyle

$19.95 Retail price
$ 1.45 Tax for Illinois residents
$ 3.50 Postage and handling
Make check payable to Junior League Publications
ISBN 0-9624788-0-6

INN-DESCRIBABLY DELICIOUS

by Tracy & Phyllis Winters
P. O. Box 501
Greensburg, IN 47240   812-663-4948

With everything from Cinnamon-Apple French Toast to Norwegian Coffee Cake, Seafood Soufflé to White Chocolate Cheesecake, this book features 82 favorite B&B recipes from throughout the state. This 112-page book includes complete information about each participating inn.

$ 9.95 Retail price
$ 2.00 Postage and handling
Make check payable to Winters Publishing
ISBN 0-9625329-5-9

JUBILEE COOKBOOK

Emmanuel Memorial Episcopal Church
208 West University Avenue
Champaign, IL 61820   217-352-9827

Our *JUBILEE Cookbook* was compiled for the Jubilee Celebration of Emmanuel Memorial Episcopal Church, Champaign. The cover is an original and pictures only grown-in-Illinois produce. The recipes include personal stories from the contributor that relate to the recipe. Sometimes these stories are the most special ingredient.

$ 8.00 Retail price
$ 2.00 Postage and handling
Make check payable to Emmanuel Memorial
Episcopal Church

THE LUCY MIELE 6-5-4 COOKBOOK: 6-INGREDIENTS, 5-MINUTES OR 4-GET IT!

by Lucy Miele/Hill House Publishers
11010 East Morseville Road
Stockton, IL 61085   815-947-3433

Today's busy woman—juggling home, family and career—needs shortcuts. There lurks in all of us the desire to put something wonderful on the table. 6*5*4 satisfies these two basic needs; the contemporary need for quick cooking, and the historic, human need for great food. 223 pages. 222 recipes.

$13.95 Retail price
$ .87 Tax for Illinois residents
$ 2.38 Postage and handling
Make check payable to Hill House Publishers

THE LUCY MIELE TOO GOOD TO BE LOW-FAT, BUT IT IS, COOKBOOK

by Lucy Miele/Hill House Publishers
11010 East Morseville Road
Stockton, IL 61085   815-947-3433

At last...the flavor-filled, low-fat cookbook you've been hoping for! Every recipe fairly bursts with flavor, plus you needn't search for exotic ingredients. If Lucy can't spell it, she doesn't use it. She loves food, and she won't waste her time (or yours) if it isn't GREAT. 256 pages. 322 recipes.

$16.95 Retail price
$ 1.06 Tax for Illinois residents
$ 2.19 Postage and handling
Make check payable to Hill House Publishers

MORE TO LOVE... RECIPES AND REMINISCENCE FROM THE MANSION OF GOLCONDA

by Marilyn Kunz
Box 339
Golconda, IL 62938   618-683-4400

Hardcover, spiralbound, 206 pages, over 250 recipes. Humorous anecdotes from the experiences of a small town country inn owner, plus restaurant business lessons and things Mama never taught. Cheesecake recipe alone is worth price of book! This is one to read while you cook.

$14.95 Retail price
$ .95 Tax for Illinois residents
$ 2.50 Postage and handling
Make check payable to *More to Love*

MUFFINS—104 RECIPES FROM A TO Z

by Dorothy Jean Publishing
62 Williamsburg Road
Evanston, IL 60203   312-252-6294

Going far beyond the basic muffin recipes, this book provides stimulating recipes: anise, kiwi mango, nectarine, plum, rice pudding, and zucchini and chocolate. The recipes don't stop at breakfast—the ham and cheese, spicy Italian pizza, or parsley potato muffins are the perfect accompaniment for lunch or dinner.

$ 9.95 Retail price
$ .79 Tax for Illinois residents
$ 4.00 Postage and handling
Make check payable to Dorothy Jean Publishing
ISBN 1-884627-00-5

NOTEWORTHY, A COLLECTION OF RECIPES FROM THE RAVINIA FESTIVAL

Women's Board of the Ravinia Festival
1575 Oakwood Avenue
Highland Park, IL 60035   708-266-5043

Beautiful, hard-bound collection of more than 600 twice-tested recipes, including 46 prepared dishes pictured on 16 full-color pages. Over 140,000 copies sold, it was awarded the McIlhenny Hall of Fame Award for community cookbooks. An all-time favorite of experienced hostesses and novice cooks alike.

$15.95 Retail price
$ 1.05 Tax for Illinois residents
$ 3.25 Postage and handling
Make check payable to *NOTEWORTHY* (Visa or MC)
ISBN 0-9615803-0-5

Old-Fashioned Cooking

Raleigh Historical Society
Raleigh, Illinois

OLD FASHIONED COOKING

Raleigh Historical Society
P. O. Box 82
Raleigh, IL 62977-0082

This cookbook consists of almost 200 tried and proven favorite recipes from the little old fashioned cooks, in the little old fashioned village of Raleigh in the Southern part of Illinois. There are 70 pages filled with recipes, plus 10 divider pages full of valuable information.

$ 6.00 Retail price
$ 1.50 Postage and handling
Make check payable to Raleigh Historical Society

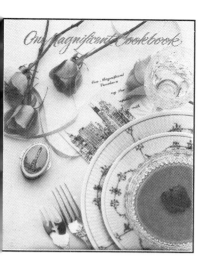

ONE MAGNIFICENT COOKBOOK

The Junior League of Chicago, Inc.
1447 North Astor Street
Chicago, IL 60610   312-664-4462

One Magnificent Cookbook is a culinary salute to Chicago. Winner of the 1988 Food and Beverage Book Award, it offers you: 240 triple tested recipes with a fresh and healthy focus; a "lay flat" feature in the binding for easy use; 20 menus and party ideas with Chicago events in mind; 13 illustrations and descriptions of Chicago landmarks.

$19.95 Retail price
$ 1.75 Tax for Illinois residents
$ 3.00 Postage and handling
Make check payable to The Junior League of Chicago, Inc.
ISBN 0-9611622-2-8

OPAA! GREEK COOKING CHICAGO STYLE

by George J. Gekas
160 East Illinois Street
Chicago, IL 60611   800-225-3775

Nowhere does great food, great drink, and fun mean more than the streets of Greektown in Chicago. Create the same authentic Green dishes featured in the top restaurants. Includes guide to Greek spices, herbs, and flavorings; Greek glossary and dinner combinations. Plus 2-for-1 coupons for featured restaurants.

$15.95 Retail price
$ 1.40 Tax for Illinois residents
$ 3.00 Postage and handling
Make check payable to Bonus Books, Inc.
ISBN 0-929387-31-7

OUR BEST HOME COOKING

Pearl Luttman
229 South 6th Street
Red Bud, IL 62278   618-282-3121

Our Best Home Cooking is a 82-page cookbook containing 200 recipes, some of which have been in the family for many years—others are recent favorites. But we all agree that these are special favorites of everyone in our family, plus friends who trade recipes.

$ 6.00 Retail price
$ 2.00 Postage and handling
Make check payable to Pearl Luttman

OUR CHERISHED RECIPES

West Salem Moravian Church
West Salem, IL

The West Salem Moravian Church celebrated 150 years of ministry and service in 1994. *Our Cherished Recipes* was compiled by members and friends as part of the observance. Some of the recipes are treasured family keepsakes and some are new; however, they all reflect the love of good cooking. Currently out of print.

OUR FAVORITE RECIPES

Union County Hospital Auxiliary
517 N. Main
Anna, IL 62906   618-833-4511 Ext. 202

Our Favorite Recipes is just that—a collection of treasured family keepsakes, as well as new recipes that reflect the love of good cooking.

$ 5.00 Retail price
$ 1.50 Postage and handling
Make check payable to Union County Hospital Auxiliary

PIONEER PANTRY

Telephone Pioneers of America,
Lucent Technologies Chapter #135
2600 Warrenville Road
Lisle, IL 60532   630-224-6300

Pioneer Pantry features 268 favorite recipes from the Telephone Pioneers Hawthorne Chapter 45. These recipes range from quick and easy to ethnic specialties. A special feature includes nutritional information for each recipe. Proceeds fund a wide variety of community service activities, many of which are described in this cookbook.

$ 8.00 Retail price
Make check payable to TPA
ISBN 0-87197-319-7

RIVER VALLEY RECIPES

Rock River Valley Council of Girl Scouts
2101 Auburn Street
Rockford, IL 61103   815-962-5591

River Valley Recipes has over 200 unique recipes in a hardcover, spiralbound cookbook. Everything from Crab Bisque to Playdough is featured throughout its 200 pages. As an added attraction, *River Valley Recipes* contains 16 beautiful photographs of local landmarks in Northern Illinois. Recipes submitted by Girl Scout Volunteers.

$12.50 Retail price
$ 2.00 Postage and handling
Make check payable to Rock River Valley Council of Girl Scouts
ISBN 0-87197-242-5

SEASONED WITH LOVE

Debra Rose
507 W. St. Charles
Springerton, IL 62887   618-643-3488

Seasoned with Love is a collection of traditional and contemporary recipes. We have included basic recipes for the novice cook, along with more challenging recipes for the adventuresome. The spiral ringbound book has a laminated cover with 251 pages.

$12.00 Retail price
Make check payable to RLDS Church

SOUPÇON I

The Junior League of Chicago, Inc.
Chicago, IL 60610

The best cook is the seasonal cook, utilizing what is available and fresh and "in season." Arranged accordingly, this outstanding cookbook was first published in 1974 and sold hundreds of thousands of copies before bowing to *Soupçon II*. Both currently out of print, their new cookbook, *One Magnificent Cookbook,* is now available.

SOUPÇON II

The Junior League of Chicago, Inc.
Chicago, IL 60610

More seasonal samplings! Soupçon is defined as "a little bit," in this instance a culinary little bit of everything. In Chicago, food is appreciated; food is an adventure; food is fun! And this book reflects it. Currently out of print, their new book *One Magnificent Cookbook* is now available.

STILL GATHERING: A CENTENNIAL CELEBRATION

Auxiliary to the American Osteopathic Assn.
142 East Ontario Street
Chicago, IL 60611   1-800-621-1773 ext. 8192

Gatherings are get-togethers with a primary purpose of enjoying good friends and good food. Many sample menus are based on traditional celebrations or occasions to gather together. Others reflect our changing lifestyle—gourmet meals that are quick and easy, and meals for our health concerns. 206 pages. Hardbound.

$ 6.00 Includes tax and postage
Make check payable to Auxiliary to the American Osteopathic Assn.
ISBN 0-9633542-0-5

SUGAR SNIPS AND ASPARAGUS TIPS

Infant Welfare Society of Chicago
1931 North Halsted - Dept BB
Chicago, IL 60614   312-751-2800

The 429 tested recipes reflect a return to natural foods that create exciting and memorable meals. The collection includes favorites from Infant Welfare Auxiliary members as well as contributions by 77 Chicagoland celebrity chefs. *Sugar Snips and Asparagus Tips* is a best seller because it appeals to cooks of all levels.

$22.95 Retail price
$ 1.84 Tax for Illinois residents
$ 4.00 Postage and handling
Make check payable to Infant Welfare Cookbook
ISBN 0-9630199-0-2

THANK HEAVEN FOR HOME MADE COOKS

C.H.O.S.E.N. Youth Group
South Side Church
500 South Illinois
Litchfield, IL 62056   217-324-5750

A delightful book—275 recipes, ten categories, helpful hints, basic kitchen information, Bible scriptures, and a "Kid's Korner." Church members supplied recipes and C.H.O.S.E.N. (Christlike Heavenbound Overcoming Students Experiencing Newness) compiled cookbook. Because of our hopes and prayers, this cookbook will be the perfect blessing for you and yours.

$ 6.50 Retail price
$ 1.75 Postage and handling
Make check payable to C.H.O.S.E.N. Youth Group

TRADITION IN THE KITCHEN 2

North Suburban Beth El Sisterhood
1175 Sheridan Road
Highland Park, IL 60035   847-432-8900

You need only to thumb through the 320 pages of this outstanding hardcover book with wire pages and 440 recipes, pre-tested and easy to read to fill your senses with wonderful aromas of superb cuisine. Meeting the needs of the 90s, the recipes are traditional, low cholesterol, and quickies. They are concise and great for holidays and everyday.

$19.95 Retail price
$ 1.60 Tax for Illinois residents
$ 4.00 Postage and handling
Make check payable to North Suburban Beth El Sisterhood
ISBN 0-9635594-0-0

WHAT'S COOKING "DOWN HOME"

by Eileen Mears
RR 2 Box 193
Greenfield, IL 62044   217-368-2758

What's Cooking "Down Home" (at Emerald Acres) is a 500-page cookbook by Eileen Mears, former farm wife/columnist (1972-1993) for the *Springfield, State Journal-Register.* More than recipes...Farm and family photos, essays, tips and more.

$15.00 Retail price
$ 2.00 Postage and handling
Make check payable to Eileen Mears
ISBN 0-9641341-0-1

The Illinois State Capitol. Springfield.

Preserving America's Food Heritage

BEST OF THE BEST COOKBOOK SERIES

Best of the Best from
ALABAMA
288 pages, $16.95

Best of the Best from
INDIANA
288 pages, $16.95

Best of the Best from
MISSISSIPPI
288 pages, $16.95

Best of the Best from
PENNSYLVANIA
320 pages, $16.95

Best of the Best from
ARKANSAS
288 pages, $16.95

Best of the Best from
IOWA
288 pages, $16.95

Best of the Best from
MISSOURI
304 pages, $16.95

Best of the Best from
SOUTH CAROLINA
288 pages, $16.95

Best of the Best from
COLORADO
288 pages, $16.95

Best of the Best from
KENTUCKY
288 pages, $16.95

Best of the Best from
NEW ENGLAND
368 pages, $16.95

Best of the Best from
TENNESSEE
288 pages, $16.95

Best of the Best from
FLORIDA
288 pages, $16.95

Best of the Best from
LOUISIANA
288 pages, $16.95

Best of the Best from
NEW MEXICO
288 pages, $16.95

Best of the Best from
TEXAS
352 pages, $16.95

Best of the Best from
GEORGIA
336 pages, $16.95

Best of the Best from
LOUISIANA II
288 pages, $16.95

Best of the Best from
NORTH CAROLINA
288 pages, $16.95

Best of the Best from
TEXAS II
352 pages, $16.95

Best of the Best from the
GREAT PLAINS
288 pages, $16.95

Best of the Best from
MICHIGAN
288 pages, $16.95

Best of the Best from
OHIO
352 pages, $16.95

Best of the Best from
VIRGINIA
320 pages, $16.95

Best of the Best from
ILLINOIS
288 pages, $16.95

Best of the Best from
MINNESOTA
288 pages, $16.95

Best of the Best from
OKLAHOMA
288 pages, $16.95

Best of the Best from
WISCONSIN
288 pages, $16.95

Cookbooks listed above have been completed as of January 1, 2000.

Special discount offers available!
(See previous page for details.)

To order by credit card, call toll-free **1-800-343-1583** or send check or money order to:
QUAIL RIDGE PRESS • P. O. Box 123 • Brandon, MS 39043
Visit our website at **www.quailridge.com** to order online!

- -

ℚ Order form

Send completed form and payment to:
QUAIL RIDGE PRESS • P. O. Box 123 • Brandon, MS 39043

❏ Check enclosed

Charge to: ❏ Visa ❏ MasterCard
❏ Discover   ❏ American Express

Card #_____

Expiration Date _____

Signature _____

Name _____

Address _____

City/State/Zip_____

Phone # _____

Qty.	Title of Book (State)	Total

Subtotal _____

7% Tax for MS residents _____

Postage ($3.00 any number of books) **+ 3.00**

Total _____